London
Railway Atlas

Joe Brown

Ian Allan PUBLISHING

Preface

London more than possibly any other city on earth owes its growth and continuing success to its intricate network of railways, which have been part of the landscape for 170 years and show no sign of losing their relevance or importance. Unlike much of the United Kingdom, London has lost relatively little of its passenger infrastructure during the 20th century and it could be argued that with the recent additions of the Docklands Light Railway and Croydon Tramlink to the scene along with 'heavy rail' developments such as the Channel Tunnel Rail Link and Jubilee Line Extension, London's passenger rail network is today at its zenith. Despite this, there are many long-forgotten branch lines and abandoned stations dotted around London; casualties of World Wars, route duplication, trams, buses and the car. London's freight and industrial facilities did not fare anywhere near as well as the passenger facilities during the late 20th century; changes to the way that freight was carried combined with industrial decline decimated the hundreds of goods and coal yards and the rail-served industrial sites in London.

I commenced this project in 2004 after searching for a publication like this one to no avail; one that provided a diagrammatic representation of London's railway history. What began as a light-hearted hobby has since become a serious project, which has taken up many hours' work through map-drawing, indexing and research. Despite many hours research I am the first to acknowledge that there are quite probably many omissions, particularly regarding freight facilities on which available information is often scant. I have endeavoured to provide a hopefully near-complete history of London's passenger railways, although I have chosen to omit a handful of temporary, excursion and unadvertised stations which have had little bearing on London's railway history or for which I have been unable to find any significant information.

I very much regard this as a work in progress, and I would be delighted to hear from anyone who can provide me with further information. There are question marks against some dates in the index (all freight facilities), and I would be very happy to receive locations and relevant dates for other goods, freight and industrial facilities that have been omitted, although I have to be mindful in more complex areas not to overload the map with detail to the extent that it becomes a distraction.

Please feel free to e-mail me with any further information at: atlasupdate@blueyonder.co.uk

Regarding future developments, I have included those under construction such as the Channel Tunnel Rail Link, DLR extension to Woolwich Arsenal and Heathrow Terminal 5, as well as one certain to come to fruition (Phase 1 of the East London Line Extension), But I have omitted Crossrail from this edition bearing in mind that project's track record.

I have chosen to omit the Post Office Railway and London's first piece of railway infrastructure, the Surrey Iron Railway, as I do not feel them to fit into the concept of railways in the modern sense.

Thanks / Dedications

I would firstly like to thank Gary James for his never-ending patience whilst I worked on this project, not least because it was usually on his computer! Secondly, a very warm thank-you to James Tinkler of Australia who provided me with a goldmine of information via email, his input was invaluable.

For Oscar & Jemime Thiagaraj and Max Brown.

In loving memory of Ruth Brown 1945-1989.

Joe Brown, London 2005

First published 2006
Reprinted 2006 (twice)
This impression 2007

ISBN (10) 0 7110 3137 1
ISBN (13) 978 0 7110 3137 1

© Joe Brown 2006

Published by Ian Allan Publishing

an imprint of Ian Allan Publishing Ltd, Hersham, Surrey KT12 4RG

Printed in England by Ian Allan Printing Ltd, Hersham, Surrey KT12 4RG

Code: 0611/3

Front cover:
SET Class 375/6 No 375606, Southern Class 377/6 and Southern Class 377/1 all head down Grosvenor Bank for London Victoria on 9 May 2005, while Class 460 No 4600(02) departs as the 13.15 for Gatwick Airport.
Brian Morrison

Visit the Ian Allan Publishing website at www.ianallanpublishing.com

Abbreviations

BAK	Bakerloo Line	Abbreviated form of BS&WR
BER	Blackwall Extension Railway	Absorbed by GER 1866
BR	British Rail	Formed 1948 (Nationalisation of all Main Line companies), became Railtrack 1994
BS&WR	Baker Street & Waterloo Railway	Part of UERL from opening, name later shortened to Bakerloo Line
CCE&HR	Charing Cross, Euston & Hampstead Railway	Part of UERL from opening, Merged with C&SLR to form Northern Line 1926 *
CEN	Central Line	Originally Central London Railway
CLR	Central London Railway	Absorbed by LT 1933 (Became Central Line)
C&SLR	City & South London Railway	Absorbed by UERL 1913, merged with CCE&HR to form Northern Line 1926 *
CTL	Croydon Tramlink	Opened 2000
DIS	District Line	Originally Metropolitan District Railway, absorbed by UERL 1902
DLR	Docklands Light Railway	Opened 1987
ECR	Eastern Counties Railway	Absorbed by Great Eastern Railway 1862
ELL	East London Line	Originally "Metropolitan Line-East London Section", name began being used in 1980s
ELR	East London Railway	Absorbed by LT 1948 (Became Metropolitan Line-East London Section)
ES	Eurostar	In operation since 1994
EWS	English, Welsh & Scottish Railway	Freight operator
GCR	Great Central Railway	Absorbed by LNER 1923
GER	Great Eastern Railway	Absorbed by LNER 1923
GN&CR	Great Northern & City Railway	Absorbed by Metropolitan railway 1913
GNP&BR	Great Northern, Piccadilly & Brompton Railway	Part of UERL from opening, name later shortened to Piccadilly Line
GNR	Great Northern Railway	Absorbed by LNER 1923
GWR	Great Western Railway	Became part of BR 1948
H&C	Hammersmith & City Line	Created 1990 (formerly part of Metropolitan Line)
HEX	Heathrow Express	Opened 1998, British Airports Authority and Railtrack joint venture
HJR	Hampstead Junction Railway	Absorbed by LNWR 1867
JUB	Jubilee Line	Opened 1979
L&B	London & Birmingham Railway	Became LNWR 1846
L&BR	London & Brighton Railway	Became LBSCR 1846
LBR	London & Blackwall Railway	Absorbed by GER 1866
LBSCR	London, Brighton & South Coast Railway	Formed 1846 from merging L&BR with LCR. Became part of SR 1923
LCC	London County Council	Operated Becontree Estate Railway
LCDR	London, Chatham & Dover Railway	Became SECR 1899
LCR	London & Croydon Railway	Became LBSCR 1846
L&CR	London & Continental Railway	Consortium building Channel Tunnel Rail Link
LGR	London & Greenwich Railway	Absorbed by SER 1845
LMS	London, Midland & Scottish Railway	Formed 1923 from MID, LNWR, N&SWJR, T&FG & LTSR. Became part of BR 1948
LNER	London & North-Eastern Railway	Formed 1923 from GNR, GER & GCR. Became Part of BR 1948
LNWR	London & North-Western Railway	Formed 1846, absorbed by LMS 1923.
LSWR	London & South-Western Railway	Absorbed by SR 1923
LT	London Transport	Formed 1933 **
LTSR	London, Tilbury & Southend Railway	Absorbed by LMS 1923
LUL	London Underground Limited	Formed 1985 from LT
MDR	Metropolitan District Railway	Absorbed by UERL 1902
MET	Metropolitan Railway	Absorbed by LT 1933
MID	Midland Railway	Absorbed by LMS 1923
NLR	North London Railway ***	Absorbed by LNWR 1922
NOR	Northern Line	Formed 1926 by amalgamating C&SLR and CCE&HR *
NR	Network Rail	Formed 2002 from Railtrack
N&SWJR	North & South-Western Junction Railway	Absorbed by LMS 1923
PIC	Piccadilly Line	Abbreviated form of GNP&BR
PLA	Port of London Authority	Operated some railways in London and West India Docks
PRIV	Private	Private sidings / Industrial Railways etc
RT	Railtrack	Formed 1994 from British Rail, became Network Rail 2002
SECR	South-Eastern & Chatham Railway	Formed 1899 from merging LCDR with SER. Became part of SR 1923
SER	South-Eastern Railway	Became SECR 1899. Includes Bexley Heath Railway & Mid Kent Railway
SR	Southern Railway	Formed 1923 from merging LSWR, SECR & LBSCR. Became part of BR 1948
T&FG	Tottenham & Forest Gate Railway	Absorbed by LMS 1923
T&HJ	Tottenham & Hampstead Junction Railway	Became LNER & LMS joint after 1923, BR after 1948
UERL	Underground Electric Railways of London	Formed 1902 from MDR and the then unopened CCE&HR, GNP&BR and BS&WR
VIC	Victoria Line	Opened 1968
W&C	Waterloo & City Line	Owned & operated by LSWR (later SR then BR), transferred to LUL in 1994
WCR	Wimbledon & Croydon Railway	Absorbed by LBSCR 1866
WLER	West London Extension Railway	GWR, LNWR, LSWR & LBSCR Joint. Became LMS, GWR & SR joint after 1923
WLR	West London Railway	Became LMS & GWR joint after 1923

* When the C&SLR and CCE&HR were merged in 1926, "Morden - Edgware Line" was used, "Northern Line" was not coined until 1937.

** London Passenger Transport Board formed 1933, became London Transport Executive 1948, then London Transport Board 1963, then London Regional Transport 1984. For simplicity all are referred to as 'LT'.

*** North London Railway originally "East & West India Docks & Birmingham Junction Railway", renamed 1853.

KEY TO MAP PAGES

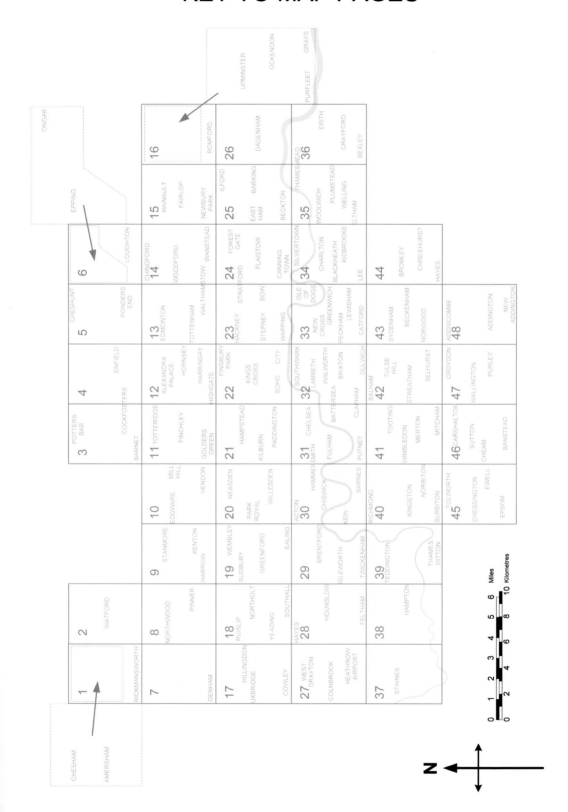

KEY TO MAP SYMBOLS

DATES INDICATE YEAR OF OPENING FOR OPEN STATIONS / LINES AND YEARS OF OPENING AND CLOSING FOR CLOSED STATIONS / LINES.
IF THE YEARS ARE FOLLOWED BY YEARS IN ITALICS, THIS INDICATES THE STATION / LINE WAS OPEN FOR FREIGHT TRAFFIC BEFORE AND /
OR AFTER IT WAS OPEN FOR PASSENGER TRAFFIC. GOODS STATIONS OPENED IN SAME YEAR AS ASSOCIATED PASSENGER STATIONS
UNLESS OTHERWISE STATED, YEAR QUOTED IS YEAR OF CLOSURE.

STATION SYMBOLS:

		GOODS / FREIGHT FACILITY (OPEN) (1900)		GOODS / FREIGHT FACILITY (CLOSED) (1900-2006)			
STATION (OPEN) (1900)	INTERCHANGE STATION (OPEN) (1900)	STATION (CLOSED) (1900-2006)	INTERCHANGE STATION (CLOSED) (1900-2006)	PROJECTED STATION (2010)	TRAINSHED (TERMINUS, DEPOT, GOODS SHED etc) (OPEN) (1900)	TRAINSHED (TERMINUS, DEPOT, GOODS SHED etc) (CLOSED) (1900-2006)

OPEN PLATFORM (INSET AND LARGE-SCALE MAPS ONLY)

CLOSED PLATFORM (INSET AND LARGE-SCALE MAPS ONLY)

LINE SYMBOLS:

1900   PAIR OF TRACKS, OPEN OR UNDER CONSTRUCTION, WITH YEAR OF OPENING

1900   SINGLE TRACK, OPEN OR UNDER CONSTRUCTION, WITH YEAR OF OPENING

1900-2006   PAIR OF TRACKS, CLOSED, WITH YEAR OF OPENING FOLLOWED BY YEAR OF CLOSING

1900-2006   SINGLE TRACK, CLOSED, WITH YEAR OF OPENING FOLLOWED BY YEAR OF CLOSING

1900   RAILWAY WHERE CONSTRUCTION COMMENCED BUT WAS ABANDONED, WITH YEAR OF ABANDONMENT

2010   PROJECTED RAILWAY WITH ANTICIPATED YEAR OF OPENING

Junction (In Use)	Junction (Dismantled)	Tunnel (Shallow Level)	Tunnel (Bored Deep Level)

NETWORK RAIL (FORMERLY RAILTRACK, BRITISH RAIL, AND PRE-NATIONALISATION MAINLINE COMPANIES)

NETWORK RAIL LINE SERVED BY LUL DISTRICT LINE TRAINS

NETWORK RAIL LINE SERVED BY LUL BAKERLOO LINE TRAINS

NETWORK RAIL LINE FORMERLY SERVED BY LUL BAKERLOO LINE TRAINS

NETWORK RAIL LINE FORMERLY OWNED AND SERVED BY LUL METROPOLITAN LINE

LUL DISTRICT LINE

LUL DISTRICT LINE SERVED BY PICCADILLY LINE TRAINS

LUL DISTRICT LINE SERVED BY CIRCLE LINE TRAINS

LUL DISTRICT LINE SERVED BY HAMMERSMITH & CITY LINE TRAINS

LUL METROPOLITAN LINE

LUL METROPOLITAN LINE SERVED BY HAMMERSMITH & CITY AND CIRCLE LINE TRAINS

LUL METROPOLITAN LINE SERVED BY MAINLINE TRAINS

LUL METROPOLITAN LINE SERVED BY PICCADILLY LINE TRAINS

LUL CIRCLE LINE

LUL HAMMERSMITH & CITY LINE

LUL HAMMERSMITH & CITY LINE SERVED BY CIRCLE LINE TRAINS

LUL EAST LONDON LINE

LUL PICCADILLY LINE

LUL VICTORIA LINE

LUL NORTHERN LINE

LUL BAKERLOO LINE

LUL JUBILEE LINE

LUL CENTRAL LINE

DOCKLANDS LIGHT RAILWAY (DLR)

ABANDONED DLR ON ABANDONED MAINLINE TRACK BED

LUL WATERLOO & CITY LINE

CROYDON TRAMLINK

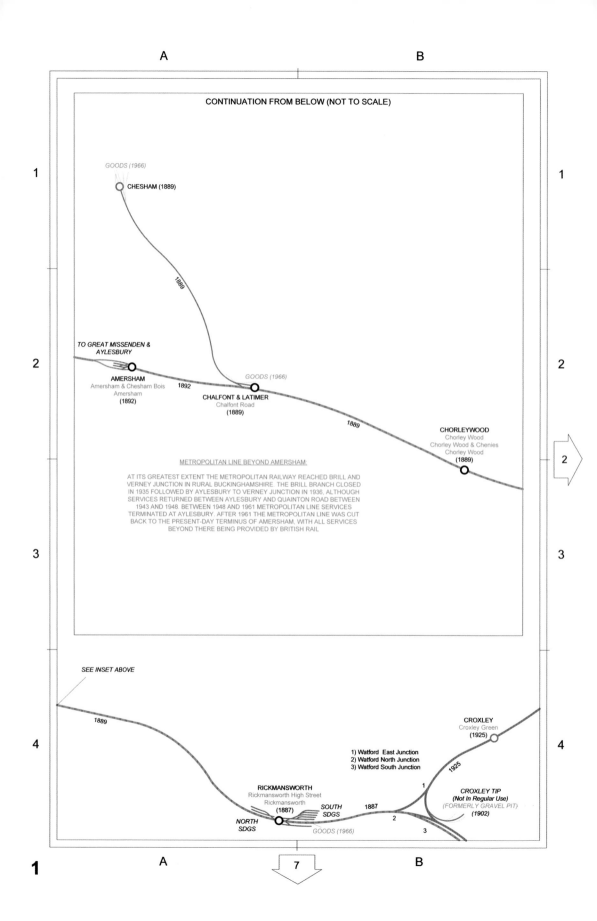

A   B

1

CONTINUATION FROM BELOW (NOT TO SCALE)

GOODS *(1966)*

○ CHESHAM (1889)

1889

TO GREAT MISSENDEN &
AYLESBURY

○
AMERSHAM
Amersham & Chesham Bois
Amersham
(1892)

1892

GOODS *(1966)*

○
CHALFONT & LATIMER
Chalfont Road
(1889)

1889

CHORLEYWOOD
Chorley Wood
Chorley Wood & Chenies
Chorley Wood
(1889)
○

METROPOLITAN LINE BEYOND AMERSHAM:

AT ITS GREATEST EXTENT THE METROPOLITAN RAILWAY REACHED BRILL AND
VERNEY JUNCTION IN RURAL BUCKINGHAMSHIRE. THE BRILL BRANCH CLOSED
IN 1935 FOLLOWED BY AYLESBURY TO VERNEY JUNCTION IN 1936, ALTHOUGH
SERVICES RETURNED BETWEEN AYLESBURY AND QUAINTON ROAD BETWEEN
1943 AND 1948. BETWEEN 1948 AND 1961 METROPOLITAN LINE SERVICES
TERMINATED AT AYLESBURY. AFTER 1961 THE METROPOLITAN LINE WAS CUT
BACK TO THE PRESENT-DAY TERMINUS OF AMERSHAM, WITH ALL SERVICES
BEYOND THERE BEING PROVIDED BY BRITISH RAIL

SEE INSET ABOVE

1889

CROXLEY
Croxley Green
(1925)
○

1) Watford East Junction
2) Watford North Junction
3) Watford South Junction

1925

1

RICKMANSWORTH
Rickmansworth High Street
Rickmansworth
(1887)
○

*SOUTH
SDGS*

1887

CROXLEY TIP
(Not In Regular Use)
(FORMERLY GRAVEL PIT)
(1902)

2

*NORTH
SDGS*

GOODS *(1966)*

3

A   B

1

7

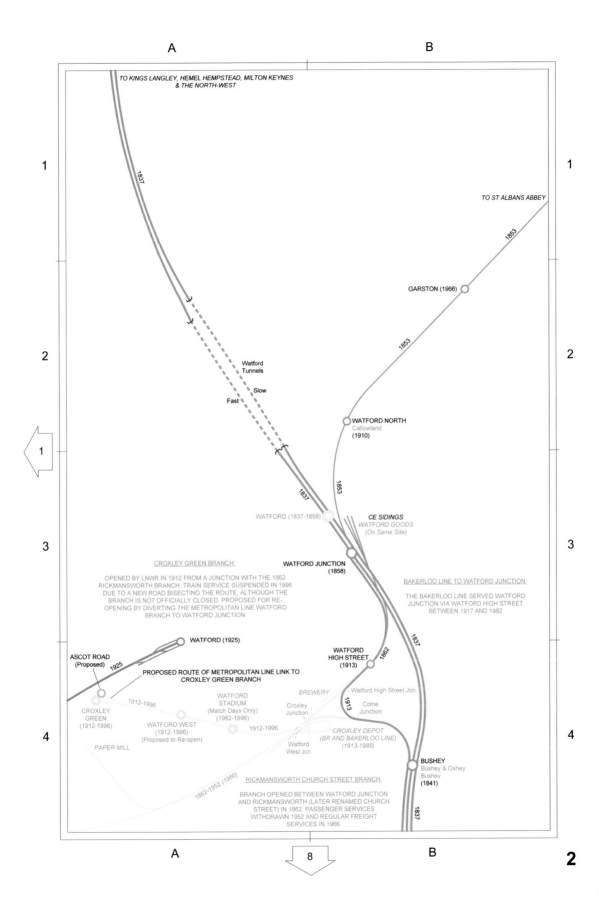

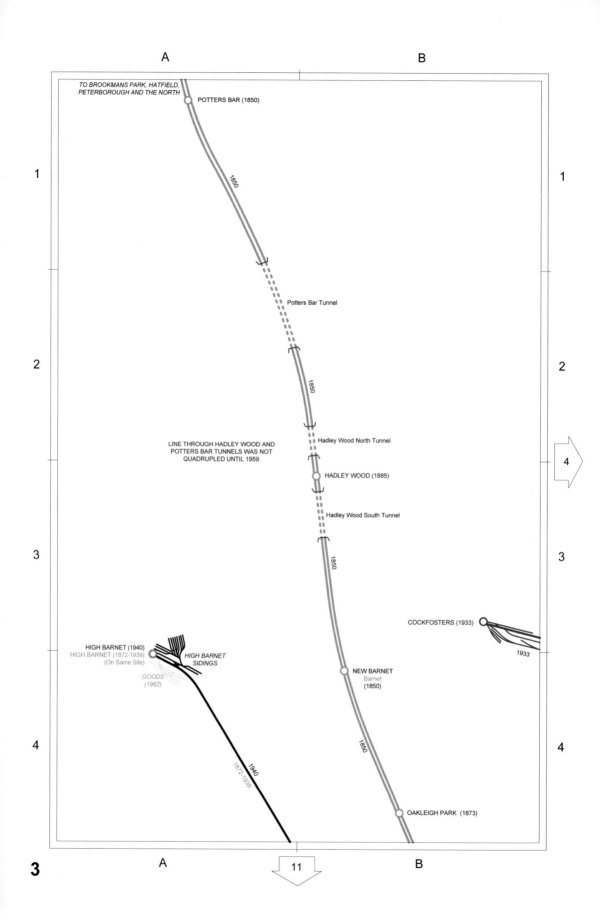

A

B

TO BROOKMANS PARK, HATFIELD,
PETERBOROUGH AND THE NORTH

POTTERS BAR (1850)

1850

1

Potters Bar Tunnel

2

LINE THROUGH HADLEY WOOD AND
POTTERS BAR TUNNELS WAS NOT
QUADRUPLED UNTIL 1959

1850

Hadley Wood North Tunnel

HADLEY WOOD (1885)

Hadley Wood South Tunnel

3

1850

COCKFOSTERS (1933)

HIGH BARNET (1940)
HIGH BARNET (1872-1939)
(On Same Site)

HIGH BARNET
SIDINGS

GOODS
(1962)

1933

NEW BARNET
Barnet
(1850)

1940

1872-1939

1850

4

OAKLEIGH PARK (1873)

A

B

3

11

4

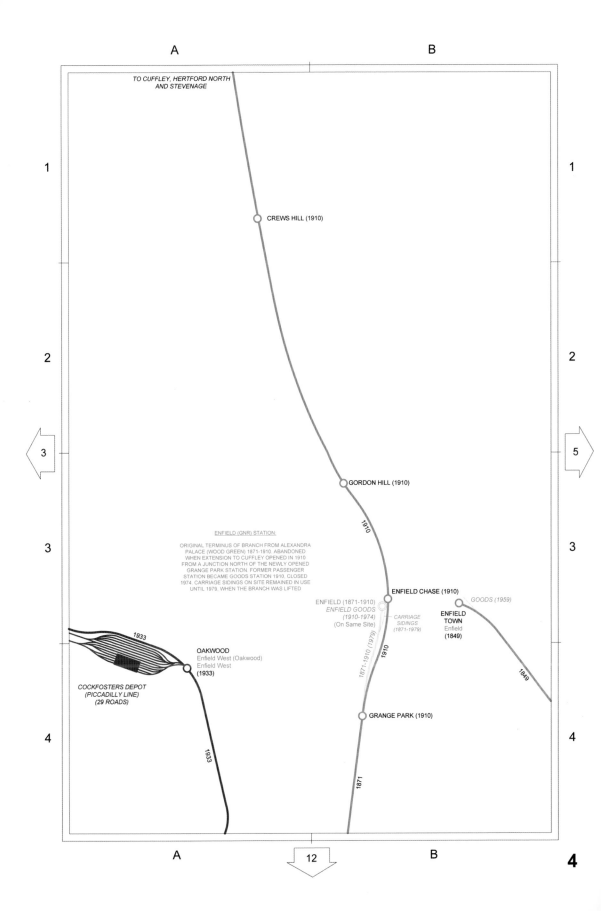

A   B

1   1

TO CUFFLEY, HERTFORD NORTH AND STEVENAGE

○ CREWS HILL (1910)

2   2

◁ 3   5 ▷

○ GORDON HILL (1910)

1910

3   3

ENFIELD (GNR) STATION:

ORIGINAL TERMINUS OF BRANCH FROM ALEXANDRA PALACE (WOOD GREEN) 1871-1910. ABANDONED WHEN EXTENSION TO CUFFLEY OPENED IN 1910 FROM A JUNCTION NORTH OF THE NEWLY OPENED GRANGE PARK STATION. FORMER PASSENGER STATION BECAME GOODS STATION 1910, CLOSED 1974. CARRIAGE SIDINGS ON SITE REMAINED IN USE UNTIL 1979, WHEN THE BRANCH WAS LIFTED

ENFIELD CHASE (1910)

GOODS (1959)

ENFIELD (1871-1910)
*ENFIELD GOODS
(1910-1974)*
(On Same Site)

*CARRIAGE
SIDINGS
(1871-1979)*

**ENFIELD
TOWN**
Enfield
(1849)

1871-1910 (1979)

1910

OAKWOOD
Enfield West (Oakwood)
Enfield West
(1933)

1933

CARRIAGE

1849

*COCKFOSTERS DEPOT
(PICCADILLY LINE)
(29 ROADS)*

○ GRANGE PARK (1910)

1933

1871

4   4

A   B

▽ 12

4

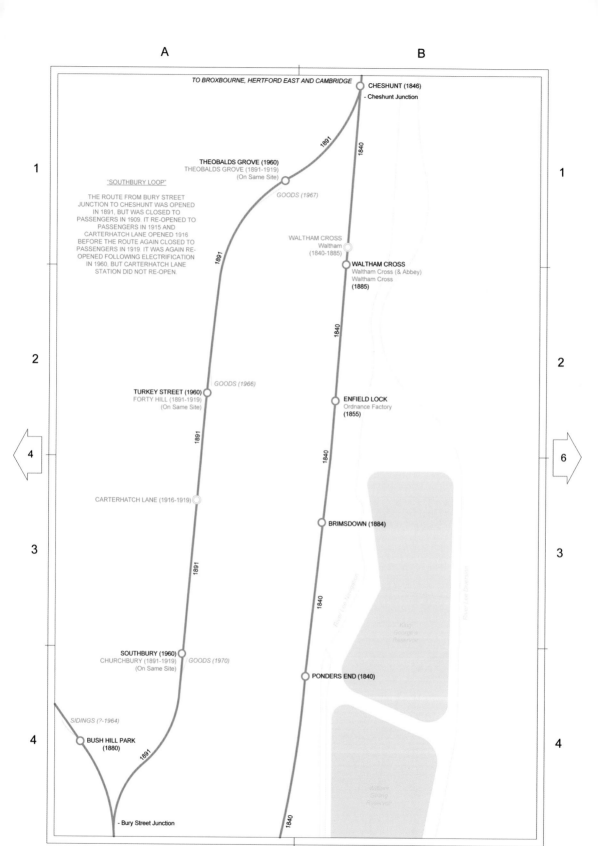

1   1

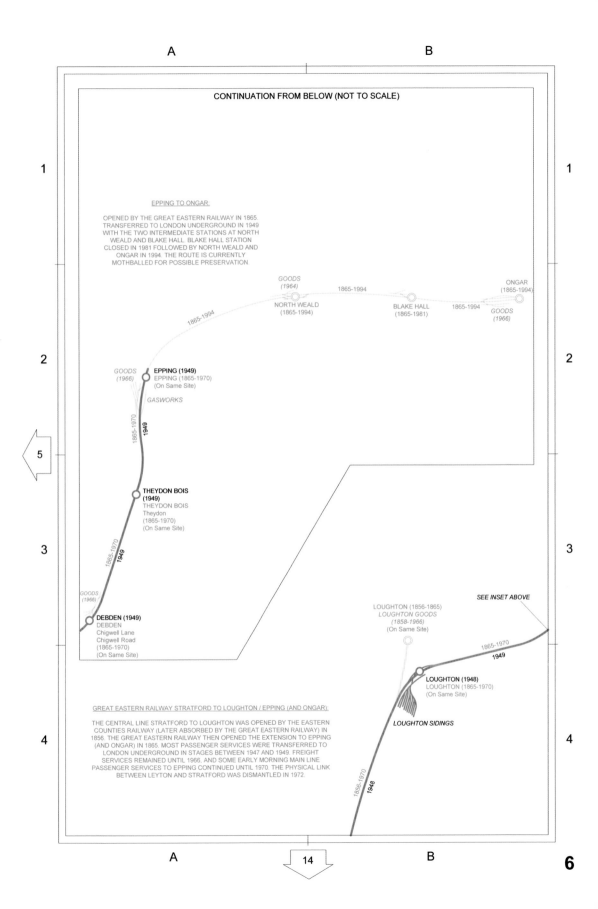

CONTINUATION FROM BELOW (NOT TO SCALE)

EPPING TO ONGAR:

OPENED BY THE GREAT EASTERN RAILWAY IN 1865.
TRANSFERRED TO LONDON UNDERGROUND IN 1949
WITH THE TWO INTERMEDIATE STATIONS AT NORTH
WEALD AND BLAKE HALL. BLAKE HALL STATION
CLOSED IN 1981 FOLLOWED BY NORTH WEALD AND
ONGAR IN 1994. THE ROUTE IS CURRENTLY
MOTHBALLED FOR POSSIBLE PRESERVATION.

GOODS
(1964)

1865-1994

ONGAR
(1865-1994)

NORTH WEALD
(1865-1994)

BLAKE HALL
(1865-1981)

1865-1994

GOODS
(1966)

GOODS
(1966)

EPPING (1949)
EPPING (1865-1970)
(On Same Site)

GASWORKS

1865-1970

1949

2   2

5

**THEYDON BOIS
(1949)**
THEYDON BOIS
Theydon
(1865-1970)
(On Same Site)

1865-1970

1949

SEE INSET ABOVE

LOUGHTON (1856-1865)
LOUGHTON GOODS
(1858-1966)
(On Same Site)

1865-1970

1949

3   3

GOODS
(1966)

DEBDEN (1949)
DEBDEN
Chigwell Lane
Chigwell Road
(1865-1970)
(On Same Site)

LOUGHTON (1948)
LOUGHTON (1865-1970)
(On Same Site)

LOUGHTON SIDINGS

GREAT EASTERN RAILWAY STRATFORD TO LOUGHTON / EPPING (AND ONGAR):

THE CENTRAL LINE STRATFORD TO LOUGHTON WAS OPENED BY THE EASTERN
COUNTIES RAILWAY (LATER ABSORBED BY THE GREAT EASTERN RAILWAY) IN
1856. THE GREAT EASTERN RAILWAY THEN OPENED THE EXTENSION TO EPPING
(AND ONGAR) IN 1865. MOST PASSENGER SERVICES WERE TRANSFERRED TO
LONDON UNDERGROUND IN STAGES BETWEEN 1947 AND 1949. FREIGHT
SERVICES REMAINED UNTIL 1966, AND SOME EARLY MORNING MAIN LINE
PASSENGER SERVICES TO EPPING CONTINUED UNTIL 1970. THE PHYSICAL LINK
BETWEEN LEYTON AND STRATFORD WAS DISMANTLED IN 1972.

1856-1970

1948

4   4

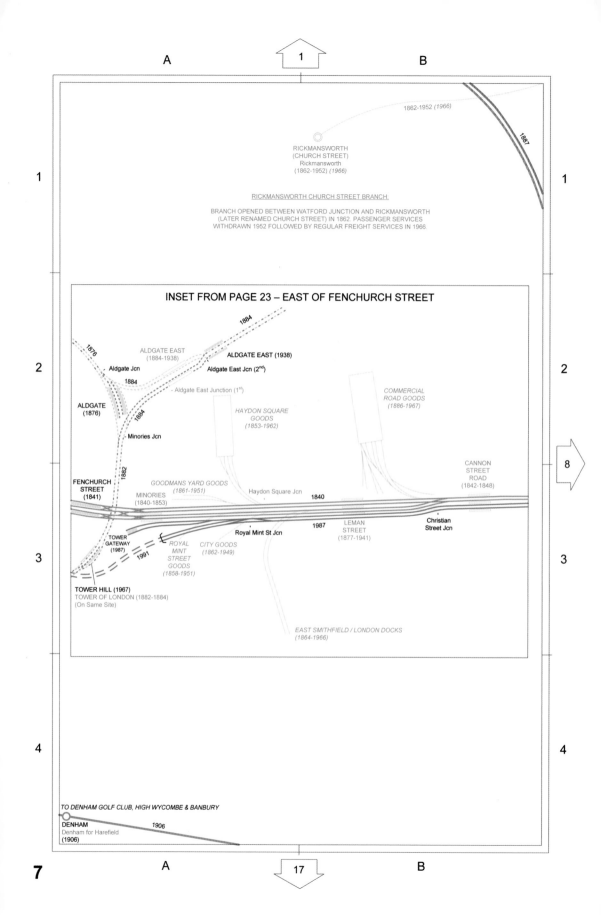

1862-1952 *(1966)*

1887

RICKMANSWORTH
(CHURCH STREET)
Rickmansworth
(1862-1952) *(1966)*

<u>RICKMANSWORTH CHURCH STREET BRANCH:</u>

BRANCH OPENED BETWEEN WATFORD JUNCTION AND RICKMANSWORTH
(LATER RENAMED CHURCH STREET) IN 1862. PASSENGER SERVICES
WITHDRAWN 1952 FOLLOWED BY REGULAR FREIGHT SERVICES IN 1966.

INSET FROM PAGE 23 – EAST OF FENCHURCH STREET

1884

1876

ALDGATE EAST
(1884-1938)   **ALDGATE EAST (1938)**

Aldgate Jcn

Aldgate East Jcn (2nd)

1884

- Aldgate East Junction (1st)

*COMMERCIAL
ROAD GOODS
(1886-1967)*

**ALDGATE
(1876)**

1884

*HAYDON SQUARE
GOODS
(1853-1962)*

Minories Jcn

1882

**CANNON
STREET
ROAD
(1842-1848)**

**FENCHURCH
STREET
(1841)**

MINORIES
(1840-1853)

*GOODMANS YARD GOODS
(1861-1951)*

Haydon Square Jcn   1840

→ 8

**TOWER
GATEWAY
(1987)**

1991

*ROYAL
MINT
STREET
GOODS
(1858-1951)*

Royal Mint St Jcn

*CITY GOODS
(1862-1949)*

1987

**LEMAN
STREET
(1877-1941)**

Christian
Street Jcn

TOWER HILL (1967)
TOWER OF LONDON (1882-1884)
(On Same Site)

*EAST SMITHFIELD / LONDON DOCKS
(1864-1966)*

TO DENHAM GOLF CLUB, HIGH WYCOMBE & BANBURY

○ **DENHAM**
Denham for Harefield
(1906)   1906

7

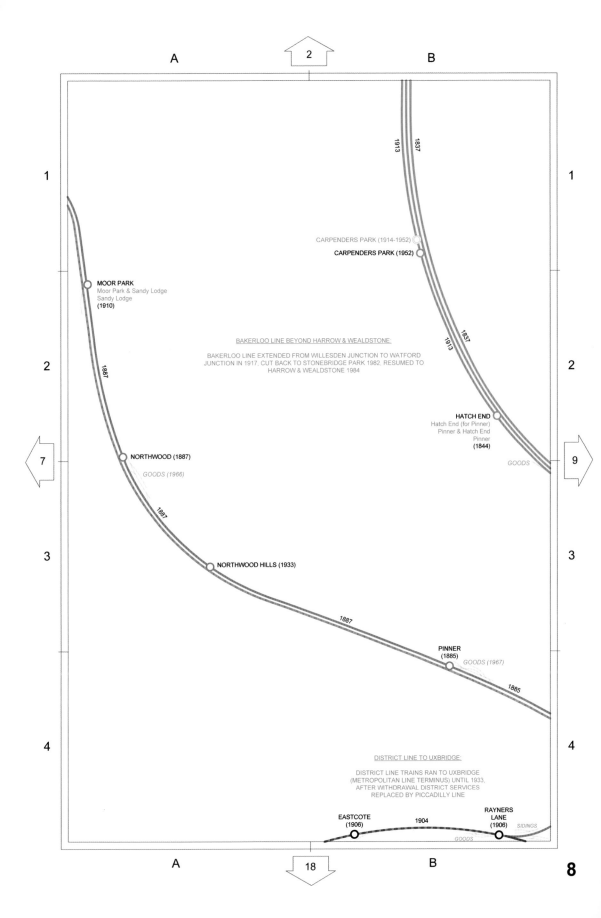

1   1

1913   1837

CARPENDERS PARK (1914-1952)
CARPENDERS PARK (1952)

MOOR PARK
Moor Park & Sandy Lodge
Sandy Lodge
(1910)

BAKERLOO LINE BEYOND HARROW & WEALDSTONE:

BAKERLOO LINE EXTENDED FROM WILLESDEN JUNCTION TO WATFORD
JUNCTION IN 1917, CUT BACK TO STONEBRIDGE PARK 1982, RESUMED TO
HARROW & WEALDSTONE 1984

1837

1913

2   2

1887

HATCH END
Hatch End (for Pinner)
Pinner & Hatch End
Pinner
(1844)

GOODS

7   **NORTHWOOD (1887)**   9

GOODS (1966)

1887

3   **NORTHWOOD HILLS (1933)**   3

1887

PINNER
(1885)   *GOODS (1967)*

1885

4   4

DISTRICT LINE TO UXBRIDGE:

DISTRICT LINE TRAINS RAN TO UXBRIDGE
(METROPOLITAN LINE TERMINUS) UNTIL 1933,
AFTER WITHDRAWAL DISTRICT SERVICES
REPLACED BY PICCADILLY LINE

EASTCOTE   **RAYNERS**
(1906)   1904   **LANE**
                                          (1906)   *SIDINGS*

                                                   GOODS

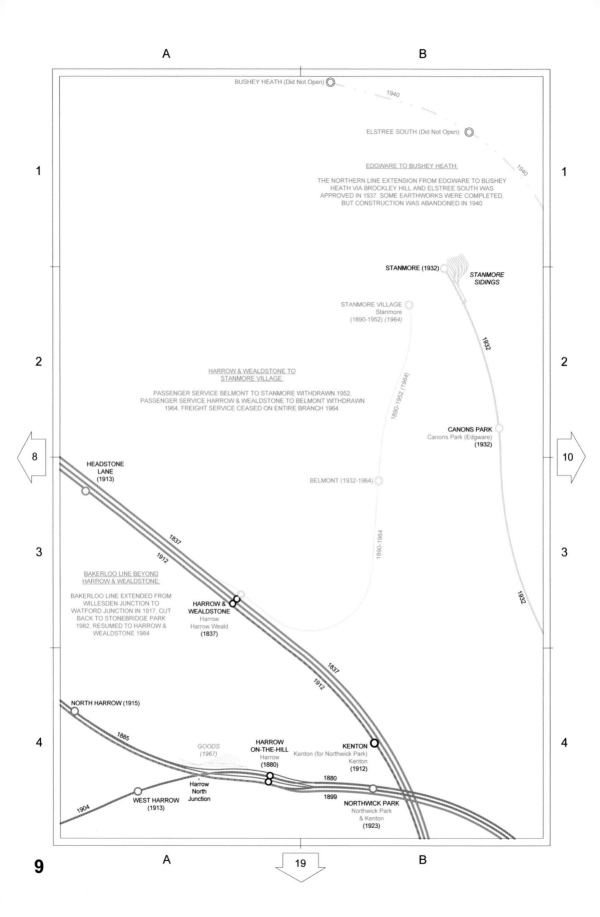

BUSHEY HEATH (Did Not Open)

1940

ELSTREE SOUTH (Did Not Open)

1940

EDGWARE TO BUSHEY HEATH:

THE NORTHERN LINE EXTENSION FROM EDGWARE TO BUSHEY HEATH VIA BROCKLEY HILL AND ELSTREE SOUTH WAS APPROVED IN 1937. SOME EARTHWORKS WERE COMPLETED, BUT CONSTRUCTION WAS ABANDONED IN 1940

STANMORE (1932)

STANMORE SIDINGS

STANMORE VILLAGE
Stanmore
(1890-1952) *(1964)*

1932

HARROW & WEALDSTONE TO STANMORE VILLAGE:

PASSENGER SERVICE BELMONT TO STANMORE WITHDRAWN 1952. PASSENGER SERVICE HARROW & WEALDSTONE TO BELMONT WITHDRAWN 1964. FREIGHT SERVICE CEASED ON ENTIRE BRANCH 1964.

1890-1952 *(1964)*

CANONS PARK
Canons Park (Edgware)
(1932)

HEADSTONE
LANE
(1913)

BELMONT (1932-1964)

8

10

1837

1912

1890-1964

1932

BAKERLOO LINE BEYOND HARROW & WEALDSTONE:

BAKERLOO LINE EXTENDED FROM WILLESDEN JUNCTION TO WATFORD JUNCTION IN 1917, CUT BACK TO STONEBRIDGE PARK 1982, RESUMED TO HARROW & WEALDSTONE 1984

HARROW &
WEALDSTONE
Harrow
Harrow Weald
(1837)

1837

1912

NORTH HARROW (1915)

1885

*GOODS
(1967)*

HARROW
ON-THE-HILL
Harrow
(1880)

KENTON
Kenton (for Northwick Park)
Kenton
(1912)

Harrow
North
Junction

1880

1904

WEST HARROW
(1913)

1899

NORTHWICK PARK
Northwick Park
& Kenton
(1923)

19

9

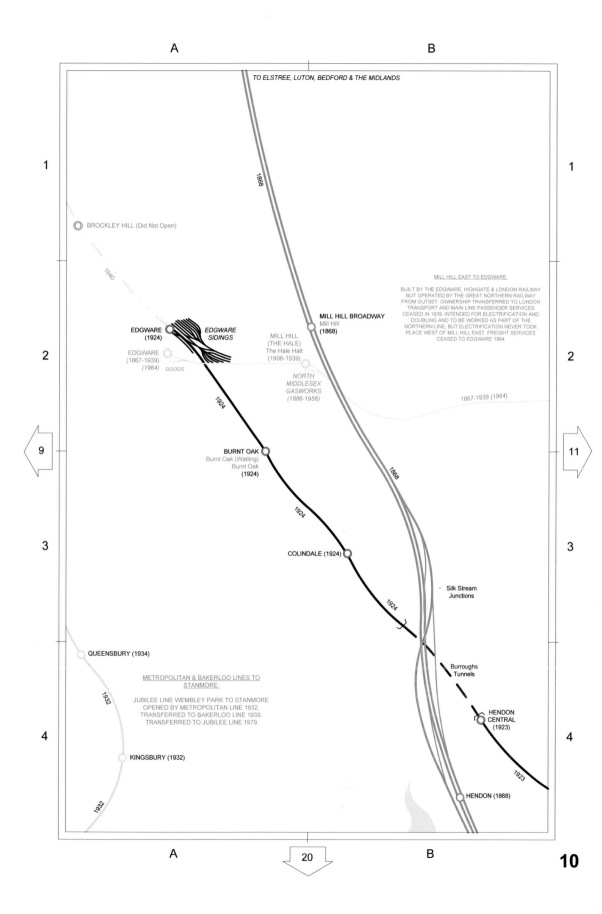

TO ELSTREE, LUTON, BEDFORD & THE MIDLANDS

1868

1

BROCKLEY HILL (Did Not Open)

1940

MILL HILL EAST TO EDGWARE:

BUILT BY THE EDGWARE, HIGHGATE & LONDON RAILWAY
BUT OPERATED BY THE GREAT NORTHERN RAILWAY
FROM OUTSET. OWNERSHIP TRANSFERRED TO LONDON
TRANSPORT AND MAIN LINE PASSENGER SERVICES
CEASED IN 1939. INTENDED FOR ELECTRIFICATION AND
DOUBLING AND TO BE WORKED AS PART OF THE
NORTHERN LINE, BUT ELECTRIFICATION NEVER TOOK
PLACE WEST OF MILL HILL EAST. FREIGHT SERVICES
CEASED TO EDGWARE 1964

MILL HILL BROADWAY
Mill Hill
(1868)

EDGWARE
(1924)

*EDGWARE
SIDINGS*

EDGWARE
(1867-1939)
(1964)   *GOODS*

MILL HILL
(THE HALE)
The Hale Halt
(1906-1939)

*NORTH
MIDDLESEX
GASWORKS
(1886-1956)*

2

1867-1939 *(1964)*

1924

9

11

BURNT OAK
Burnt Oak (Watling)
Burnt Oak
(1924)

1868

1924

3

COLINDALE (1924)

1924

- Silk Stream
  Junctions

QUEENSBURY (1934)

METROPOLITAN & BAKERLOO LINES TO
STANMORE:

JUBILEE LINE WEMBLEY PARK TO STANMORE
OPENED BY METROPOLITAN LINE 1932,
TRANSFERRED TO BAKERLOO LINE 1939,
TRANSFERRED TO JUBILEE LINE 1979

Burroughs
Tunnels

1932

HENDON
CENTRAL
(1923)

4

KINGSBURY (1932)

1932

1923

HENDON (1868)

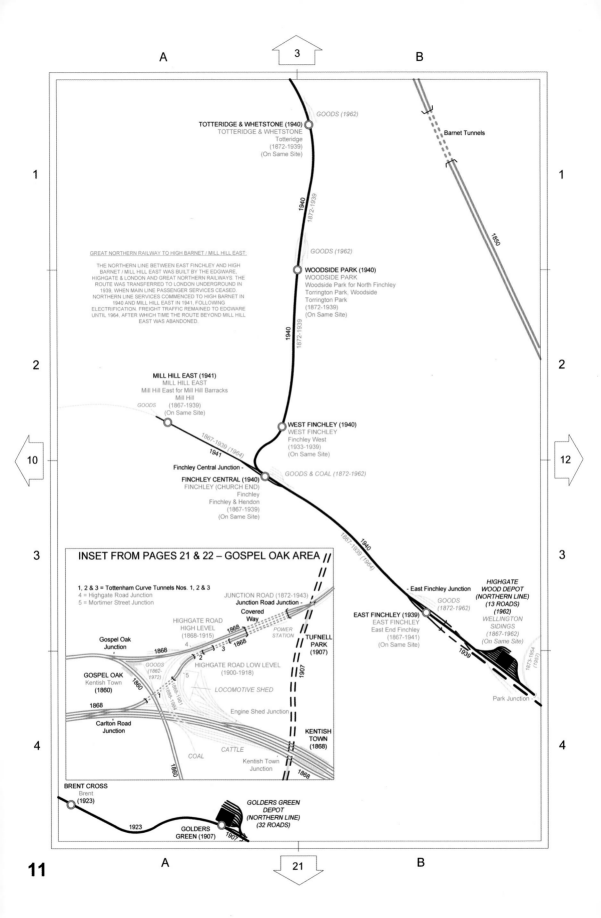

TOTTERIDGE & WHETSTONE (1940)
TOTTERIDGE & WHETSTONE
Totteridge
(1872-1939)
(On Same Site)

GOODS (1962)

Barnet Tunnels

1940

1872-1939

1850

1

GOODS (1962)

GREAT NORTHERN RAILWAY TO HIGH BARNET / MILL HILL EAST:

THE NORTHERN LINE BETWEEN EAST FINCHLEY AND HIGH
BARNET / MILL HILL EAST WAS BUILT BY THE EDGWARE,
HIGHGATE & LONDON AND GREAT NORTHERN RAILWAYS. THE
ROUTE WAS TRANSFERRED TO LONDON UNDERGROUND IN
1939, WHEN MAIN LINE PASSENGER SERVICES CEASED.
NORTHERN LINE SERVICES COMMENCED TO HIGH BARNET IN
1940 AND MILL HILL EAST IN 1941, FOLLOWING
ELECTRIFICATION. FREIGHT TRAFFIC REMAINED TO EDGWARE
UNTIL 1964, AFTER WHICH TIME THE ROUTE BEYOND MILL HILL
EAST WAS ABANDONED.

WOODSIDE PARK (1940)
WOODSIDE PARK
Woodside Park for North Finchley
Torrington Park, Woodside
Torrington Park
(1872-1939)
(On Same Site)

1940

1872-1939

MILL HILL EAST (1941)
MILL HILL EAST
Mill Hill East for Mill Hill Barracks
Mill Hill
GOODS
(1867-1939)
(On Same Site)

1867-1939 (1964)

1941

WEST FINCHLEY (1940)
WEST FINCHLEY
Finchley West
(1933-1939)
(On Same Site)

Finchley Central Junction -

FINCHLEY CENTRAL (1940)
FINCHLEY (CHURCH END)
Finchley
Finchley & Hendon
(1867-1939)
(On Same Site)

GOODS & COAL (1872-1962)

1867-1939 (1964)

1940

2

10

12

3

HIGHGATE
WOOD DEPOT
(NORTHERN LINE)
(13 ROADS)
(1962)
WELLINGTON
SIDINGS
(1867-1962)
(On Same Site)

- East Finchley Junction

EAST FINCHLEY (1939)
EAST FINCHLEY
East End Finchley
(1867-1941)
(On Same Site)

GOODS
(1872-1962)

1939

1873-1954
(1957)

Park Junction -

INSET FROM PAGES 21 & 22 – GOSPEL OAK AREA

1, 2 & 3 = Tottenham Curve Tunnels Nos. 1, 2 & 3
4 = Highgate Road Junction
5 = Mortimer Street Junction

JUNCTION ROAD (1872-1943)
Junction Road Junction -
Covered
Way

HIGHGATE
ROAD
HIGH LEVEL
(1868-1915)

1868

POWER
STATION

TUFNELL
PARK
(1907)

Gospel Oak
Junction

4

1868

3

1868

Gospel Oak
Junction

1868

2

HIGHGATE ROAD LOW LEVEL
(1900-1918)

1868-1981

GOSPEL OAK
Kentish Town
(1860)

GOODS
(1862-
1972)

1860

5

LOCOMOTIVE SHED

1907

1868-1964

1

1868

**Carlton Road
Junction**

Engine Shed Junction

**KENTISH
TOWN
(1868)**

1860

COAL

CATTLE

Kentish Town
Junction

1868

BRENT CROSS
Brent
(1923)

1923

**GOLDERS
GREEN (1907)**

1907

GOLDERS GREEN
DEPOT
(NORTHERN LINE)
(32 ROADS)

4

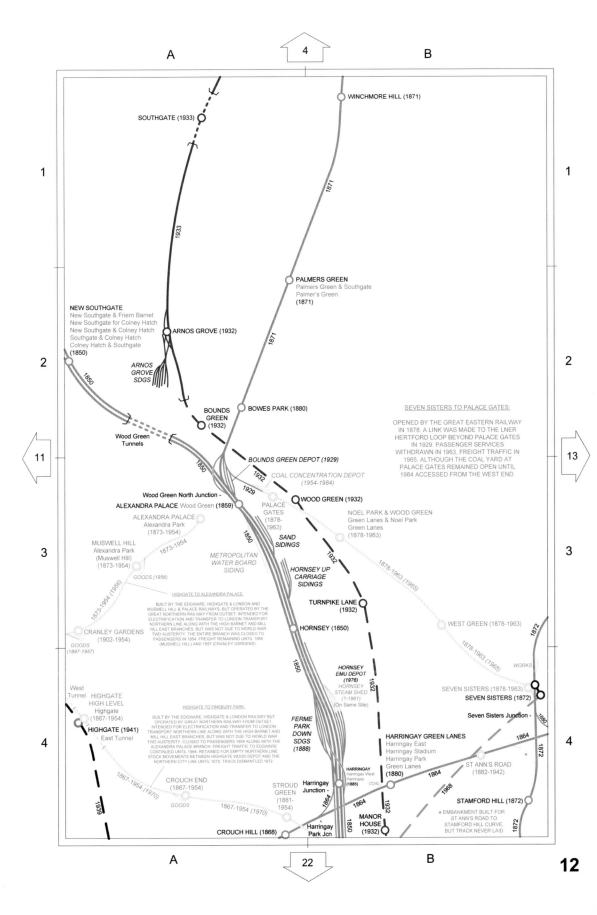

WINCHMORE HILL (1871)

SOUTHGATE (1933)

1933

PALMERS GREEN
Palmers Green & Southgate
Palmer's Green
(1871)

1871

NEW SOUTHGATE
New Southgate & Friern Barnet
New Southgate for Colney Hatch
New Southgate & Colney Hatch
Southgate & Colney Hatch
Colney Hatch & Southgate
(1850)

ARNOS GROVE (1932)

ARNOS GROVE SDGS

1871

1850

Wood Green Tunnels

BOWES PARK (1880)

BOUNDS GREEN (1932)

BOUNDS GREEN DEPOT (1929)

1850

1932

1929

COAL CONCENTRATION DEPOT (1954-1984)

WOOD GREEN (1932)

Wood Green North Junction -
ALEXANDRA PALACE Wood Green **(1859)**

PALACE GATES (1878-1963)

NOEL PARK & WOOD GREEN
Green Lanes & Noel Park
Green Lanes
(1878-1963)

ALEXANDRA PALACE
Alexandra Park
(1873-1954)

MUSWELL HILL
Alexandra Park
(Muswell Hill)
(1873-1954)

1873-1954

GOODS (1956)

1873-1954 (1956)

SAND SIDINGS

METROPOLITAN WATER BOARD SIDING

1850

HORNSEY UP CARRIAGE SIDINGS

1932

1878-1963 (1965)

TURNPIKE LANE (1932)

WEST GREEN (1878-1963)

1872

CRANLEY GARDENS
(1902-1954)

GOODS (1897-1957)

HORNSEY (1850)

HIGHGATE TO ALEXANDRA PALACE:
BUILT BY THE EDGWARE, HIGHGATE AND
MUSWELL HILL & PALACE RAILWAYS, BUT OPERATED BY THE
GREAT NORTHERN RAILWAY FROM OUTSET. INTENDED FOR
ELECTRIFICATION AND TRANSFER TO LONDON TRANSPORT
NORTHERN LINE ALONG WITH THE HIGH BARNET AND MILL
HILL EAST BRANCHES, BUT WAS NOT DUE TO WORLD WAR
TWO AUSTERITY. THE ENTIRE BRANCH WAS CLOSED TO
PASSENGERS IN 1954, FREIGHT REMAINING UNTIL 1956
(MUSWELL HILL) AND 1957 (CRANLEY GARDENS).

1878-1963 (1965)

WORKS

SEVEN SISTERS (1878-1963)
SEVEN SISTERS (1872)

Seven Sisters Junction -

1880

West Tunnel **HIGHGATE HIGH LEVEL**
Highgate
(1867-1954)

HIGHGATE (1941)
East Tunnel

HORNSEY EMU DEPOT (1976)
HORNSEY STEAM SHED (?-1961) (On Same Site)

1932

HIGHGATE TO FINSBURY PARK:
BUILT BY THE EDGWARE, HIGHGATE & LONDON RAILWAY BUT
OPERATED BY GREAT NORTHERN RAILWAY FROM OUTSET.
INTENDED FOR ELECTRIFICATION AND TRANSFER TO LONDON
TRANSPORT NORTHERN LINE ALONG WITH THE HIGH BARNET AND
MILL HILL EAST BRANCHES, BUT WAS NOT DUE TO WORLD WAR
TWO AUSTERITY. CLOSED TO PASSENGERS 1954 ALONG WITH THE
ALEXANDRA PALACE BRANCH. FREIGHT TRAFFIC TO EDGWARE
CONTINUED UNTIL 1964. RETAINED FOR EMPTY NORTHERN LINE
STOCK MOVEMENTS BETWEEN HIGHGATE WOOD DEPOT AND THE
NORTHERN CITY LINE UNTIL 1970. TRACK DISMANTLED 1972.

FERME PARK DOWN SDGS (1888)

HARRINGAY GREEN LANES
Harringay East
Harringay Stadium
Harringay Park
Green Lanes
(1880)

1864

ST ANN'S ROAD
(1882-1942)

1867-1954 (1970)

CROUCH END
(1867-1954)

GOODS

1867-1954 (1970)

STROUD GREEN
(1881-1954)

Harringay Junction -

HARRINGAY
Harringay West
Harringay
(1885)

COAL

1864

1968

STAMFORD HILL (1872)

1939

1864

1864

1850

1932

MANOR HOUSE (1932)

1872

* EMBANKMENT BUILT FOR
ST ANN'S ROAD TO
STAMFORD HILL CURVE,
BUT TRACK NEVER LAID

Harringay Park Jcn

CROUCH HILL (1868)

← 11 · 13 → · ← 1 · 2 · 3 · 4 →

SEVEN SISTERS TO PALACE GATES:

OPENED BY THE GREAT EASTERN RAILWAY
IN 1878. A LINK WAS MADE TO THE LNER
HERTFORD LOOP BEYOND PALACE GATES
IN 1929. PASSENGER SERVICES
WITHDRAWN IN 1963, FREIGHT TRAFFIC IN
1965, ALTHOUGH THE COAL YARD AT
PALACE GATES REMAINED OPEN UNTIL
1984 ACCESSED FROM THE WEST END

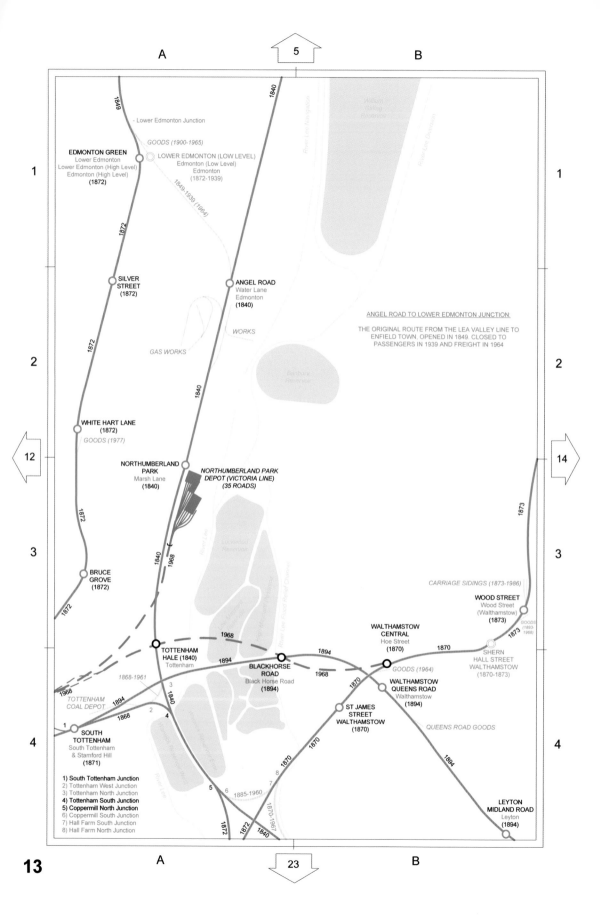

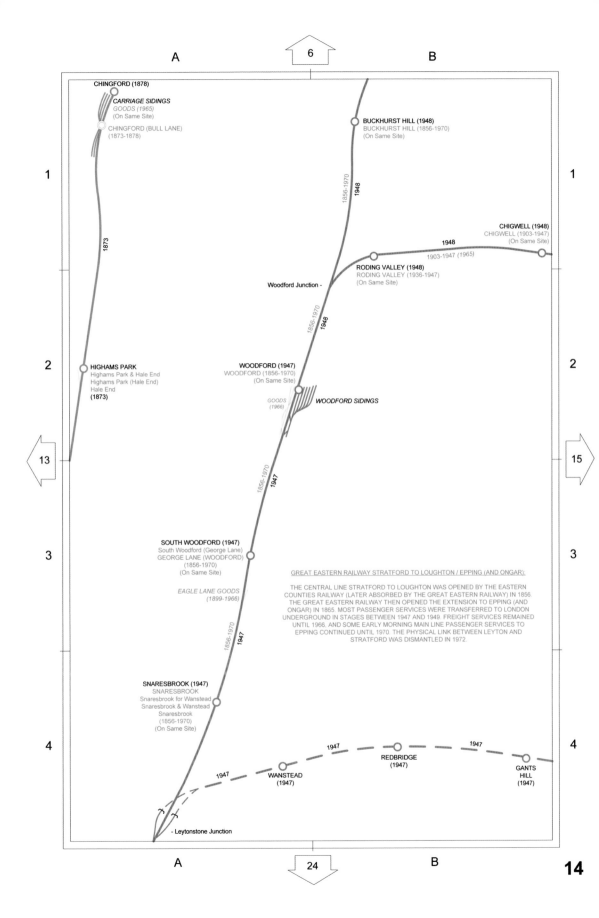

CHINGFORD (1878)
CARRIAGE SIDINGS
GOODS (1965)
(On Same Site)
CHINGFORD (BULL LANE)
(1873-1878)

BUCKHURST HILL (1948)
BUCKHURST HILL (1856-1970)
(On Same Site)

1856-1970

1948

1873

CHIGWELL (1948)
CHIGWELL (1903-1947)
(On Same Site)

1948

1903-1947 (1965)

RODING VALLEY (1948)
RODING VALLEY (1936-1947)
(On Same Site)

Woodford Junction -

1856-1970

1948

HIGHAMS PARK
Highams Park & Hale End
Highams Park (Hale End)
Hale End
(1873)

WOODFORD (1947)
WOODFORD (1856-1970)
(On Same Site)

GOODS (1966)   *WOODFORD SIDINGS*

1856-1970

1947

SOUTH WOODFORD (1947)
South Woodford (George Lane)
GEORGE LANE (WOODFORD)
(1856-1970)
(On Same Site)

EAGLE LANE GOODS (1899-1966)

GREAT EASTERN RAILWAY STRATFORD TO LOUGHTON / EPPING (AND ONGAR):

THE CENTRAL LINE STRATFORD TO LOUGHTON WAS OPENED BY THE EASTERN
COUNTIES RAILWAY (LATER ABSORBED BY THE GREAT EASTERN RAILWAY) IN 1856.
THE GREAT EASTERN RAILWAY THEN OPENED THE EXTENSION TO EPPING (AND
ONGAR) IN 1865. MOST PASSENGER SERVICES WERE TRANSFERRED TO LONDON
UNDERGROUND IN STAGES BETWEEN 1947 AND 1949. FREIGHT SERVICES REMAINED
UNTIL 1966, AND SOME EARLY MORNING MAIN LINE PASSENGER SERVICES TO
EPPING CONTINUED UNTIL 1970. THE PHYSICAL LINK BETWEEN LEYTON AND
STRATFORD WAS DISMANTLED IN 1972.

1856-1970

1947

SNARESBROOK (1947)
SNARESBROOK
Snaresbrook for Wanstead
Snaresbrook & Wanstead
Snaresbrook
(1856-1970)
(On Same Site)

1947

REDBRIDGE
(1947)

1947

GANTS
HILL
(1947)

1947

WANSTEAD
(1947)

- Leytonstone Junction

13
15
24

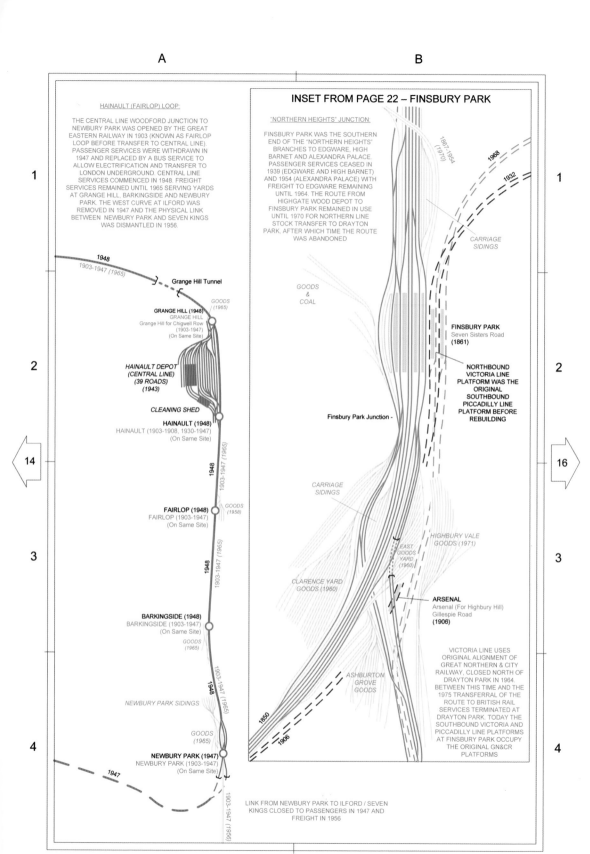

1

HAINAULT (FAIRLOP) LOOP:

THE CENTRAL LINE WOODFORD JUNCTION TO NEWBURY PARK WAS OPENED BY THE GREAT EASTERN RAILWAY IN 1903 (KNOWN AS FAIRLOP LOOP BEFORE TRANSFER TO CENTRAL LINE). PASSENGER SERVICES WERE WITHDRAWN IN 1947 AND REPLACED BY A BUS SERVICE TO ALLOW ELECTRIFICATION AND TRANSFER TO LONDON UNDERGROUND. CENTRAL LINE SERVICES COMMENCED IN 1948. FREIGHT SERVICES REMAINED UNTIL 1965 SERVING YARDS AT GRANGE HILL, BARKINGSIDE AND NEWBURY PARK. THE WEST CURVE AT ILFORD WAS REMOVED IN 1947 AND THE PHYSICAL LINK BETWEEN NEWBURY PARK AND SEVEN KINGS WAS DISMANTLED IN 1956.

INSET FROM PAGE 22 – FINSBURY PARK

"NORTHERN HEIGHTS" JUNCTION:

FINSBURY PARK WAS THE SOUTHERN END OF THE "NORTHERN HEIGHTS" BRANCHES TO EDGWARE, HIGH BARNET AND ALEXANDRA PALACE. PASSENGER SERVICES CEASED IN 1939 (EDGWARE AND HIGH BARNET) AND 1954 (ALEXANDRA PALACE) WITH FREIGHT TO EDGWARE REMAINING UNTIL 1964. THE ROUTE FROM HIGHGATE WOOD DEPOT TO FINSBURY PARK REMAINED IN USE UNTIL 1970 FOR NORTHERN LINE STOCK TRANSFER TO DRAYTON PARK, AFTER WHICH TIME THE ROUTE WAS ABANDONED

1867-1954 (1970)

1968

1932

CARRIAGE SIDINGS

1948
1903-1947 (1965)

Grange Hill Tunnel

GOODS (1965)

GRANGE HILL (1948)
GRANGE HILL
Grange Hill for Chigwell Row
(1903-1947)
(On Same Site)

HAINAULT DEPOT (CENTRAL LINE) (39 ROADS) (1943)

CLEANING SHED

HAINAULT (1948)
HAINAULT (1903-1908, 1930-1947)
(On Same Site)

1948
1903-1947 (1965)

GOODS & COAL

FINSBURY PARK
Seven Sisters Road
(1861)

NORTHBOUND VICTORIA LINE PLATFORM WAS THE ORIGINAL SOUTHBOUND PICCADILLY LINE PLATFORM BEFORE REBUILDING

Finsbury Park Junction -

CARRIAGE SIDINGS

HIGHBURY VALE GOODS (1971)

EAST GOODS YARD (1960)

CLARENCE YARD GOODS (1960)

ARSENAL
Arsenal (For Highbury Hill)
Gillespie Road
(1906)

2

FAIRLOP (1948)
FAIRLOP (1903-1947)
(On Same Site)

GOODS (1958)

1948
1903-1947 (1965)

3

BARKINGSIDE (1948)
BARKINGSIDE (1903-1947)
(On Same Site)

GOODS (1965)

1903-1947 (1965)

NEWBURY PARK SIDINGS

1948
1903-1947 (1965)

ASHBURTON GROVE GOODS

VICTORIA LINE USES ORIGINAL ALIGNMENT OF GREAT NORTHERN & CITY RAILWAY, CLOSED NORTH OF DRAYTON PARK IN 1964. BETWEEN THIS TIME AND THE 1975 TRANSFERRAL OF THE ROUTE TO BRITISH RAIL SERVICES TERMINATED AT DRAYTON PARK. TODAY THE SOUTHBOUND VICTORIA AND PICCADILLY LINE PLATFORMS AT FINSBURY PARK OCCUPY THE ORIGINAL GN&CR PLATFORMS

4

GOODS (1965)

NEWBURY PARK (1947)
NEWBURY PARK (1903-1947)
(On Same Site)

1947

1903-1947 (1956)

1850

1906

LINK FROM NEWBURY PARK TO ILFORD / SEVEN KINGS CLOSED TO PASSENGERS IN 1947 AND FREIGHT IN 1956

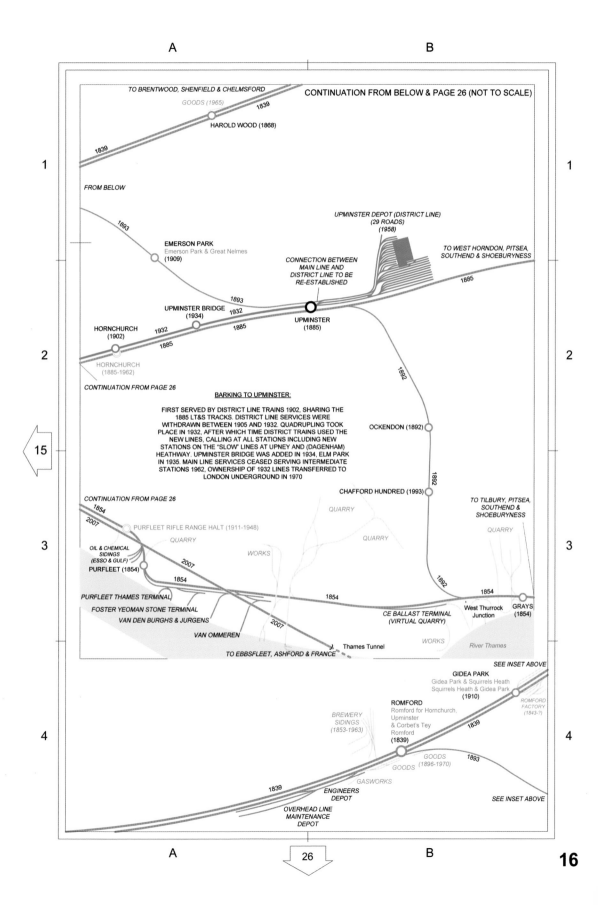

TO BRENTWOOD, SHENFIELD & CHELMSFORD

GOODS (1965)

1839

HAROLD WOOD (1868)

1839

FROM BELOW

1893

EMERSON PARK
Emerson Park & Great Nelmes
(1909)

UPMINSTER DEPOT (DISTRICT LINE)
(29 ROADS)
(1958)

CONNECTION BETWEEN
MAIN LINE AND
DISTRICT LINE TO BE
RE-ESTABLISHED

TO WEST HORNDON, PITSEA,
SOUTHEND & SHOEBURYNESS

1885

1893

UPMINSTER BRIDGE
(1934)

1932

1932

UPMINSTER
(1885)

HORNCHURCH
(1902)

1932

1885

1885

HORNCHURCH
(1885-1962)

CONTINUATION FROM PAGE 26

BARKING TO UPMINSTER:

FIRST SERVED BY DISTRICT LINE TRAINS 1902, SHARING THE
1885 LT&S TRACKS. DISTRICT LINE SERVICES WERE
WITHDRAWN BETWEEN 1905 AND 1932. QUADRUPLING TOOK
PLACE IN 1932, AFTER WHICH TIME DISTRICT TRAINS USED THE
NEW LINES, CALLING AT ALL STATIONS INCLUDING NEW
STATIONS ON THE "SLOW" LINES AT UPNEY AND (DAGENHAM)
HEATHWAY. UPMINSTER BRIDGE WAS ADDED IN 1934, ELM PARK
IN 1935. MAIN LINE SERVICES CEASED SERVING INTERMEDIATE
STATIONS 1962, OWNERSHIP OF 1932 LINES TRANSFERRED TO
LONDON UNDERGROUND IN 1970

1892

OCKENDON (1892)

1892

CHAFFORD HUNDRED (1993)

TO TILBURY, PITSEA,
SOUTHEND &
SHOEBURYNESS

QUARRY

CONTINUATION FROM PAGE 26

1854

2007

QUARRY

PURFLEET RIFLE RANGE HALT (1911-1948)

QUARRY

WORKS

QUARRY

OIL & CHEMICAL
SIDINGS
(ESSO & GULF)

PURFLEET (1854)

2007

1854

1892

1854

West Thurrock
Junction

GRAYS
(1854)

PURFLEET THAMES TERMINAL

1854

FOSTER YEOMAN STONE TERMINAL

VAN DEN BURGHS & JURGENS

CE BALLAST TERMINAL
(VIRTUAL QUARRY)

WORKS

VAN OMMEREN

2007

Thames Tunnel

River Thames

TO EBBSFLEET, ASHFORD & FRANCE

SEE INSET ABOVE

GIDEA PARK
Gidea Park & Squirrels Heath
Squirrels Heath & Gidea Park
(1910)

ROMFORD FACTORY
(1843-?)

ROMFORD
Romford for Hornchurch,
Upminster
& Corbet's Tey
Romford
(1839)

BREWERY
SIDINGS
(1853-1963)

1839

GOODS
(1896-1970)

1893

GOODS

GASWORKS

1839

ENGINEERS
DEPOT

SEE INSET ABOVE

OVERHEAD LINE
MAINTENANCE
DEPOT

15

26

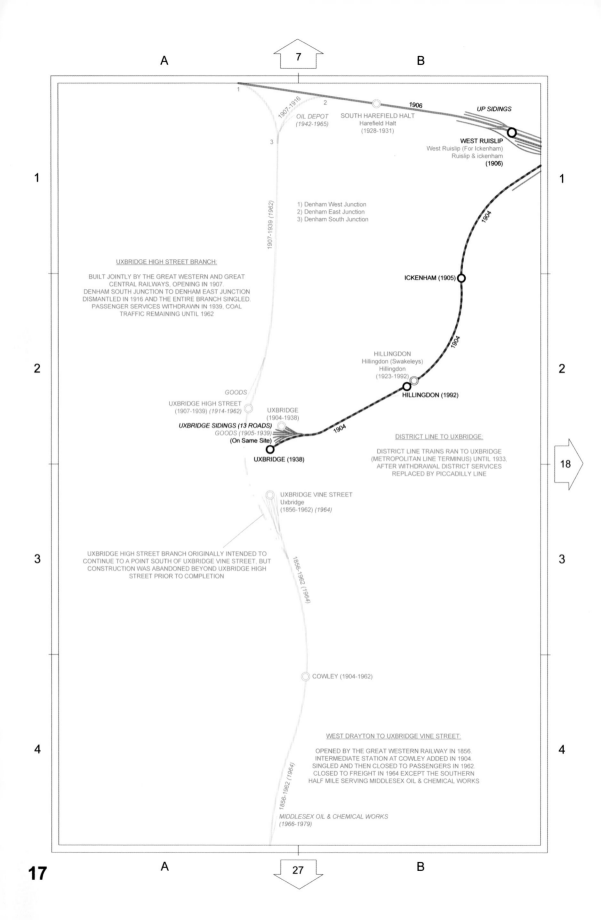

1906

UP SIDINGS

1907-1916

OIL DEPOT
(1942-1965)

SOUTH HAREFIELD HALT
Harefield Halt
(1928-1931)

WEST RUISLIP
West Ruislip (For Ickenham)
Ruislip & ickenham
(1906)

1904

1907-1939 (1962)

1) Denham West Junction
2) Denham East Junction
3) Denham South Junction

1
1

ICKENHAM (1905)

UXBRIDGE HIGH STREET BRANCH:

BUILT JOINTLY BY THE GREAT WESTERN AND GREAT
CENTRAL RAILWAYS, OPENING IN 1907.
DENHAM SOUTH JUNCTION TO DENHAM EAST JUNCTION
DISMANTLED IN 1916 AND THE ENTIRE BRANCH SINGLED.
PASSENGER SERVICES WITHDRAWN IN 1939, COAL
TRAFFIC REMAINING UNTIL 1962

1904

HILLINGDON
Hillingdon (Swakeleys)
Hillingdon
(1923-1992)

2
2

GOODS
UXBRIDGE HIGH STREET
(1907-1939) *(1914-1962)*

UXBRIDGE
(1904-1938)

HILLINGDON (1992)

UXBRIDGE SIDINGS (13 ROADS)
GOODS (1905-1939)
(On Same Site)

1904

DISTRICT LINE TO UXBRIDGE:

DISTRICT LINE TRAINS RAN TO UXBRIDGE
(METROPOLITAN LINE TERMINUS) UNTIL 1933.
AFTER WITHDRAWAL DISTRICT SERVICES
REPLACED BY PICCADILLY LINE

UXBRIDGE (1938)

18

UXBRIDGE VINE STREET
Uxbridge
(1856-1962) *(1964)*

UXBRIDGE HIGH STREET BRANCH ORIGINALLY INTENDED TO
CONTINUE TO A POINT SOUTH OF UXBRIDGE VINE STREET, BUT
CONSTRUCTION WAS ABANDONED BEYOND UXBRIDGE HIGH
STREET PRIOR TO COMPLETION

3
3

1856-1962 (1964)

COWLEY (1904-1962)

WEST DRAYTON TO UXBRIDGE VINE STREET:

OPENED BY THE GREAT WESTERN RAILWAY IN 1856.
INTERMEDIATE STATION AT COWLEY ADDED IN 1904.
SINGLED AND THEN CLOSED TO PASSENGERS IN 1962.
CLOSED TO FREIGHT IN 1964 EXCEPT THE SOUTHERN
HALF MILE SERVING MIDDLESEX OIL & CHEMICAL WORKS

4
4

1856-1962 (1964)

MIDDLESEX OIL & CHEMICAL WORKS
(1966-1979)

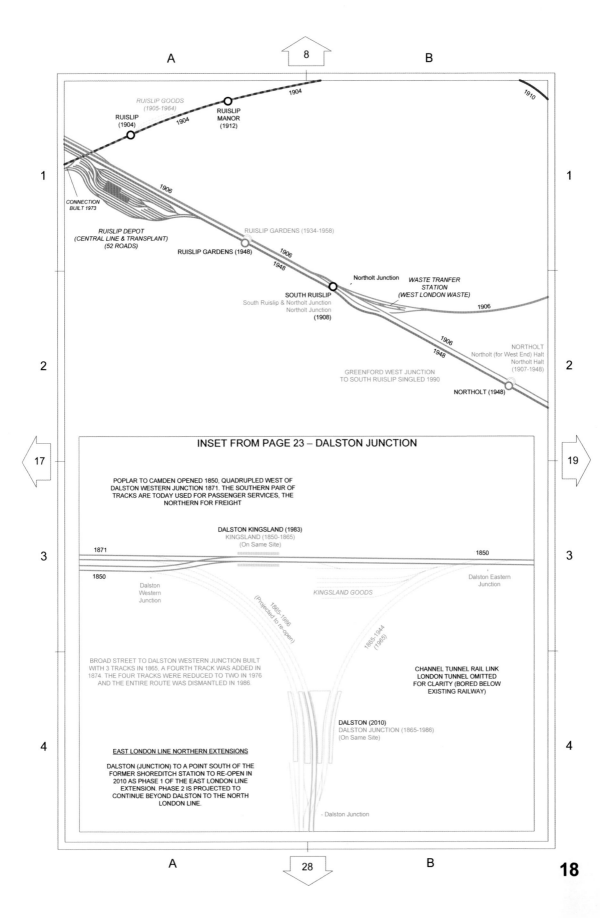

RUISLIP GOODS
(1905-1964)

RUISLIP
(1904)

RUISLIP
MANOR
(1912)

1904

1904

1904

1910

CONNECTION
BUILT 1973

1906

1   1906   **1**

RUISLIP DEPOT
(CENTRAL LINE & TRANSPLANT)
(52 ROADS)

RUISLIP GARDENS (1934-1958)

RUISLIP GARDENS (1948)

1906

1948

Northolt Junction

WASTE TRANFER
STATION
(WEST LONDON WASTE)

1906

SOUTH RUISLIP
South Ruislip & Northolt Junction
Northolt Junction
(1908)

1906

1948

NORTHOLT
Northolt (for West End) Halt
Northolt Halt
(1907-1948)

2   **2**

GREENFORD WEST JUNCTION
TO SOUTH RUISLIP SINGLED 1990

NORTHOLT (1948)

17
19

INSET FROM PAGE 23 – DALSTON JUNCTION

POPLAR TO CAMDEN OPENED 1850, QUADRUPLED WEST OF
DALSTON WESTERN JUNCTION 1871. THE SOUTHERN PAIR OF
TRACKS ARE TODAY USED FOR PASSENGER SERVICES, THE
NORTHERN FOR FREIGHT

DALSTON KINGSLAND (1983)
KINGSLAND (1850-1865)
(On Same Site)

3   1871   1850   **3**

1850

Dalston
Western
Junction

Dalston Eastern
Junction

1865-1986
(Projected to re-open)

KINGSLAND GOODS

1865-1944
(1965)

BROAD STREET TO DALSTON WESTERN JUNCTION BUILT
WITH 3 TRACKS IN 1865, A FOURTH TRACK WAS ADDED IN
1874. THE FOUR TRACKS WERE REDUCED TO TWO IN 1976
AND THE ENTIRE ROUTE WAS DISMANTLED IN 1986.

CHANNEL TUNNEL RAIL LINK
LONDON TUNNEL OMITTED
FOR CLARITY (BORED BELOW
EXISTING RAILWAY)

DALSTON (2010)
DALSTON JUNCTION (1865-1986)
(On Same Site)

4   **4**

<u>EAST LONDON LINE NORTHERN EXTENSIONS</u>

DALSTON (JUNCTION) TO A POINT SOUTH OF THE
FORMER SHOREDITCH STATION TO RE-OPEN IN
2010 AS PHASE 1 OF THE EAST LONDON LINE
EXTENSION. PHASE 2 IS PROJECTED TO
CONTINUE BEYOND DALSTON TO THE NORTH
LONDON LINE.

- Dalston Junction

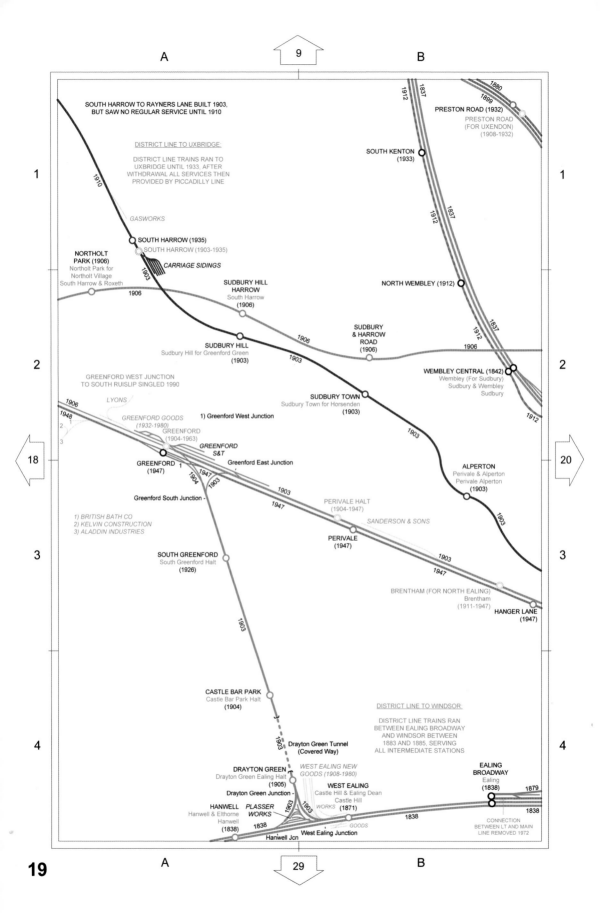

SOUTH HARROW TO RAYNERS LANE BUILT 1903,
BUT SAW NO REGULAR SERVICE UNTIL 1910

DISTRICT LINE TO UXBRIDGE:

DISTRICT LINE TRAINS RAN TO
UXBRIDGE UNTIL 1933, AFTER
WITHDRAWAL ALL SERVICES THEN
PROVIDED BY PICCADILLY LINE

GASWORKS

1910

1

PRESTON ROAD (1932)
PRESTON ROAD
(FOR UXENDON)
(1908-1932)

SOUTH KENTON
(1933)

NORTHOLT
PARK (1906)
Northolt Park for
Northolt Village
South Harrow & Roxeth

SOUTH HARROW (1935)
SOUTH HARROW (1903-1935)
CARRIAGE SIDINGS

1903

1906

SUDBURY HILL
HARROW
South Harrow
(1906)

NORTH WEMBLEY (1912)

SUDBURY HILL
Sudbury Hill for Greenford Green
(1903)

1906

SUDBURY &
HARROW
ROAD
(1906)

1906

WEMBLEY CENTRAL (1842)
Wembley (For Sudbury)
Sudbury & Wembley
Sudbury

2

GREENFORD WEST JUNCTION
TO SOUTH RUISLIP SINGLED 1990

LYONS

1906
1948
2
3

SUDBURY TOWN
Sudbury Town for Horsenden
(1903)

1903

1912

*GREENFORD GOODS
(1932-1980)*
GREENFORD
(1904-1963)
*GREENFORD
S&T*

1) Greenford West Junction

GREENFORD
(1947)

1904

1947

Greenford East Junction

1903

1903

ALPERTON
Perivale & Alperton
Perivale Alperton
(1903)

18

Greenford South Junction

1903

1947

PERIVALE HALT
(1904-1947)

SANDERSON & SONS

1903

20

*1) BRITISH BATH CO
2) KELVIN CONSTRUCTION
3) ALADDIN INDUSTRIES*

PERIVALE
(1947)

1903

1947

3

SOUTH GREENFORD
South Greenford Halt
(1926)

BRENTHAM (FOR NORTH EALING)
Brentham
(1911-1947)

HANGER LANE
(1947)

1903

CASTLE BAR PARK
Castle Bar Park Halt
(1904)

DISTRICT LINE TO WINDSOR:

DISTRICT LINE TRAINS RAN
BETWEEN EALING BROADWAY
AND WINDSOR BETWEEN
1883 AND 1885, SERVING
ALL INTERMEDIATE STATIONS

4

1903

Drayton Green Tunnel
(Covered Way)

*WEST EALING NEW
GOODS (1908-1980)*

DRAYTON GREEN
Drayton Green Ealing Halt
(1905)
Drayton Green Junction

WEST EALING
Castle Hill & Ealing Dean
Castle Hill
WORKS (1871)

EALING
BROADWAY
Ealing
(1838)

1879

1903

1903

HANWELL
Hanwell & Elthorne
Hanwell
(1838)

*PLASSER
WORKS*

1838

GOODS

1838

1838

CONNECTION
BETWEEN LT AND MAIN
LINE REMOVED 1972

Hanwell Jcn

West Ealing Junction

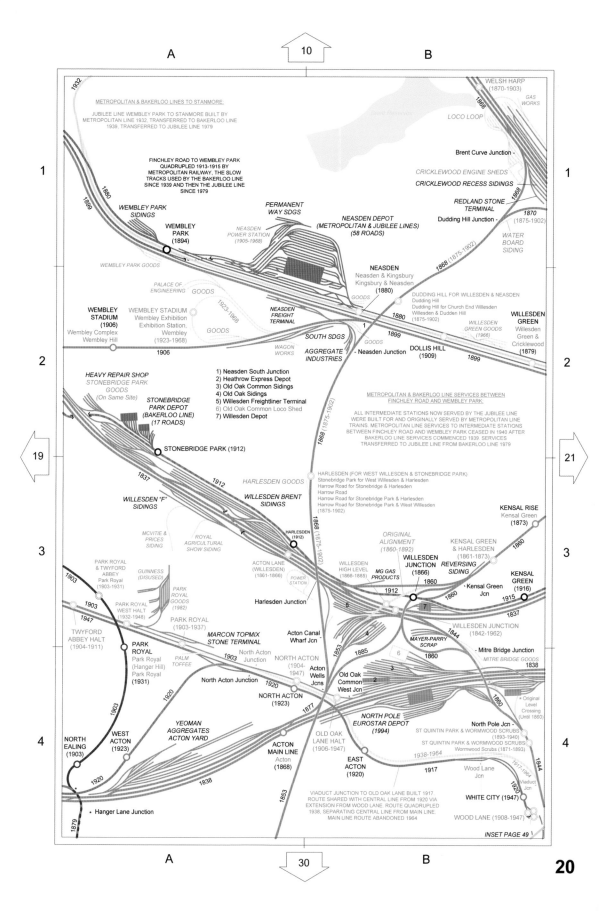

1932

WELSH HARP
(1870-1903)
GAS WORKS

LOCO LOOP

1868

Brent Curve Junction -

METROPOLITAN & BAKERLOO LINES TO STANMORE:

JUBILEE LINE WEMBLEY PARK TO STANMORE BUILT BY
METROPOLITAN LINE 1932, TRANSFERRED TO BAKERLOO LINE
1939, TRANSFERRED TO JUBILEE LINE 1979

1

CRICKLEWOOD ENGINE SHEDS
CRICKLEWOOD RECESS SIDINGS

1868

REDLAND STONE
TERMINAL

FINCHLEY ROAD TO WEMBLEY PARK
QUADRUPLED 1913-1915 BY
METROPOLITAN RAILWAY, THE SLOW
TRACKS USED BY THE BAKERLOO LINE
SINCE 1939 AND THEN THE JUBILEE LINE
SINCE 1979

1880

1899

Dudding Hill Junction -

1870
(1875-1902)

WATER
BOARD
SIDING

1

WEMBLEY PARK
SIDINGS

PERMANENT
WAY SDGS

WEMBLEY
PARK
(1894)

NEASDEN
POWER STATION
(1905-1968)

NEASDEN DEPOT
(METROPOLITAN & JUBILEE LINES)
(58 ROADS)

1868 (1875-1902)

WEMBLEY PARK GOODS

PALACE OF
ENGINEERING

GOODS

NEASDEN
FREIGHT
TERMINAL

NEASDEN
Neasden & Kingsbury
Kingsbury & Neasden
(1880)

GOODS

DUDDING HILL FOR WILLESDEN & NEASDEN
Dudding Hill
Dudding Hill for Church End Willesden
Willesden & Dudden Hill
(1875-1902)

WILLESDEN
GREEN
Willesden
Green &
Cricklewood
(1879)

1923-1968

WEMBLEY
STADIUM
(1906)
Wembley Complex
Wembley Hill

WEMBLEY STADIUM
Wembley Exhibition
Exhibition Station,
Wembley (1923-1968)

GOODS

1880

1899

WILLESDEN
GREEN GOODS
(1966)

2

1906

WAGON
WORKS

SOUTH SDGS

AGGREGATE
INDUSTRIES

GOODS

- Neasden Junction

DOLLIS HILL
(1909)

1899

2

HEAVY REPAIR SHOP
STONEBRIDGE PARK
GOODS
(On Same Site)

STONEBRIDGE
PARK DEPOT
(BAKERLOO LINE)
(17 ROADS)

1) Neasden South Junction
2) Heathrow Express Depot
3) Old Oak Common Sidings
4) Old Oak Sidings
5) Willesden Freightliner Terminal
6) Old Oak Common Loco Shed
7) Willesden Depot

**METROPOLITAN & BAKERLOO LINE SERVICES BETWEEN
FINCHLEY ROAD AND WEMBLEY PARK:**

ALL INTERMEDIATE STATIONS NOW SERVED BY THE JUBILEE LINE
WERE BUILT FOR AND ORIGINALLY SERVED BY METROPOLITAN LINE
TRAINS. METROPOLITAN LINE SERVICES TO INTERMEDIATE STATIONS
BETWEEN FINCHLEY ROAD AND WEMBLEY PARK CEASED IN 1940 AFTER
BAKERLOO LINE SERVICES COMMENCED 1939. SERVICES
TRANSFERRED TO JUBILEE LINE FROM BAKERLOO LINE 1979

19

STONEBRIDGE PARK (1912)

1837

1912

WILLESDEN "F"
SIDINGS

WILLESDEN BRENT
SIDINGS

HARLESDEN (FOR WEST WILLESDEN & STONEBRIDGE PARK)
Stonebridge Park for West Willesden & Harlesden
Harrow Road for Stonebridge & Harlesden
Harrow Road
Harrow Road for Stonebridge Park & Harlesden
Harrow Road for Stonebridge Park & West Willesden
(1875-1902)

KENSAL RISE
Kensal Green
(1873)

1860

21

MCVITIE &
PRICES
SIDING

ROYAL
AGRICULTURAL
SHOW SIDING

HARLESDEN GOODS

1868 (1875-1902)

HARLESDEN
(1912)

ORIGINAL
ALIGNMENT
(1860-1892)

WILLESDEN
HIGH LEVEL
(1866-1885)

MG GAS
PRODUCTS

WILLESDEN
JUNCTION
(1866)

REVERSING
SIDING

KENSAL GREEN
& HARLESDEN
(1861-1873)

KENSAL
GREEN
(1916)

3

PARK ROYAL
& TWYFORD
ABBEY
Park Royal
(1903-1931)

GUINNESS
(DISUSED)

ACTON LANE
(WILLESDEN)
(1861-1866)

POWER
STATION

Harlesden Junction

1912

1860

Kensal Green
Jcn

1860

1915

1837

3

1903

1903

PARK ROYAL
GOODS
(1982)

PARK ROYAL
(1903-1937)

5

WILLESDEN JUNCTION
(1842-1962)

1844

1947

PARK ROYAL
WEST HALT
(1932-1948)

MARCON TOPMIX
STONE TERMINAL

Acton Canal
Wharf Jcn

MAYER-PARRY
SCRAP

- Mitre Bridge Junction
MITRE BRIDGE GOODS
1838

TWYFORD
ABBEY HALT
(1904-1911)

PARK
ROYAL
Park Royal
(Hanger Hill)
Park Royal
(1931)

PALM
TOFFEE

1903

North Acton
Junction

NORTH ACTON
(1904-1947)

Acton
Wells
Jcns

1885

6

1860

1860

Original
Level
Crossing
(Until 1860)

4

1903

North Acton Junction

1920

NORTH ACTON
(1923)

1877

Old Oak
Common
West Jcn

2

3

North Pole Jcn
(1893-1940)

1844

WEST
ACTON
(1923)

YEOMAN
AGGREGATES
ACTON YARD

NORTH POLE
EUROSTAR DEPOT
(1994)

ST QUINTIN PARK & WORMWOOD SCRUBS
(1893-1940)
ST QUINTIN PARK & WORMWOOD SCRUBS
Wormwood Scrubs (1871-1893)

1917-1964

NORTH
EALING
(1903)

ACTON
MAIN LINE
Acton
(1868)

OLD OAK
LANE HALT
(1906-1947)

EAST
ACTON
(1920)

1938-1964

1917

Wood Lane
Jcn

Viaduct
Jcn

1920

4

1920

1838

1853

VIADUCT JUNCTION TO OLD OAK LANE BUILT 1917.
ROUTE SHARED WITH CENTRAL LINE FROM 1920 VIA
EXTENSION FROM WOOD LANE. ROUTE QUADRUPLED
1938, SEPARATING CENTRAL LINE FROM MAIN LINE.
MAIN LINE ROUTE ABANDONED 1964

WHITE CITY (1947)

WOOD LANE (1908-1947)

1879

- Hanger Lane Junction

INSET PAGE 49

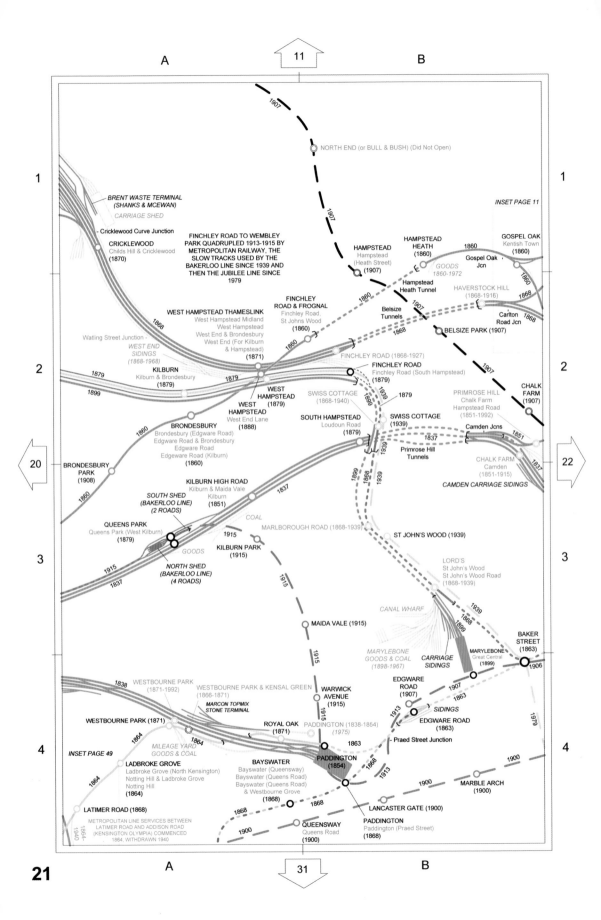

1

INSET PAGE 11

NORTH END (or BULL & BUSH) (Did Not Open)

1907

BRENT WASTE TERMINAL
(SHANKS & MCEWAN)
CARRIAGE SHED

- Cricklewood Curve Junction
CRICKLEWOOD
Childs Hill & Cricklewood
(1870)

FINCHLEY ROAD TO WEMBLEY
PARK QUADRUPLED 1913-1915 BY
METROPOLITAN RAILWAY, THE
SLOW TRACKS USED BY THE
BAKERLOO LINE SINCE 1939 AND
THEN THE JUBILEE LINE SINCE
1979

HAMPSTEAD
HEATH
(1860)

HAMPSTEAD
Hampstead
(Heath Street)
(1907)

GOODS
1860-1972

GOSPEL OAK
Kentish Town
(1860)

Gospel Oak
Jcn

1860

Hampstead
Heath Tunnel

HAVERSTOCK HILL
(1868-1916)

Carlton
Road Jcn

1868

1868

Belsize
Tunnels

1907

BELSIZE PARK (1907)

1868

2

1879

1899

Watling Street Junction -
WEST END
SIDINGS
(1868-1968)

1868

WEST HAMPSTEAD THAMESLINK
West Hampstead Midland
West Hampstead
West End & Brondesbury
West End (For Kilburn
& Hampstead)
(1871)

FINCHLEY
ROAD & FROGNAL
Finchley Road,
St Johns Wood
(1860)

1860

1860

FINCHLEY ROAD (1868-1927)

FINCHLEY ROAD
Finchley Road (South Hampstead)
(1879)

1907

KILBURN
Kilburn & Brondesbury
(1879)

1879

WEST
HAMPSTEAD
(1879)

WEST
HAMPSTEAD
West End Lane
(1888)

SWISS COTTAGE
(1868-1940)

SOUTH HAMPSTEAD
Loudoun Road
(1879)

1939

1879

1899

SWISS
COTTAGE
(1939)

PRIMROSE HILL
Chalk Farm
Hampstead Road
(1851-1992)

CHALK
FARM
(1907)

1851

BRONDESBURY
Brondesbury (Edgware Road)
Edgware Road & Brondesbury
Edgware Road
Edgware Road (Kilburn)
(1860)

1860

1837

Camden Jcns

1837

20

BRONDESBURY
PARK
(1908)

1860

KILBURN HIGH ROAD
Kilburn & Maida Vale
Kilburn
(1851)

1837

1939

1868

1939

Primrose Hill
Tunnels

CHALK FARM
Camden
(1851-1915)

CAMDEN CARRIAGE SIDINGS

22

SOUTH SHED
(BAKERLOO LINE)
(2 ROADS)

QUEENS PARK
Queens Park (West Kilburn)
(1879)

GOODS

COAL

MARLBOROUGH ROAD (1868-1939)

1899

1868

1939

ST JOHN'S WOOD (1939)

3

1915

1837

NORTH SHED
(BAKERLOO LINE)
(4 ROADS)

KILBURN PARK
(1915)

1915

LORD'S
St John's Wood
St John's Wood Road
(1868-1939)

1939

1868

3

MAIDA VALE (1915)

CANAL WHARF

1915

MARYLEBONE
GOODS & COAL
(1898-1967)

CARRIAGE
SIDINGS

MARYLEBONE
Great Central
(1899)

BAKER
STREET
(1863)

1906

1838

WESTBOURNE PARK
(1871-1992)

WESTBOURNE PARK & KENSAL GREEN
(1866-1871)

MARCON TOPMIX
STONE TERMINAL

WARWICK
AVENUE
(1915)

1915

EDGWARE
ROAD
(1907)

1907

1863

1913

SIDINGS

EDGWARE ROAD
(1863)

1979

4

WESTBOURNE PARK (1871)

1864

1864

MILEAGE YARD
GOODS & COAL

ROYAL OAK
(1871)

PADDINGTON (1838-1854)
(1975)

1863

- Praed Street Junction

INSET PAGE 49

LADBROKE GROVE
Ladbroke Grove (North Kensington)
Notting Hill & Ladbroke Grove
Notting Hill
(1864)

BAYSWATER
Bayswater (Queensway)
Bayswater (Queens Road)
Bayswater (Queens Road)
& Westbourne Grove
(1868)

PADDINGTON
(1854)

1868

1913

MARBLE ARCH
(1900)

1900

1864

LATIMER ROAD (1868)

1864-
1940

METROPOLITAN LINE SERVICES BETWEEN
LATIMER ROAD AND ADDISON ROAD
(KENSINGTON OLYMPIA) COMMENCED
1864, WITHDRAWN 1940

1868

1868

1868

LANCASTER GATE (1900)

PADDINGTON
Paddington (Praed Street)
(1868)

1900

QUEENSWAY
Queens Road
(1900)

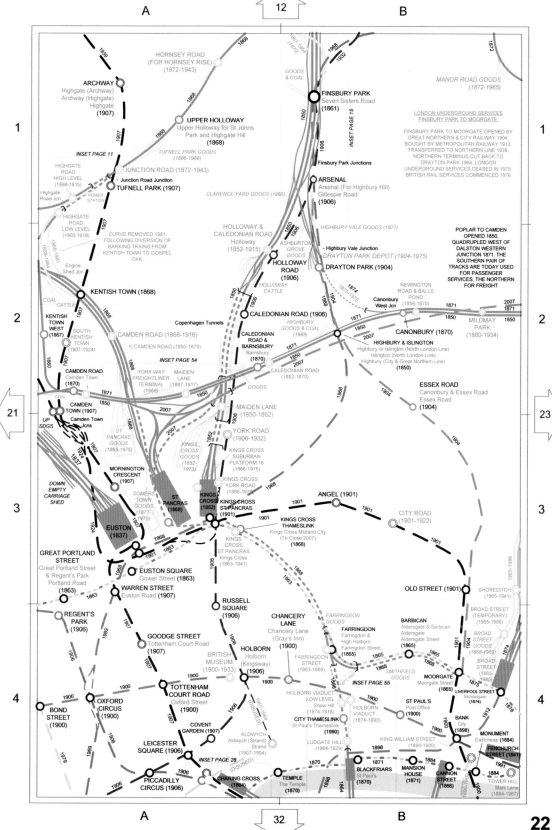

HORNSEY ROAD
(FOR HORNSEY RISE)
(1872-1943)

GOODS
& COAL

MANOR ROAD GOODS
(1872-1965)

ARCHWAY
Highgate (Archway)
Archway (Highgate)
Highgate
(1907)

FINSBURY PARK
Seven Sisters Road
(1861)

INSET PAGE 15

UPPER HOLLOWAY
Upper Holloway for St Johns
Park and Highgate Hill
(1868)

TUFNELL PARK GOODS
(1886-1968)

Finsbury Park Junctions

LONDON UNDERGROUND SERVICES
FINSBURY PARK TO MOORGATE:

FINSBURY PARK TO MOORGATE OPENED BY
GREAT NORTHERN & CITY RAILWAY 1904
BOUGHT BY METROPOLITAN RAILWAY 1913,
TRANSFERRED TO NORTHERN LINE 1939.
NORTHERN TERMINUS CUT BACK TO
DRAYTON PARK 1964. LONDON
UNDERGROUND SERVICES CEASED IN 1975,
BRITISH RAIL SERVICES COMMENCED 1976

INSET PAGE 11

HIGHGATE
ROAD
HIGH LEVEL
(1858-1915)

JUNCTION ROAD (1872-1943)

Junction Road Junction

TUFNELL PARK (1907)

Highgate
Road Jcn

POWER
STATION

ARSENAL
Arsenal (For Highbury Hill)
Gillespie Road
(1906)

CLARENCE YARD GOODS (1960)

HIGHGATE
ROAD
LOW LEVEL
(1900-1918)

CURVE REMOVED 1981
FOLLOWING DIVERSION
OF BARKING TRAINS FROM
KENTISH TOWN TO GOSPEL
OAK

HOLLOWAY &
CALEDONIAN ROAD
Holloway
(1852-1915)

HIGHBURY VALE GOODS (1971)

POPLAR TO CAMDEN
OPENED 1850,
QUADRUPLED WEST OF
DALSTON WESTERN
JUNCTION 1871. THE
SOUTHERN PAIR OF
TRACKS ARE TODAY USED
FOR PASSENGER
SERVICES, THE NORTHERN
FOR FREIGHT

Engine
Shed Jcn

ASHBURTON
GROVE
GOODS

- Highbury Vale Junction

DRAYTON PARK DEPOT (1904-1975)

HOLLOWAY
ROAD
(1906)

DRAYTON PARK (1904)

KENTISH TOWN (1868)

NEWINGTON
ROAD & BALLS
POND
(1858-1870)

COAL &
CATTLE

HOLLOWAY
CATTLE

Canonbury
West Jcn

CALEDONIAN ROAD (1906)

MILDMAY
PARK
(1880-1934)

KENTISH
TOWN
WEST
(1867)

SOUTH
KENTISH
TOWN
(1907-1924)

CAMDEN ROAD (1868-1916)

1) CAMDEN ROAD (1850-1870)

Copenhagen Tunnels

HIGHBURY
GOODS & COAL
(1969)

CALEDONIAN
ROAD &
BARNSBURY
Barnsbury
(1870)

CANONBURY (1870)

HIGHBURY & ISLINGTON
Highbury or Islington (North London Line)
Islington (North London Line)
Highbury (City & Great Northern Line)
(1850)

CAMDEN ROAD
Camden Town
(1870)

CALEDONIAN ROAD
(1852-1870)

ESSEX ROAD
Canonbury & Essex Road
Essex Road
(1904)

COAL

MAIDEN
LANE
(1887-1917)

GOODS

CAMDEN
TOWN (1907)

YORK WAY
FREIGHTLINER
TERMINAL
(1968)

Camden Town
Jcns

ST
PANCRAS
GOODS
(1865-1975)

MAIDEN LANE
(1850-1852)

YORK ROAD
(1906-1932)

MORNINGTON
CRESCENT
(1907)

DOWN
EMPTY
CARRIAGE
SHED

UP
SDGS

KINGS
CROSS
GOODS
(1852-
1973)

KINGS CROSS
SUBURBAN
PLATFORM 16
(1866-1976)

KINGS CROSS
YORK ROAD
(1866-1976)

ANGEL (1901)

CITY ROAD
(1901-1922)

SOMERS
TOWN
GOODS
(1877-
1975)

ST
PANCRAS
(1868)

KINGS
CROSS
(1852)

KINGS CROSS
ST PANCRAS
(1901)

EUSTON
(1837)

KINGS CROSS
THAMESLINK
Kings Cross Midland City
(To Close 2007)
(1868)

KINGS
CROSS
ST PANCRAS
Kings Cross
(1863-1941)

GREAT PORTLAND
STREET
Great Portland Street
& Regent's Park
Portland Road
(1863)

EUSTON SQUARE
Gower Street (1863)

OLD STREET (1901)

SHOREDITCH
(1865-1941)

WARREN STREET
Euston Road (1907)

REGENT'S
PARK
(1906)

GOODGE STREET
Tottenham Court Road
(1907)

RUSSELL
SQUARE
(1906)

CHANCERY
LANE
Chancery Lane
(Gray's Inn)
(1900)

FARRINGDON
GOODS

BARBICAN
Aldersgate & Barbican
Aldersgate
Aldersgate Street
(1865)

BROAD
STREET
(TEMPORARY)
(1985-1986)

BROAD
STREET
(1868-1969)

FARRINGDON
Farringdon &
High Holborn
Farringdon Street
(1865)

BOND
STREET
(1900)

OXFORD
CIRCUS
(1900)

TOTTENHAM
COURT ROAD
Oxford Street
(1900)

BRITISH
MUSEUM
(1900-1933)

HOLBORN
Holborn
(Kingsway)
(1906)

FARRINGDON
STREET
(1863-1865)

SMITHFIELD
GOODS

MOORGATE
Moorgate Street
(1865)

BROAD
STREET
(1865-
1985)

INSET PAGE 55

LIVERPOOL STREET
Bishopsgate
(1874)

COVENT
GARDEN (1907)

HOLBORN VIADUCT
LOW LEVEL
Snow Hill
(1874-1916)

ST PAUL'S
Post Office
(1900)

BANK
City
(1898)

LEICESTER
SQUARE (1906)

ALDWYCH
(Strand)
Strand
(1907-1994)

HOLBORN
VIADUCT
(1874-1990)

CITY THAMESLINK
St Paul's Thameslink
(1990)

MONUMENT
Eastcheap
(1884)

FENCHURCH
STREET
(1841)

INSET PAGE 28

LUDGATE HILL
(1864-1929)

KING WILLIAM STREET
(1890-1900)

PICCADILLY
CIRCUS (1906)

CHARING CROSS
(1884)

TEMPLE
The Temple
(1870)

BLACKFRIARS
St Paul's
(1870)

MANSION
HOUSE
(1871)

CANNON
STREET
(1866)

TOWER
HILL
Mark Lane
(1884-1967)

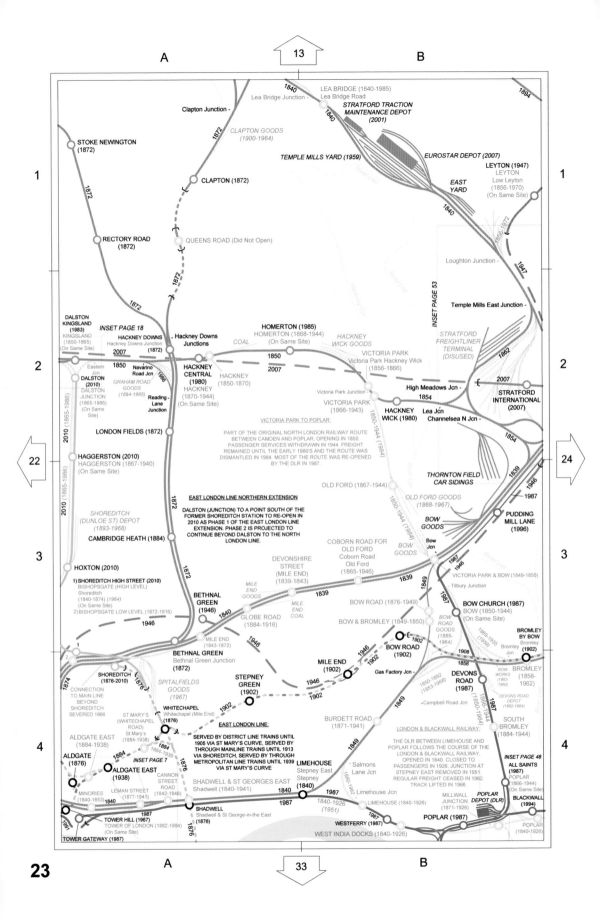

1

LEA BRIDGE (1840-1985)
Lea Bridge Road
Lea Bridge Junction -
Clapton Junction -
**STRATFORD TRACTION
MAINTENANCE DEPOT
(2001)**
1840

*CLAPTON GOODS
(1900-1964)*

TEMPLE MILLS YARD (1959)

EUROSTAR DEPOT (2007)

**EAST
YARD**

LEYTON (1947)
LEYTON
Low Leyton
(1856-1970)
(On Same Site)

STOKE NEWINGTON
(1872)

CLAPTON (1872)
1840

RECTORY ROAD
(1872)

QUEENS ROAD (Did Not Open)

1872

Loughton Junction -

1947

Temple Mills East Junction -

DALSTON
KINGSLAND
(1983)
KINGSLAND
(1850-1865)
(On Same Site)

INSET PAGE 18

HACKNEY DOWNS
(2007)
Hackney Downs Junction -

- Hackney Downs
Junctions
(1872)

HOMERTON (1985)
HOMERTON (1868-1944)
(On Same Site)

*HACKNEY
WICK GOODS*

*STRATFORD
FREIGHTLINER
TERMINAL
(DISUSED)*

1862

INSET PAGE 53

COAL

VICTORIA PARK
Victoria Park Hackney Wick
(1856-1866)

1850
2007

High Meadows Jcn -

2007

**STRATFORD
INTERNATIONAL
(2007)**

Eastern
Jcn

DALSTON
(2010)
DALSTON
JUNCTION
(1865-1986)
(On Same Site)

1850

Navarino
Road Jcn

*GRAHAM ROAD
GOODS
(1894-1965)*

Reading -
Lane
Junction

HACKNEY
CENTRAL
(1980)
HACKNEY
(1870-1944)
(On Same Site)

HACKNEY
(1850-1870)

Victoria Park Junction -

VICTORIA PARK
(1866-1943)

HACKNEY
WICK (1980)

1854

Lea Jcn
Channelsea N Jcn -

1854

LONDON FIELDS (1872)

VICTORIA PARK TO POPLAR:
PART OF THE ORIGINAL NORTH LONDON RAILWAY ROUTE
BETWEEN CAMDEN AND POPLAR, OPENING IN 1850.
PASSENGER SERVICES WITHDRAWN IN 1944. FREIGHT
REMAINED UNTIL THE EARLY 1980'S AND THE ROUTE WAS
DISMANTLED IN 1984. MOST OF THE ROUTE WAS RE-OPENED
BY THE DLR IN 1987.

HAGGERSTON (2010)
HAGGERSTON (1867-1940)
(On Same Site)

*THORNTON FIELD
CAR SIDINGS*

1839

1946

1987

PUDDING
MILL LANE
(1996)

*SHOREDITCH
(DUNLOE ST) DEPOT
(1893-1968)*

EAST LONDON LINE NORTHERN EXTENSION
DALSTON (JUNCTION) TO A POINT SOUTH OF THE
FORMER SHOREDITCH STATION TO RE-OPEN IN
2010 AS PHASE 1 OF THE EAST LONDON LINE
EXTENSION. PHASE 2 IS PROJECTED TO
CONTINUE BEYOND DALSTON TO THE NORTH
LONDON LINE.

OLD FORD (1867-1944)

*OLD FORD GOODS
(1868-1967)*

*BOW
GOODS*

CAMBRIDGE HEATH (1884)

DEVONSHIRE
STREET
(MILE END)
(1839-1843)

COBORN ROAD FOR
OLD FORD
Coborn Road
Old Ford
(1865-1946)

*BOW
GOODS*

Bow
Jcn

VICTORIA PARK & BOW (1849-1850)

HOXTON (2010)

1) SHOREDITCH HIGH STREET (2010)
BISHOPSGATE (HIGH LEVEL)
Shoreditch
(1840-1874) (1964)
(On Same Site)
2) BISHOPSGATE LOW LEVEL (1872-1916)

1839

Tilbury Junction -

BOW CHURCH (1987)
BOW (1850-1944)
(On Same Site)

*MILE
END
GOODS*

BETHNAL
GREEN
(1946)

1840

GLOBE ROAD
(1884-1916)

*MILE
END
COAL*

1839

BOW ROAD (1876-1949)

*BOW
ROAD
GOODS
(1885-
1964)*

BROMLEY
BY BOW
Bromley
(1902)

BOW & BROMLEY (1849-1850)

1946

*MILE END
(1843-1872)*

1946

BOW ROAD
(1902)

1902

1908

Bromley
Jcn

BETHNAL GREEN
Bethnal Green Junction
(1872)

1858

BROMLEY
(1858-
1962)

1874

SHOREDITCH
(1876-2010)
1876

*SPITALFIELDS
GOODS
(1967)*

STEPNEY
GREEN
(1902)

1902

MILE END
(1902)

1946

1902

Gas Factory Jcn -

DEVONS
ROAD
(1987)

*BOW
WORKS
(1863-
1950)*

*DEVONS ROAD
DEPOT
(1882-1964)*

CONNECTION
TO MAIN LINE
BEYOND
SHOREDITCH
SEVERED 1966

ST MARY'S
(WHITECHAPEL
ROAD)
St Mary's
(1884-1938)

WHITECHAPEL
Whitechapel (Mile End)
(1876)

1902

BURDETT
ROAD
(1871-1941)

1849

Campbell Road Jcn -

SOUTH
BROMLEY
(1884-1944)

ALDGATE EAST
(1884-1938)

EAST LONDON LINE:
SERVED BY DISTRICT LINE TRAINS UNTIL
1905 VIA ST MARY'S CURVE, SERVED BY
THROUGH MAINLINE TRAINS UNTIL 1913
VIA SHOREDITCH, SERVED BY THROUGH
METROPOLITAN LINE TRAINS UNTIL 1939
VIA ST MARY'S CURVE.

LONDON & BLACKWALL RAILWAY

INSET PAGE 48

ALL SAINTS
(1987)
POPLAR
(1866-1944)
(On Same Site)

ALDGATE
(1876)

1884

ALDGATE EAST
(1938)

1884-1939

1876

CANNON
STREET
ROAD
(1842-1848)

LIMEHOUSE
Stepney East
Stepney
(1840)

Salmons
Lane Jcn

THE DLR BETWEEN LIMEHOUSE AND
POPLAR FOLLOWS THE COURSE OF THE
LONDON & BLACKWALL RAILWAY,
OPENED IN 1840. CLOSED TO
PASSENGERS IN 1926. JUNCTION AT
STEPNEY EAST REMOVED IN 1951.
REGULAR FREIGHT CEASED IN 1962.
TRACK LIFTED IN 1966.

BLACKWALL
(1994)

MINORIES
(1840-1853)

LEMAN
STREET
(1877-1941)

1840

SHADWELL & ST GEORGES EAST
Shadwell (1840-1941)

1840

1987

LIMEHOUSE (1840-1926)
(1951)

MILLWALL
JUNCTION
(1871-1926)

*POPLAR
DEPOT (DLR)*

POPLAR (1987)

POPLAR
(1840-1926)

TOWER HILL (1967)
TOWER OF LONDON (1882-1884)
(On Same Site)

SHADWELL
Shadwell & St George-in-the-East
(1876)

1876

WESTFERRY (1987)

WEST INDIA DOCKS (1840-1926)

WESTFERRY (1987)

TOWER GATEWAY (1987)

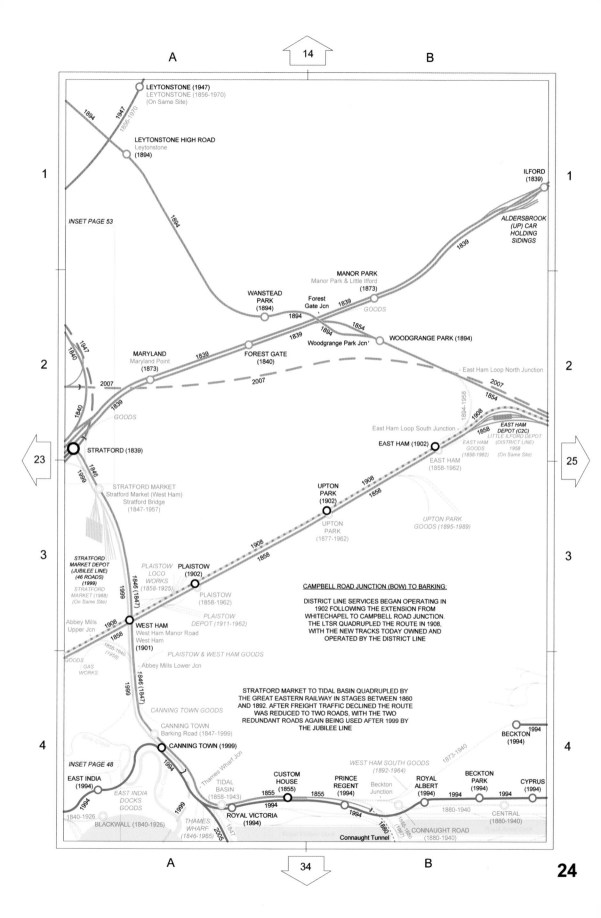

LEYTONSTONE (1947)
LEYTONSTONE (1856-1970)
(On Same Site)

1894
1947
1856-1970

LEYTONSTONE HIGH ROAD
Leytonstone
(1894)

1

INSET PAGE 53

1894

1894

ILFORD
(1839)

ALDERSBROOK
(UP) CAR
HOLDING
SIDINGS

1839

MANOR PARK
Manor Park & Little Ilford
(1873)

WANSTEAD
PARK
(1894)

Forest
Gate Jcn

1839

GOODS

1894

1839

1894

1854

WOODGRANGE PARK (1894)

Woodgrange Park Jcn

2

1840
1947

MARYLAND
Maryland Point
(1873)

1839

FOREST GATE
(1840)

1894

East Ham Loop North Junction

2007

2007

1854

2

2007

2007

1839

GOODS

1840

1839

East Ham Loop South Junction

1894-1958

1908

1858

EAST HAM
DEPOT (C2C)
LITTLE ILFORD DEPOT
(DISTRICT LINE)
1958
(On Same Site)

STRATFORD (1839)

1846

EAST HAM (1902)

EAST HAM
GOODS
(1858-1962)

EAST HAM
(1858-1962)

23

1999

STRATFORD MARKET
Stratford Market (West Ham)
Stratford Bridge
(1847-1957)

UPTON
PARK
(1902)

1908

1858

25

3

STRATFORD MARKET
DEPOT (JUBILEE LINE)
(46 ROADS)
(1999)
STRATFORD MARKET (1988)
(On Same Site)

PLAISTOW
LOCO
WORKS
(1858-1925)

PLAISTOW
(1902)

PLAISTOW
(1858-1962)

UPTON
PARK
(1877-1962)

UPTON PARK
GOODS (1895-1989)

1908

1858

3

1846
(1847)

1999

PLAISTOW
DEPOT (1911-1962)

CAMPBELL ROAD JUNCTION (BOW) TO BARKING:

DISTRICT LINE SERVICES BEGAN OPERATING IN
1902 FOLLOWING THE EXTENSION FROM
WHITECHAPEL TO CAMPBELL ROAD JUNCTION.
THE LTSR QUADRUPLED THE ROUTE IN 1908,
WITH THE NEW TRACKS TODAY OWNED AND
OPERATED BY THE DISTRICT LINE

Abbey Mills
Upper Jcn

1908

1858

WEST HAM
West Ham Manor Road
West Ham
(1901)

PLAISTOW & WEST HAM GOODS

1858-1940
(1958)

GOODS
GAS
WORKS

Abbey Mills Lower Jcn

1846
(1847)

1999

CANNING TOWN GOODS

STRATFORD MARKET TO TIDAL BASIN QUADRUPLED BY
THE GREAT EASTERN RAILWAY IN STAGES BETWEEN 1860
AND 1892. AFTER FREIGHT TRAFFIC DECLINED THE ROUTE
WAS REDUCED TO TWO ROADS, WITH THE TWO
REDUNDANT ROADS AGAIN BEING USED AFTER 1999 BY
THE JUBILEE LINE

CANNING TOWN
Barking Road (1847-1999)

CANNING TOWN (1999)

BECKTON
(1994)

1994

4

INSET PAGE 48

EAST INDIA
(1994)

EAST INDIA
DOCKS
GOODS

1994

BLACKWALL (1840-1926)

1840-1926

1994

Thames Wharf Jcn

TIDAL
BASIN
(1858-1943)

THAMES
WHARF
(1846-1965)

1999

ROYAL
VICTORIA
(1994)

2005

1847

CUSTOM
HOUSE
(1855)

1855

1994

WEST HAM SOUTH GOODS
(1892-1964)

PRINCE
REGENT
(1994)

1855

Beckton
Junction

1994

Connaught Tunnel

1880
(1847)

1858-1880
(1847)

ROYAL
ALBERT
(1994)

1880

CONNAUGHT ROAD
(1880-1940)

1873-1940

BECKTON
PARK
(1994)

1994

1880-1940

CENTRAL
(1880-1940)

1994

CYPRUS
(1994)

4

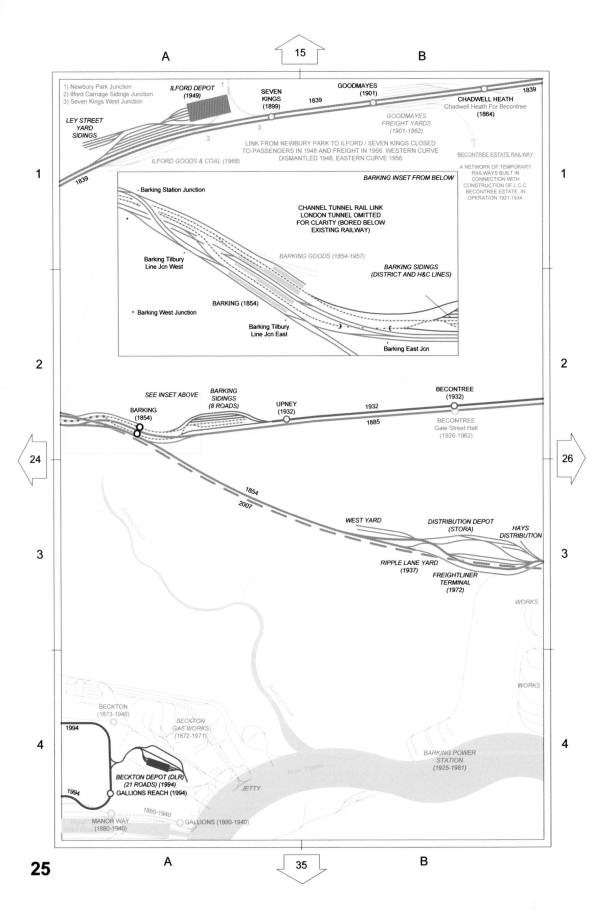

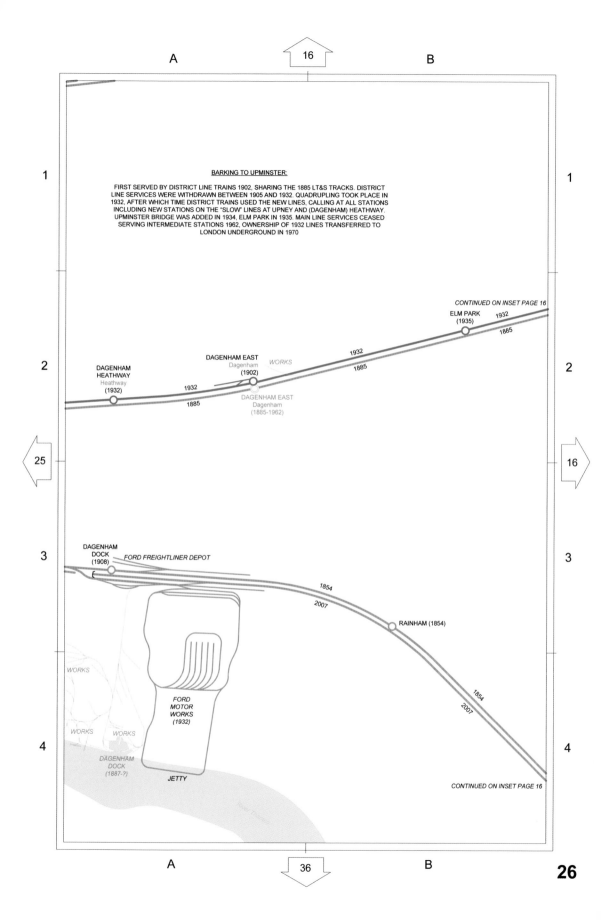

16

1   1

BARKING TO UPMINSTER:

FIRST SERVED BY DISTRICT LINE TRAINS 1902, SHARING THE 1885 LT&S TRACKS. DISTRICT
LINE SERVICES WERE WITHDRAWN BETWEEN 1905 AND 1932. QUADRUPLING TOOK PLACE IN
1932, AFTER WHICH TIME DISTRICT TRAINS USED THE NEW LINES, CALLING AT ALL STATIONS
INCLUDING NEW STATIONS ON THE "SLOW" LINES AT UPNEY AND (DAGENHAM) HEATHWAY.
UPMINSTER BRIDGE WAS ADDED IN 1934, ELM PARK IN 1935. MAIN LINE SERVICES CEASED
SERVING INTERMEDIATE STATIONS 1962, OWNERSHIP OF 1932 LINES TRANSFERRED TO
LONDON UNDERGROUND IN 1970

CONTINUED ON INSET PAGE 16

ELM PARK
(1935)

1932

1885

1932

1885

DAGENHAM EAST
Dagenham
(1902)

WORKS

2   2

DAGENHAM
HEATHWAY
Heathway
(1932)

1932

1885

DAGENHAM EAST
Dagenham
(1885-1962)

25

16

DAGENHAM
DOCK
(1908)

3   *FORD FREIGHTLINER DEPOT*   3

1854

2007

RAINHAM (1854)

WORKS

**FORD
MOTOR
WORKS
(1932)**

1854

2007

WORKS   *WORKS*

4   4

*DAGENHAM
DOCK
(1887-?)*

JETTY

CONTINUED ON INSET PAGE 16

36

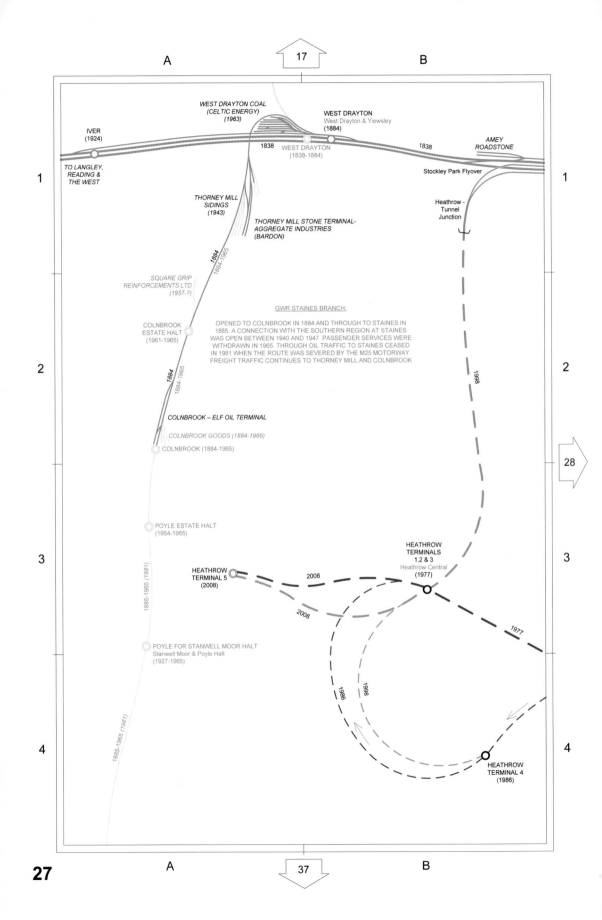

A   B

IVER
(1924)

WEST DRAYTON COAL
(CELTIC ENERGY)
(1963)

WEST DRAYTON
West Drayton & Yiewsley
(1884)

1838

WEST DRAYTON
(1838-1884)

1838

AMEY
ROADSTONE

TO LANGLEY,
READING &
THE WEST

Stockley Park Flyover

THORNEY MILL
SIDINGS
(1943)

Heathrow -
Tunnel
Junction

THORNEY MILL STONE TERMINAL-
AGGREGATE INDUSTRIES
(BARDON)

1884
1884-1965

SQUARE GRIP
REINFORCEMENTS LTD
(1957-?)

GWR STAINES BRANCH:

OPENED TO COLNBROOK IN 1884 AND THROUGH TO STAINES IN
1885. A CONNECTION WITH THE SOUTHERN REGION AT STAINES
WAS OPEN BETWEEN 1940 AND 1947. PASSENGER SERVICES WERE
WITHDRAWN IN 1965. THROUGH OIL TRAFFIC TO STAINES CEASED
IN 1981 WHEN THE ROUTE WAS SEVERED BY THE M25 MOTORWAY.
FREIGHT TRAFFIC CONTINUES TO THORNEY MILL AND COLNBROOK

COLNBROOK
ESTATE HALT
(1961-1965)

1884
1884-1965

1998

COLNBROOK – ELF OIL TERMINAL

COLNBROOK GOODS (1884-1966)

COLNBROOK (1884-1965)

POYLE ESTATE HALT
(1954-1965)

1885-1965 (1981)

HEATHROW
TERMINALS
1,2 & 3
Heathrow Central
(1977)

HEATHROW
TERMINAL 5
(2008)

2008

2008

1977

POYLE FOR STANWELL MOOR HALT
Stanwell Moor & Poyle Halt
(1927-1965)

1986

1998

1885-1965 (1981)

HEATHROW
TERMINAL 4
(1986)

A   B

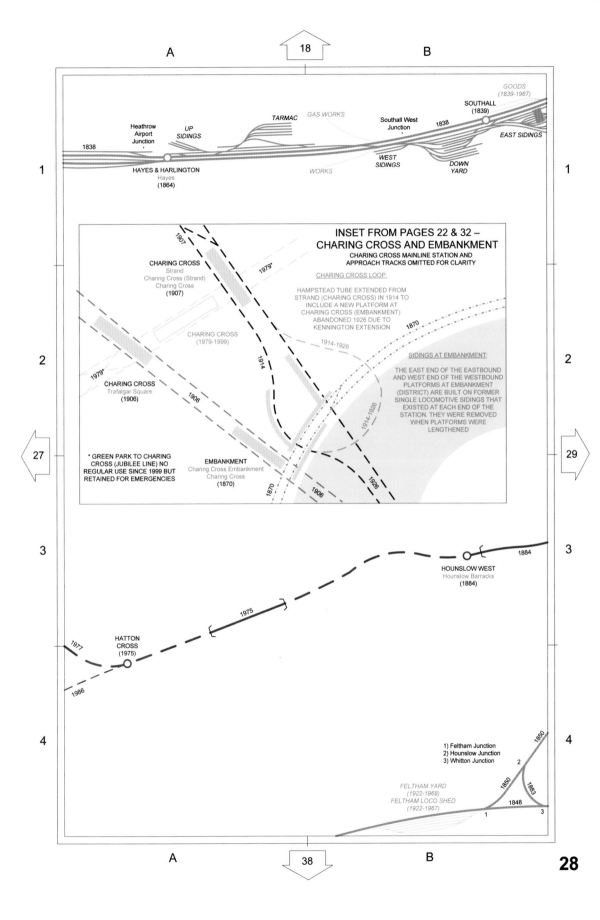

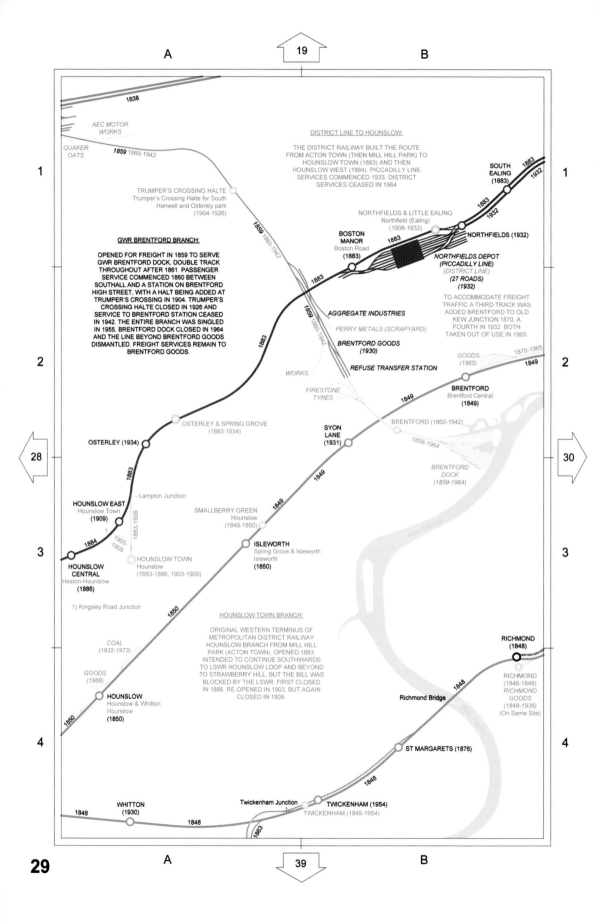

1838

AEC MOTOR
WORKS

QUAKER
OATS

1859   1860-1942

1

TRUMPER'S CROSSING HALTE
Trumper's Crossing Halte for South
Hanwell and Osterley park
(1904-1926)

DISTRICT LINE TO HOUNSLOW:

THE DISTRICT RAILWAY BUILT THE ROUTE
FROM ACTON TOWN (THEN MILL HILL PARK) TO
HOUNSLOW TOWN (1883) AND THEN
HOUNSLOW WEST (1884). PICCADILLY LINE
SERVICES COMMENCED 1933, DISTRICT
SERVICES CEASED IN 1964

SOUTH
EALING
(1883)

1883
1932

1883
1932

NORTHFIELDS & LITTLE EALING
Northfield (Ealing)
(1908-1932)

NORTHFIELDS (1932)

GWR BRENTFORD BRANCH:

OPENED FOR FREIGHT IN 1859 TO SERVE
GWR BRENTFORD DOCK, DOUBLE TRACK
THROUGHOUT AFTER 1861. PASSENGER
SERVICE COMMENCED 1860 BETWEEN
SOUTHALL AND A STATION ON BRENTFORD
HIGH STREET, WITH A HALT BEING ADDED AT
TRUMPER'S CROSSING IN 1904. TRUMPER'S
CROSSING HALTE CLOSED IN 1926 AND
SERVICE TO BRENTFORD STATION CEASED
IN 1942. THE ENTIRE BRANCH WAS SINGLED
IN 1955. BRENTFORD DOCK CLOSED IN 1964
AND THE LINE BEYOND BRENTFORD GOODS
DISMANTLED. FREIGHT SERVICES REMAIN TO
BRENTFORD GOODS.

BOSTON
MANOR
Boston Road
(1883)

1883

**NORTHFIELDS DEPOT
(PICCADILLY LINE)**
(DISTRICT LINE)
(27 ROADS)
(1932)

TO ACCOMMODATE FREIGHT
TRAFFIC A THIRD TRACK WAS
ADDED BRENTFORD TO OLD
KEW JUNCTION 1870, A
FOURTH IN 1932. BOTH
TAKEN OUT OF USE IN 1965.

1859 1860-1942

1883

AGGREGATE INDUSTRIES

PERRY METALS (SCRAPYARD)

**BRENTFORD GOODS
(1930)**

REFUSE TRANSFER STATION

GOODS
(1965)

1870-1965

1849

1849

WORKS

1883

*FIRESTONE
TYRES*

BRENTFORD
Brentford Central
(1849)

2

OSTERLEY & SPRING GROVE
(1883-1934)

SYON
LANE
(1931)

BRENTFORD (1860-1942)

1849

1859-1964

*BRENTFORD
DOCK
(1859-1964)*

OSTERLEY (1934)

1883

1849

28   **30**

- Lampton Junction

SMALLBERRY GREEN
Hounslow
(1849-1850)

River Thames

HOUNSLOW EAST
Hounslow Town
(1909)

1883-1909

1849

ISLEWORTH
Spring Grove & Isleworth
Isleworth
(1850)

1884

1905-
1909

3

HOUNSLOW TOWN
Hounslow
(1883-1886, 1903-1909)

**HOUNSLOW
CENTRAL**
Heston-Hounslow
(1886)

1) Kingsley Road Junction

1850

HOUNSLOW TOWN BRANCH:

ORIGINAL WESTERN TERMINUS OF
METROPOLITAN DISTRICT RAILWAY
HOUNSLOW BRANCH FROM MILL HILL
PARK (ACTON TOWN). OPENED 1883
INTENDED TO CONTINUE SOUTHWARDS
TO LSWR HOUNSLOW LOOP AND BEYOND
TO STRAWBERRY HILL, BUT THE BILL WAS
BLOCKED BY THE LSWR. FIRST CLOSED
IN 1886. RE-OPENED IN 1903, BUT AGAIN
CLOSED IN 1909.

**RICHMOND
(1848)**

*COAL
(1932-1973)*

*GOODS
(1968)*

*RICHMOND
(1846-1848)
RICHMOND
GOODS
(1848-1936)
(On Same Site)*

Richmond Bridge

1846

HOUNSLOW
Hounslow & Whitton
Hounslow
(1850)

1850

4

ST MARGARETS (1876)

1848

**WHITTON
(1930)**

Twickenham Junction

TWICKENHAM (1954)
TWICKENHAM (1849-1954)

1848

1848

1863

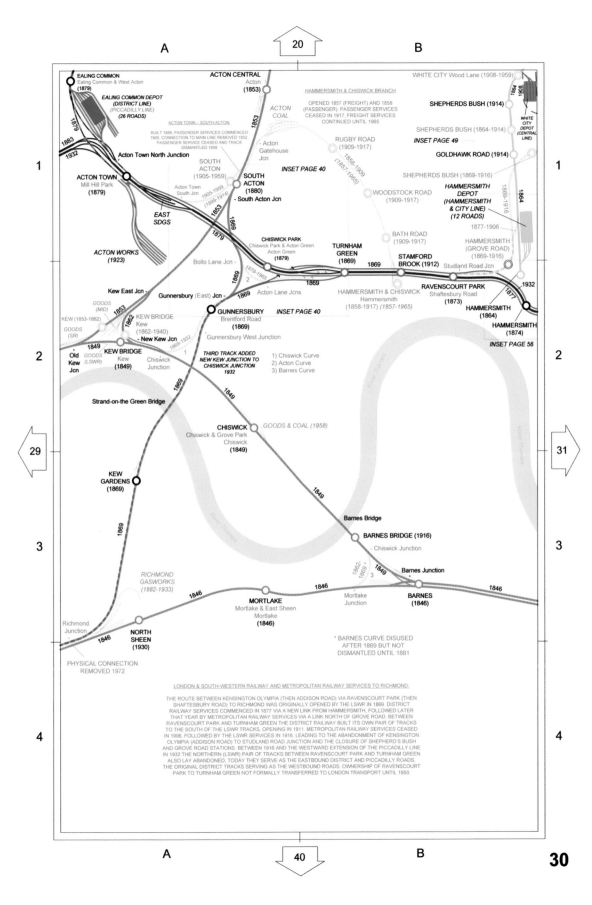

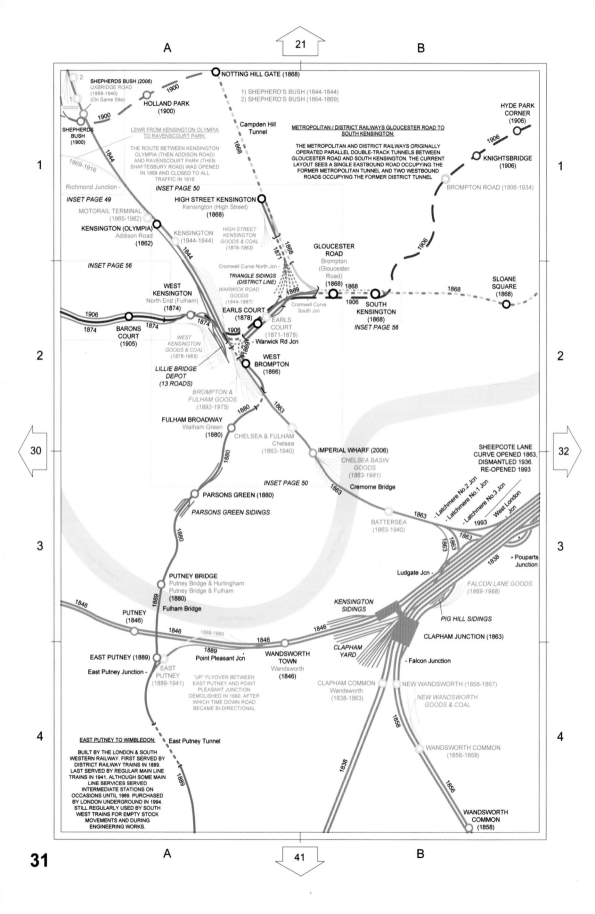

SHEPHERDS BUSH (2006)
UXBRIDGE ROAD
(1869-1940)
(On Same Site)
GOODS

SHEPHERDS
BUSH
(1900)

HOLLAND PARK
(1900)

NOTTING HILL GATE (1868)

1) SHEPHERD'S BUSH (1844-1844)
2) SHEPHERD'S BUSH (1864-1869)

HYDE PARK
CORNER
(1906)

KNIGHTSBRIDGE
(1906)

Camden Hill
Tunnel

METROPOLITAN / DISTRICT RAILWAYS GLOUCESTER ROAD TO SOUTH KENSINGTON:

THE METROPOLITAN AND DISTRICT RAILWAYS ORIGINALLY OPERATED PARALLEL DOUBLE-TRACK TUNNELS BETWEEN GLOUCESTER ROAD AND SOUTH KENSINGTON. THE CURRENT LAYOUT SEES A SINGLE EASTBOUND ROAD OCCUPYING THE FORMER METROPOLITAN TUNNEL AND TWO WESTBOUND ROADS OCCUPYING THE FORMER DISTRICT TUNNEL.

BROMPTON ROAD (1906-1934)

LSWR FROM KENSINGTON OLYMPIA TO RAVENSCOURT PARK:

THE ROUTE BETWEEN KENSINGTON OLYMPIA (THEN ADDISON ROAD) AND RAVENSCOURT PARK (THEN SHAFTESBURY ROAD) WAS OPENED IN 1869 AND CLOSED TO ALL TRAFFIC IN 1916

Richmond Junction -

INSET PAGE 49

HIGH STREET KENSINGTON
Kensington (High Street)
(1868)

HIGH STREET KENSINGTON GOODS & COAL (1878-1963)

MOTORAIL TERMINAL
(1965-1982)

KENSINGTON (OLYMPIA)
Addison Road
(1862)

KENSINGTON
(1844-1844)

GLOUCESTER
ROAD
Brompton
(Gloucester
Road)
(1868)

SLOANE
SQUARE
(1868)

INSET PAGE 56

Cromwell Curve North Jcn -

TRIANGLE SIDINGS (DISTRICT LINE)

WARWICK ROAD GOODS (1844-1967)

WEST
KENSINGTON
North End (Fulham)
(1874)

EARLS COURT
(1878)

EARLS
COURT
(1871-1878)

Cromwell Curve
South Jcn -

SOUTH
KENSINGTON
(1868)

INSET PAGE 56

BARONS
COURT
(1905)

WEST KENSINGTON GOODS & COAL (1878-1965)

- Warwick Rd Jcn

WEST
BROMPTON
(1866)

LILLIE BRIDGE DEPOT (13 ROADS)

BROMPTON & FULHAM GOODS (1892-1975)

FULHAM BROADWAY
Walham Green
(1880)

CHELSEA & FULHAM
Chelsea
(1863-1940)

IMPERIAL WHARF (2006)

CHELSEA BASIN GOODS (1863-1981)

SHEEPCOTE LANE
CURVE OPENED 1863,
DISMANTLED 1936.
RE-OPENED 1993

Cremorne Bridge

INSET PAGE 50

PARSONS GREEN (1880)

PARSONS GREEN SIDINGS

- Latchmere No.2 Jcn
- Latchmere No.1 Jcn
- Latchmere No.3 Jcn
West London
Jcn
1993

BATTERSEA
(1863-1940)

• Pouparts
Junction

FALCON LANE GOODS (1869-1968)

Ludgate Jcn -

PUTNEY BRIDGE
Putney Bridge & Hurlingham
Putney Bridge & Fulham
(1880)
Fulham Bridge

KENSINGTON SIDINGS

PIG HILL SIDINGS

CLAPHAM JUNCTION (1863)

PUTNEY
(1846)

1889-1990

1846

1846

CLAPHAM YARD

- Falcon Junction

EAST PUTNEY (1889)

East Putney Junction -

EAST
PUTNEY
(1889-1941)

Point Pleasant Jcn

WANDSWORTH
TOWN
Wandsworth
(1846)

CLAPHAM COMMON
Wandsworth
(1838-1863)

NEW WANDSWORTH (1858-1867)

NEW WANDSWORTH GOODS & COAL

'UP' FLYOVER BETWEEN EAST PUTNEY AND POINT PLEASANT JUNCTION DEMOLISHED IN 1990, AFTER WHICH TIME DOWN ROAD BECAME BI-DIRECTIONAL

WANDSWORTH COMMON
(1856-1858)

EAST PUTNEY TO WIMBLEDON:

BUILT BY THE LONDON & SOUTH WESTERN RAILWAY. FIRST SERVED BY DISTRICT RAILWAY TRAINS IN 1889. LAST SERVED BY REGULAR MAIN LINE TRAINS IN 1941, ALTHOUGH SOME MAIN LINE SERVICES SERVED INTERMEDIATE STATIONS ON OCCASIONS UNTIL 1969. PURCHASED BY LONDON UNDERGROUND IN 1994. STILL REGULARLY USED BY SOUTH WEST TRAINS FOR EMPTY STOCK MOVEMENTS AND DURING ENGINEERING WORKS.

East Putney Tunnel

WANDSWORTH
COMMON
(1858)

30
32

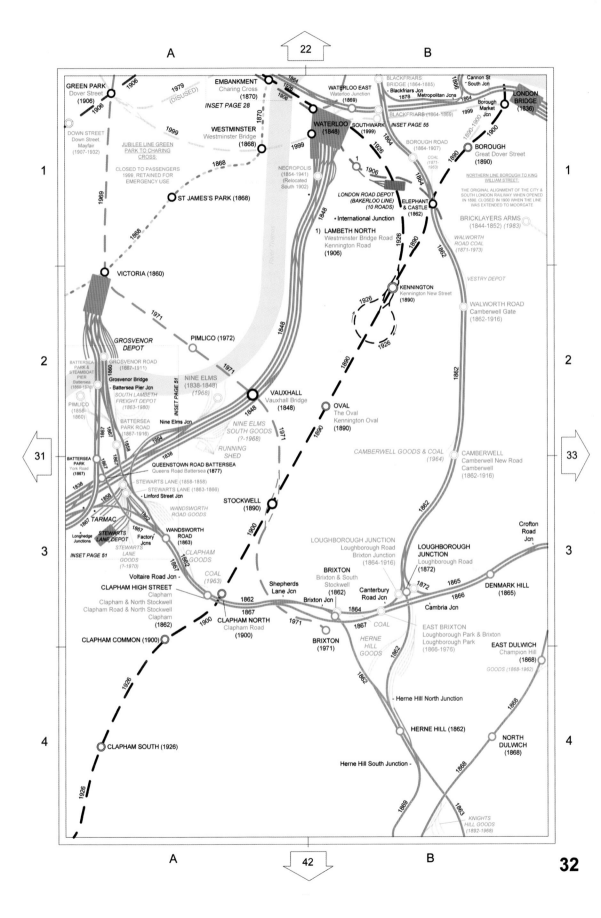

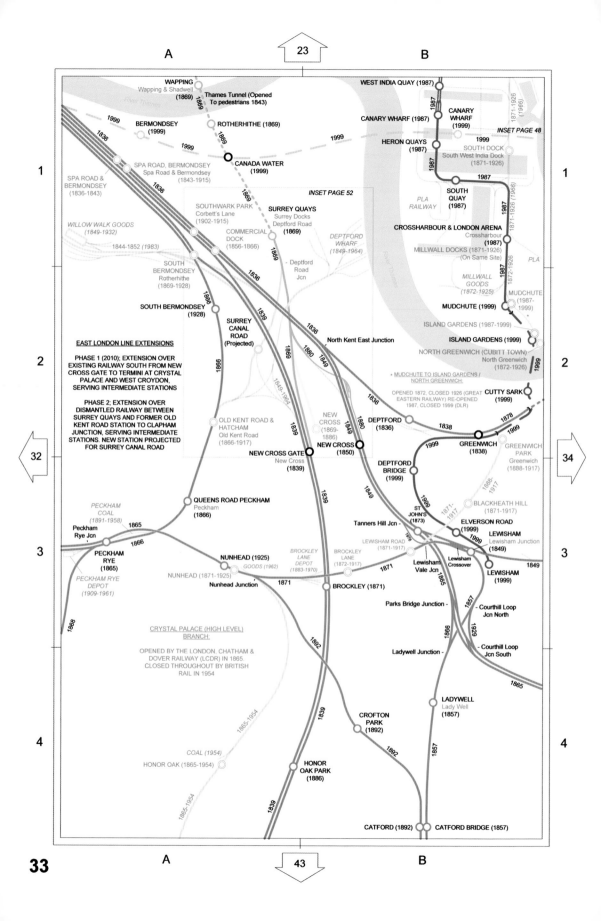

WAPPING
Wapping & Shadwell
(1869)

Thames Tunnel (Opened
To pedestrians 1843)

1869

BERMONDSEY
(1999)

1999

ROTHERHITHE (1869)

1869

1999

WEST INDIA QUAY (1987)

1987

CANARY WHARF (1987)

CANARY
WHARF
(1999)

1987

1871-1926
(1966)

INSET PAGE 48

HERON QUAYS
(1987)

1987

1999

SOUTH DOCK
South West India Dock
(1871-1926)

1999

CANADA WATER
(1999)

1836

1999

SPA ROAD, BERMONDSEY
Spa Road & Bermondsey
(1843-1915)

SPA ROAD &
BERMONDSEY
(1836-1843)

1

1836

SOUTH
QUAY
(1987)

1987

PLA
RAILWAY

1871-1926 (1966)

WILLOW WALK GOODS
(1849-1932)

SOUTHWARK PARK
Corbett's Lane
(1902-1915)

1836

SURREY QUAYS
Surrey Docks
Deptford Road
(1869)

INSET PAGE 52

CROSSHARBOUR & LONDON ARENA
(1987)
Crossharbour

1987

1844-1852 (1983)

COMMERCIAL
DOCK
(1856-1866)

1869

DEPTFORD
WHARF
(1849-1964)

MILLWALL DOCKS (1871-1926)
(On Same Site)

PLA

1872-1926

SOUTH
BERMONDSEY
Rotherhithe
(1869-1928)

1836

MILLWALL
GOODS
(1872-1925)

MUDCHUTE
(1987-1999)

1866

Deptford
Road
Jcn

MUDCHUTE (1999)

SOUTH BERMONDSEY
(1928)

1869

1839

1836

North Kent East Junction

ISLAND GARDENS (1987-1999)

1987

ISLAND GARDENS (1999)

EAST LONDON LINE EXTENSIONS

SURREY
CANAL
ROAD
(Projected)

1866

1869

1890

1849

NORTH GREENWICH (CUBITT TOWN)
North Greenwich
(1872-1926)

1999

PHASE 1 (2010); EXTENSION OVER
EXISTING RAILWAY SOUTH FROM NEW
CROSS GATE TO TERMINI AT CRYSTAL
PALACE AND WEST CROYDON,
SERVING INTERMEDIATE STATIONS

1836

· MUDCHUTE TO ISLAND GARDENS /
NORTH GREENWICH.

2

PHASE 2; EXTENSION OVER
DISMANTLED RAILWAY BETWEEN
SURREY QUAYS AND FORMER OLD
KENT ROAD STATION TO CLAPHAM
JUNCTION, SERVING INTERMEDIATE
STATIONS. NEW STATION PROJECTED
FOR SURREY CANAL ROAD

1849-1964

OLD KENT ROAD &
HATCHAM
Old Kent Road
(1866-1917)

NEW
CROSS
(1869-
1886)

NEW CROSS
(1850)

1849

1880

DEPTFORD
(1836)

1838

OPENED 1872, CLOSED 1926 (GREAT
EASTERN RAILWAY) RE-OPENED
1987, CLOSED 1999 (DLR)

1878

CUTTY SARK
(1999)

1999

1999

GREENWICH
(1838)

GREENWICH
PARK
Greenwich
(1888-1917)

32

1839

NEW CROSS GATE
New Cross
(1839)

DEPTFORD
BRIDGE
(1999)

1838

1999

34

PECKHAM
COAL
(1891-1958)

QUEENS ROAD PECKHAM
Peckham
(1866)

1839

1849

ST
JOHN'S
(1873)

1871-
1917

1888-
1917

BLACKHEATH HILL
(1871-1917)

Peckham
Rye Jcn

1865

Tanners Hill Jcn

1976

ELVERSON ROAD
(1999)

1866

PECKHAM
RYE
(1865)

NUNHEAD (1925)

BROCKLEY
LANE
DEPOT
(1883-1970)

BROCKLEY
LANE
(1872-1917)

LEWISHAM ROAD
(1871-1917)

Lewisham
Vale Jcn

1999

Lewisham
Crossover

LEWISHAM
Lewisham Junction
(1849)

3

PECKHAM RYE
DEPOT
(1909-1961)

NUNHEAD (1871-1925)
GOODS (1962)

Nunhead Junction

1871

1871

1865

LEWISHAM
(1999)

1849

1868

CRYSTAL PALACE (HIGH LEVEL)
BRANCH:

1892

BROCKLEY (1871)

Parks Bridge Junction -

1866

1857

Courthill Loop
Jcn North

OPENED BY THE LONDON, CHATHAM &
DOVER RAILWAY (LCDR) IN 1865.
CLOSED THROUGHOUT BY BRITISH
RAIL IN 1954.

Ladywell Junction -

1829

Courthill Loop
Jcn South

1865

COAL (1954)

1865-1954

LADYWELL
Lady Well
(1857)

HONOR OAK (1865-1954)

CROFTON
PARK
(1892)

1839

1892

1857

4

1865-1954

HONOR
OAK PARK
(1886)

1892

1839

CATFORD (1892)

CATFORD BRIDGE (1857)

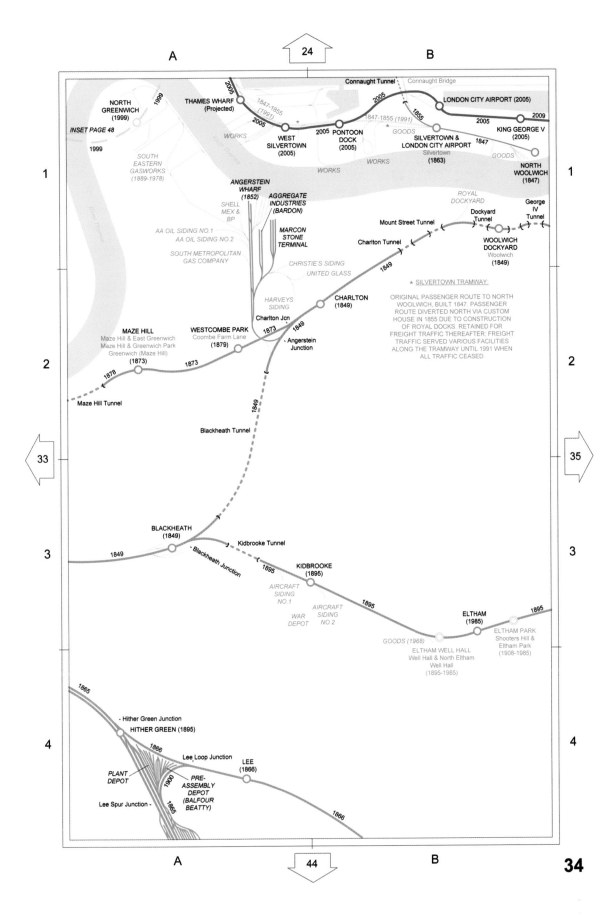

NORTH GREENWICH (1999)

INSET PAGE 48

1999

1999

SOUTH EASTERN GASWORKS (1889-1978)

THAMES WHARF (Projected)

2005

2005

1847-1855 (1991)

WORKS

WEST SILVERTOWN (2005)

2005

PONTOON DOCK (2005)

Connaught Tunnel

Connaught Bridge

2005

1847-1855 (1991)

GOODS

SILVERTOWN & LONDON CITY AIRPORT
Silvertown
(1863)

1855

LONDON CITY AIRPORT (2005)

2005

1847

GOODS

2009

KING GEORGE V (2005)

NORTH WOOLWICH (1847)

WORKS

ANGERSTEIN WHARF (1852)

SHELL MEX & BP

AA OIL SIDING NO.1
AA OIL SIDING NO.2

SOUTH METROPOLITAN GAS COMPANY

AGGREGATE INDUSTRIES (BARDON)

MARCON STONE TERMINAL

CHRISTIE'S SIDING
UNITED GLASS

ROYAL DOCKYARD

Mount Street Tunnel

Dockyard Tunnel

George IV Tunnel

Charlton Tunnel

1849

WOOLWICH DOCKYARD
Woolwich
(1849)

HARVEYS SIDING

Charlton Jcn

CHARLTON (1849)

* SILVERTOWN TRAMWAY.

ORIGINAL PASSENGER ROUTE TO NORTH WOOLWICH, BUILT 1847. PASSENGER ROUTE DIVERTED NORTH VIA CUSTOM HOUSE IN 1855 DUE TO CONSTRUCTION OF ROYAL DOCKS. RETAINED FOR FREIGHT TRAFFIC THEREAFTER; FREIGHT TRAFFIC SERVED VARIOUS FACILITIES ALONG THE TRAMWAY UNTIL 1991 WHEN ALL TRAFFIC CEASED.

MAZE HILL
Maze Hill & East Greenwich
Maze Hill & Greenwich Park
Greenwich (Maze Hill)
(1873)

WESTCOMBE PARK
Coombe Farm Lane
(1879)

1873

1849

Charlton Jcn

1873

Angerstein Junction

1878

1873

Maze Hill Tunnel

1849

Blackheath Tunnel

BLACKHEATH (1849)

1849

Blackheath Junction

Kidbrooke Tunnel

1895

KIDBROOKE (1895)

AIRCRAFT SIDING NO.1

WAR DEPOT

AIRCRAFT SIDING NO.2

1895

GOODS (1968)

ELTHAM WELL HALL
Well Hall & North Eltham
Well Hall
(1895-1985)

ELTHAM (1985)

1895

ELTHAM PARK
Shooters Hill & Eltham Park
(1908-1985)

1865

Hither Green Junction

HITHER GREEN (1895)

1866

Lee Loop Junction

LEE (1866)

PLANT DEPOT

1900

PRE-ASSEMBLY DEPOT (BALFOUR BEATTY)

Lee Spur Junction

1865

1866

33

35

44

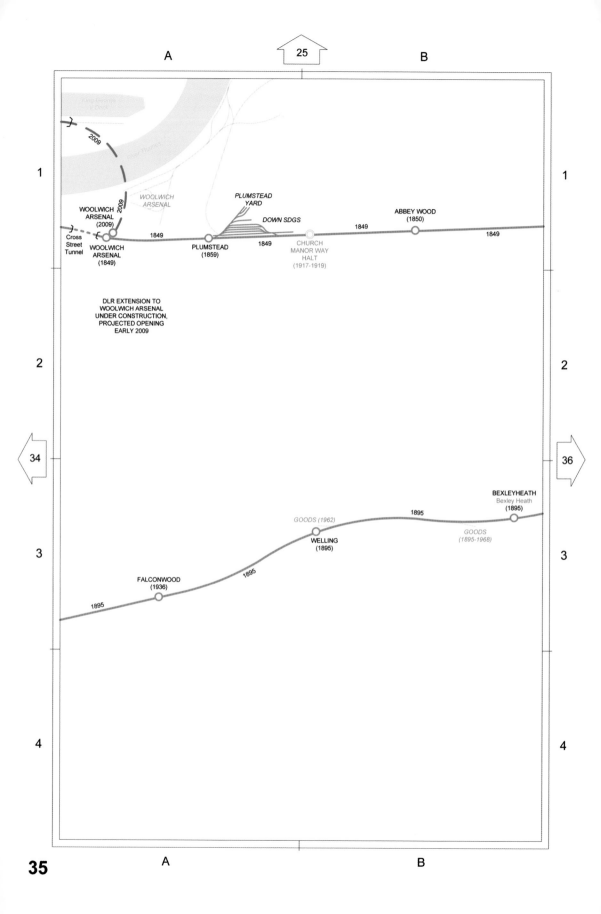

1

Woolwich K George
V Dock

2009

2009

WOOLWICH
ARSENAL
(2009)

Cross
Street
Tunnel

WOOLWICH
ARSENAL
(1849)

*WOOLWICH
ARSENAL*

1849

*PLUMSTEAD
YARD*

DOWN SDGS

PLUMSTEAD
(1859)

1849

CHURCH
MANOR WAY
HALT
(1917-1919)

1849

ABBEY WOOD
(1850)

1849

1

DLR EXTENSION TO
WOOLWICH ARSENAL
UNDER CONSTRUCTION,
PROJECTED OPENING
EARLY 2009

2

2

34

36

BEXLEYHEATH
Bexley Heath
(1895)

GOODS (1962)

1895

WELLING
(1895)

*GOODS
(1895-1968)*

FALCONWOOD
(1936)

1895

1895

3

3

1895

4

4

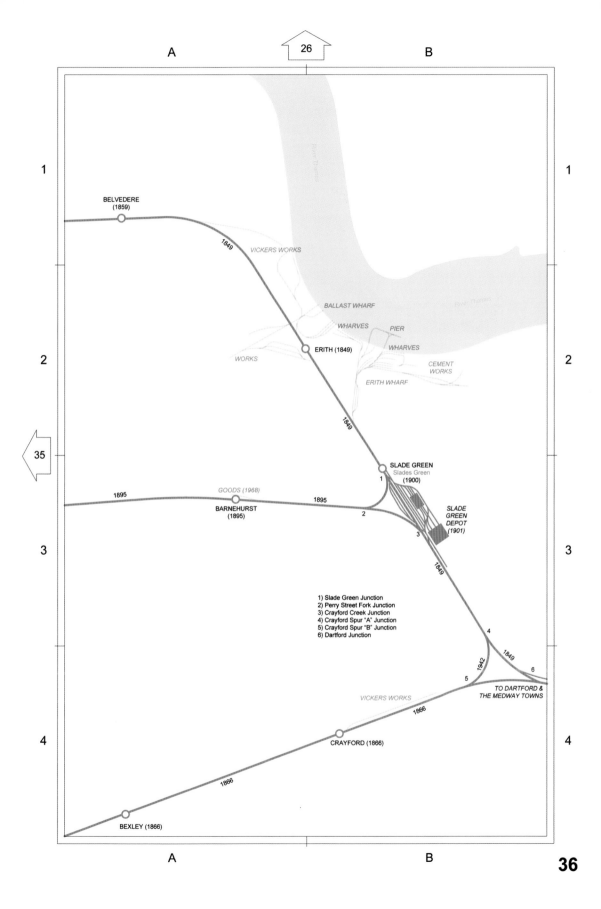

1) Slade Green Junction
2) Perry Street Fork Junction
3) Crayford Creek Junction
4) Crayford Spur "A" Junction
5) Crayford Spur "B" Junction
6) Dartford Junction

BELVEDERE (1859)

1849

VICKERS WORKS

BALLAST WHARF

WHARVES

PIER

WHARVES

WORKS

CEMENT WORKS

ERITH (1849)

1849

ERITH WHARF

River Thames

SLADE GREEN
Slades Green
(1900)

1895

GOODS (1968)

BARNEHURST
(1895)

1895

SLADE GREEN DEPOT (1901)

1849

1942

1849

TO DARTFORD &
THE MEDWAY TOWNS

VICKERS WORKS

1866

CRAYFORD (1866)

1866

BEXLEY (1866)

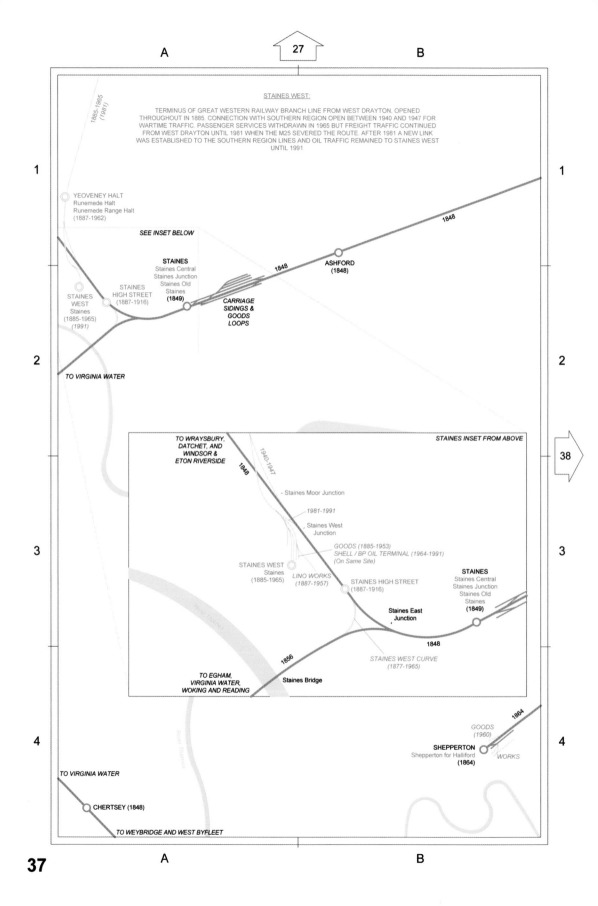

STAINES WEST:

TERMINUS OF GREAT WESTERN RAILWAY BRANCH LINE FROM WEST DRAYTON, OPENED
THROUGHOUT IN 1885. CONNECTION WITH SOUTHERN REGION OPEN BETWEEN 1940 AND 1947 FOR
WARTIME TRAFFIC. PASSENGER SERVICES WITHDRAWN IN 1965 BUT FREIGHT TRAFFIC CONTINUED
FROM WEST DRAYTON UNTIL 1981 WHEN THE M25 SEVERED THE ROUTE. AFTER 1981 A NEW LINK
WAS ESTABLISHED TO THE SOUTHERN REGION LINES AND OIL TRAFFIC REMAINED TO STAINES WEST
UNTIL 1991

1885-1965
(1981)

1848

1

YEOVENEY HALT
Runemede Halt
Runemede Range Halt
(1887-1962)

SEE INSET BELOW

STAINES
Staines Central
Staines Junction
Staines Old
Staines
(1849)

ASHFORD
(1848)

1848

STAINES
WEST
Staines
(1885-1965)
(1991)

STAINES
HIGH STREET
(1887-1916)

CARRIAGE
SIDINGS &
GOODS
LOOPS

2

TO VIRGINIA WATER

TO WRAYSBURY,
DATCHET, AND
WINDSOR &
ETON RIVERSIDE

STAINES INSET FROM ABOVE

38

1848

1940-1947

- Staines Moor Junction

1981-1991

Staines West
Junction

GOODS (1885-1953)
SHELL / BP OIL TERMINAL (1964-1991)
(On Same Site)

3

STAINES WEST
Staines
(1885-1965)

LINO WORKS
(1887-1957)

STAINES HIGH STREET
(1887-1916)

STAINES
Staines Central
Staines Junction
Staines Old
Staines
(1849)

Staines East
Junction

1848

STAINES WEST CURVE
(1877-1965)

1856

TO EGHAM,
VIRGINIA WATER,
WOKING AND READING

Staines Bridge

River Thames

1864

GOODS
(1960)

4

SHEPPERTON
Shepperton for Halliford
(1864)

WORKS

TO VIRGINIA WATER

River Thames

CHERTSEY (1848)

TO WEYBRIDGE AND WEST BYFLEET

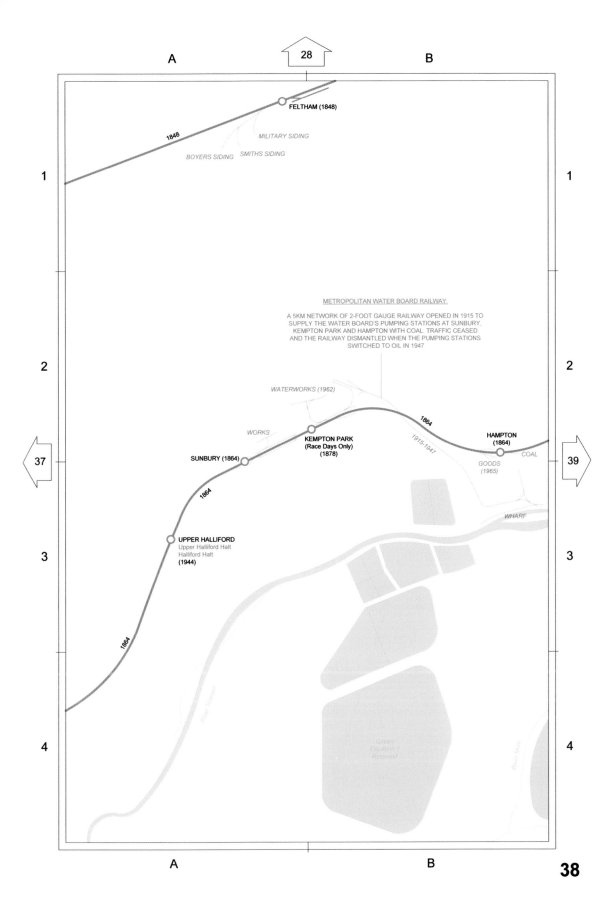

1

FELTHAM (1848)

1848

MILITARY SIDING

BOYERS SIDING   *SMITHS SIDING*

1

METROPOLITAN WATER BOARD RAILWAY:

A 5KM NETWORK OF 2-FOOT GAUGE RAILWAY OPENED IN 1915 TO
SUPPLY THE WATER BOARD'S PUMPING STATIONS AT SUNBURY,
KEMPTON PARK AND HAMPTON WITH COAL. TRAFFIC CEASED
AND THE RAILWAY DISMANTLED WHEN THE PUMPING STATIONS
SWITCHED TO OIL IN 1947

2

WATERWORKS (1962)

1864

WORKS

KEMPTON PARK
(Race Days Only)
(1878)

1915-1947

HAMPTON
(1864)

COAL

SUNBURY (1864)

1864

*GOODS
(1965)*

37

39

WHARF

2

UPPER HALLIFORD
Upper Halliford Halt
Halliford Halt
(1944)

1864

3

1864

River Thames

*Queen
Elizabeth II
Reservoir*

River Ash

4

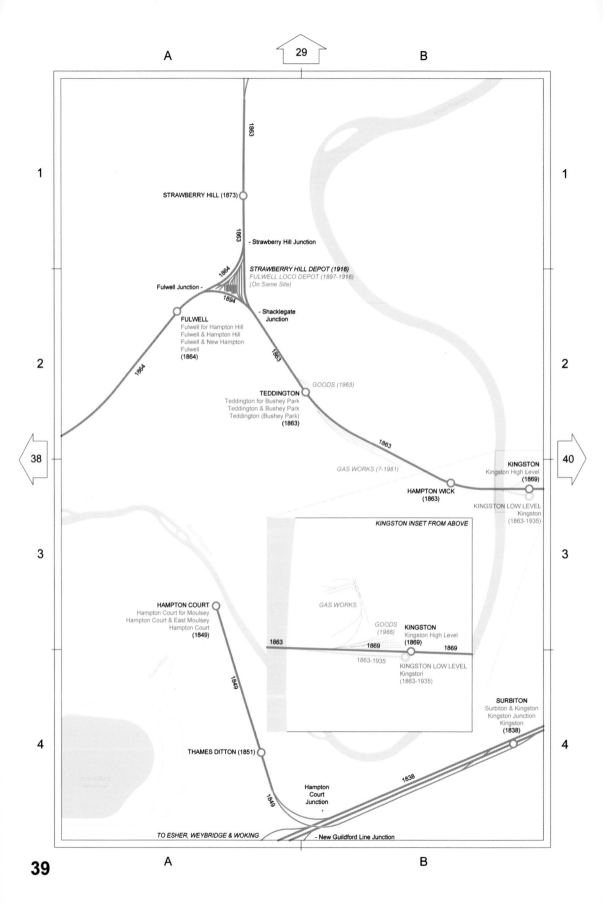

1   1

1863

STRAWBERRY HILL (1873)

1863

- Strawberry Hill Junction

1864

STRAWBERRY HILL DEPOT (1916)
*FULWELL LOCO DEPOT (1897-1916)
(On Same Site)*

Fulwell Junction -

1894

- Shacklegate
Junction

FULWELL
Fulwell for Hampton Hill
Fulwell & Hampton Hill
Fulwell & New Hampton
Fulwell
(1864)

1863

1864

2   2

GOODS (1965)

TEDDINGTON
Teddington for Bushey Park
Teddington & Bushey Park
Teddington (Bushey Park)
(1863)

1863

GAS WORKS (?-1961)

KINGSTON
Kingston High Level
(1869)

38   40

HAMPTON WICK
(1863)

KINGSTON LOW LEVEL
Kingston
(1863-1935)

KINGSTON INSET FROM ABOVE

3   3

GAS WORKS

HAMPTON COURT
Hampton Court for Moulsey
Hampton Court & East Moulsey
Hampton Court
(1849)

*GOODS
(1966)*

KINGSTON
Kingston High Level
(1869)

1863   1869   1869

1863-1935

KINGSTON LOW LEVEL
Kingston
(1863-1935)

1849

SURBITON
Surbiton & Kingston
Kingston Junction
Kingston
(1838)

THAMES DITTON (1851)

Hampton
Court
Junction

4   4

1849

1838

TO ESHER, WEYBRIDGE & WOKING   - New Guildford Line Junction

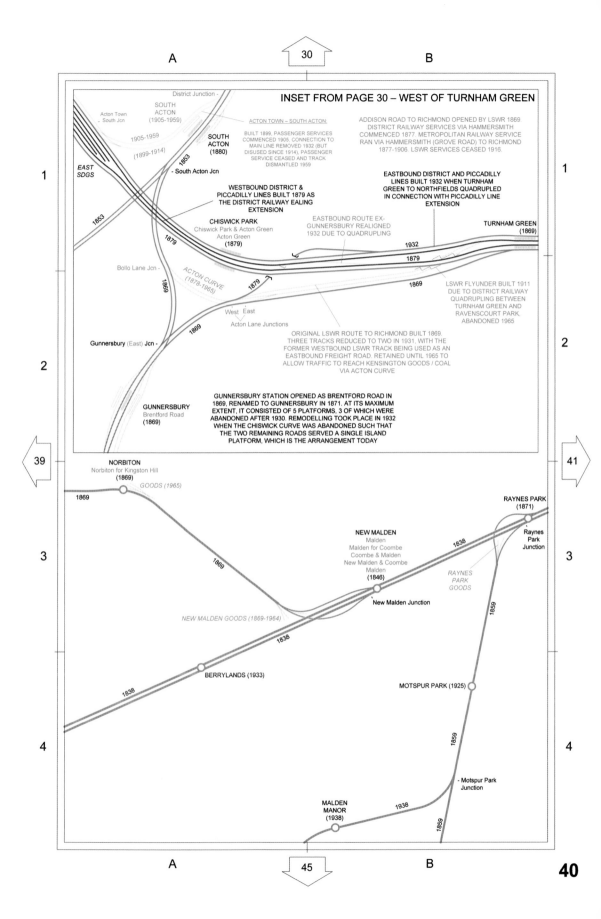

INSET FROM PAGE 30 – WEST OF TURNHAM GREEN

ADDISON ROAD TO RICHMOND OPENED BY LSWR 1869. DISTRICT RAILWAY SERVICES VIA HAMMERSMITH COMMENCED 1877. METROPOLITAN RAILWAY SERVICE RAN VIA HAMMERSMITH (GROVE ROAD) TO RICHMOND 1877-1906. LSWR SERVICES CEASED 1916.

District Junction -

SOUTH ACTON (1905-1959)

Acton Town - South Jcn

1905-1959

SOUTH ACTON (1880)

(1899-1914)

1853

EAST SDGS

1853

- South Acton Jcn

ACTON TOWN – SOUTH ACTON:
BUILT 1899, PASSENGER SERVICES COMMENCED 1905. CONNECTION TO MAIN LINE REMOVED 1932 (BUT DISUSED SINCE 1914), PASSENGER SERVICE CEASED AND TRACK DISMANTLED 1959

WESTBOUND DISTRICT & PICCADILLY LINES BUILT 1879 AS THE DISTRICT RAILWAY EALING EXTENSION

EASTBOUND DISTRICT AND PICCADILLY LINES BUILT 1932 WHEN TURNHAM GREEN TO NORTHFIELDS QUADRUPLED IN CONNECTION WITH PICCADILLY LINE EXTENSION

CHISWICK PARK
Chiswick Park & Acton Green
Acton Green
(1879)

EASTBOUND ROUTE EX-GUNNERSBURY REALIGNED 1932 DUE TO QUADRUPLING

TURNHAM GREEN (1869)

1879

1932

1879

Bollo Lane Jcn -

1879

ACTON CURVE (1878-1965)

1869

West   East
Acton Lane Junctions

1869

1869

LSWR FLYUNDER BUILT 1911 DUE TO DISTRICT RAILWAY QUADRUPLING BETWEEN TURNHAM GREEN AND RAVENSCOURT PARK, ABANDONED 1965

Gunnersbury (East) Jcn -

1869

ORIGINAL LSWR ROUTE TO RICHMOND BUILT 1869. THREE TRACKS REDUCED TO TWO IN 1931, WITH THE FORMER WESTBOUND LSWR TRACK BEING USED AS AN EASTBOUND FREIGHT ROAD. RETAINED UNTIL 1965 TO ALLOW TRAFFIC TO REACH KENSINGTON GOODS / COAL VIA ACTON CURVE

GUNNERSBURY
Brentford Road
(1869)

GUNNERSBURY STATION OPENED AS BRENTFORD ROAD IN 1869, RENAMED TO GUNNERSBURY IN 1871. AT ITS MAXIMUM EXTENT, IT CONSISTED OF 5 PLATFORMS, 3 OF WHICH WERE ABANDONED AFTER 1930. REMODELLING TOOK PLACE IN 1932 WHEN THE CHISWICK CURVE WAS ABANDONED SUCH THAT THE TWO REMAINING ROADS SERVED A SINGLE ISLAND PLATFORM, WHICH IS THE ARRANGEMENT TODAY

39
41

NORBITON
Norbiton for Kingston Hill
(1869)

GOODS (1965)

1869

1869

RAYNES PARK
(1871)

NEW MALDEN
Malden
Malden for Coombe
Coombe & Malden
New Malden & Coombe
Malden
(1846)

1838

Raynes Park Junction

RAYNES PARK GOODS

1859

NEW MALDEN GOODS (1869-1964)

New Malden Junction

1838

BERRYLANDS (1933)

MOTSPUR PARK (1925)

1838

1859

- Motspur Park Junction

MALDEN MANOR
(1938)

1938

1859

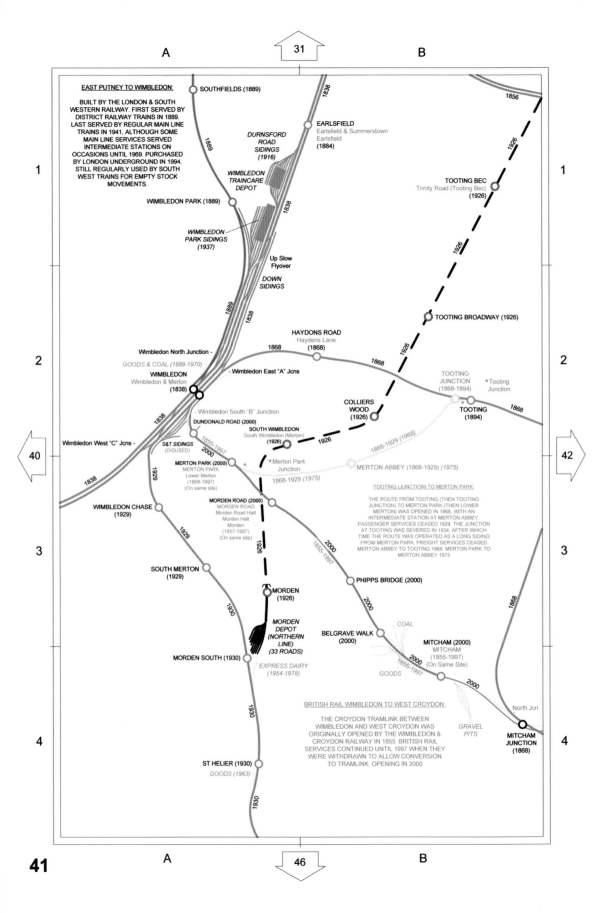

A   B

EAST PUTNEY TO WIMBLEDON:

BUILT BY THE LONDON & SOUTH WESTERN RAILWAY. FIRST SERVED BY DISTRICT RAILWAY TRAINS IN 1889. LAST SERVED BY REGULAR MAIN LINE TRAINS IN 1941, ALTHOUGH SOME MAIN LINE SERVICES SERVED INTERMEDIATE STATIONS ON OCCASIONS UNTIL 1969. PURCHASED BY LONDON UNDERGROUND IN 1994. STILL REGULARLY USED BY SOUTH WEST TRAINS FOR EMPTY STOCK MOVEMENTS.

SOUTHFIELDS (1889)

1838

EARLSFIELD
Earlsfield & Summerstown
Earlsfield
(1884)

1856

DURNSFORD ROAD SIDINGS (1916)

1889

1926

WIMBLEDON TRAINCARE DEPOT

TOOTING BEC
Trinity Road (Tooting Bec)
(1926)

WIMBLEDON PARK (1889)

1838

WIMBLEDON PARK SIDINGS (1937)

1926

Up Slow Flyover

DOWN SIDINGS

TOOTING BROADWAY (1926)

1889 1838

HAYDONS ROAD
Haydens Lane
(1868)

1926

Wimbledon North Junction -
GOODS & COAL (1889-1970)

1868

1868

WIMBLEDON
Wimbledon & Merton
(1838)

- Wimbledon East "A" Jcns

COLLIERS WOOD
(1926)

TOOTING JUNCTION
(1868-1894)

* Tooting Junction

1838

- Wimbledon South "B" Junction

TOOTING
(1894)

1868

DUNDONALD ROAD (2000)

SOUTH WIMBLEDON
South Wimbledon (Merton)
(1926)

1926

Wimbledon West "C" Jcns -

S&T SIDINGS (DISUSED)

1855-1997

1868-1929 (1968)

42

1838

2000

MERTON PARK (2000)
*MERTON PARK
Lower Merton
(1868-1997)
(On same site)*

*

* Merton Park Junction

MERTON ABBEY (1868-1929) *(1975)*

TOOTING (JUNCTION) TO MERTON PARK:

WIMBLEDON CHASE
(1929)

1929

MORDEN ROAD (2000)
*MORDEN ROAD
Morden Road Halt
Morden Halt
(1857-1997)
(On same site)*

1926

1868-1929 *(1975)*

THE ROUTE FROM TOOTING (THEN TOOTING JUNCTION) TO MERTON PARK (THEN LOWER MERTON) WAS OPENED IN 1868, WITH AN INTERMEDIATE STATION AT MERTON ABBEY. PASSENGER SERVICES CEASED 1929. THE JUNCTION AT TOOTING WAS SEVERED IN 1934, AFTER WHICH TIME THE ROUTE WAS OPERATED AS A LONG SIDING FROM MERTON PARK. FREIGHT SERVICES CEASED MERTON ABBEY TO TOOTING 1968, MERTON PARK TO MERTON ABBEY 1975

SOUTH MERTON
(1929)

1929

2000

PHIPPS BRIDGE (2000)

1868

1930

MORDEN
(1926)

2000

MORDEN DEPOT (NORTHERN LINE) (33 ROADS)

COAL

BELGRAVE WALK
(2000)

MITCHAM (2000)
*MITCHAM
(1855-1997)
(On Same Site)*

MORDEN SOUTH (1930)

EXPRESS DAIRY (1954-1978)

1855-1997

2000

GOODS

2000

North Jcn

BRITISH RAIL WIMBLEDON TO WEST CROYDON:

1930

THE CROYDON TRAMLINK BETWEEN WIMBLEDON AND WEST CROYDON WAS ORIGINALLY OPENED BY THE WIMBLEDON & CROYDON RAILWAY IN 1855. BRITISH RAIL SERVICES CONTINUED UNTIL 1997 WHEN THEY WERE WITHDRAWN TO ALLOW CONVERSION TO TRAMLINK, OPENING IN 2000

GRAVEL PITS

MITCHAM JUNCTION
(1868)

ST HELIER (1930)
GOODS (1963)

1930

A   B

40

1

2

3

4

42

1

2

3

4

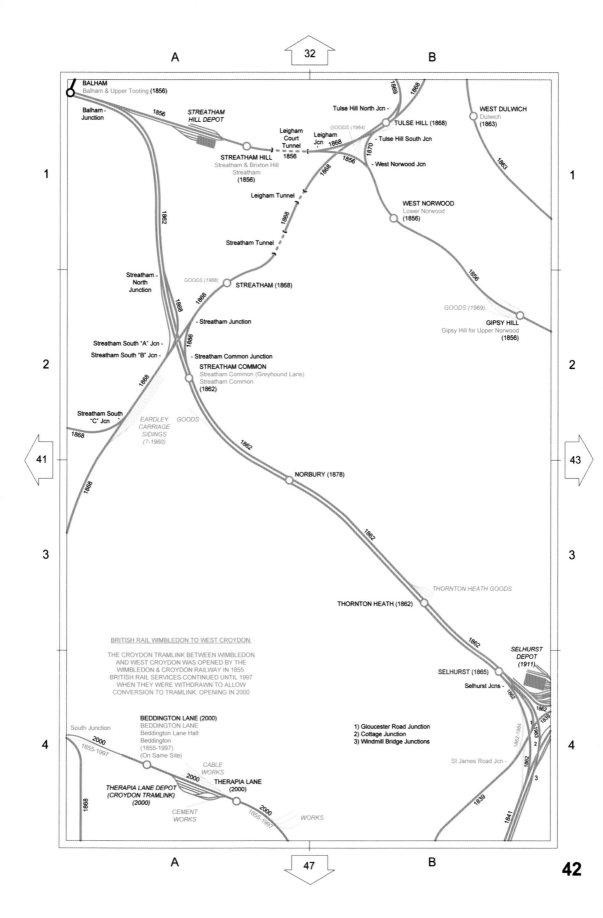

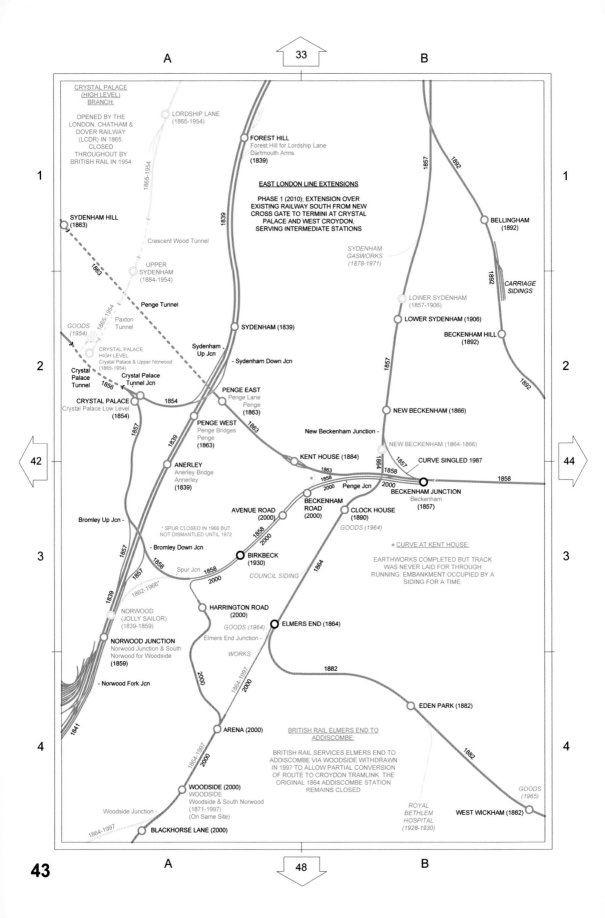

CRYSTAL PALACE
(HIGH LEVEL)
BRANCH:

OPENED BY THE
LONDON, CHATHAM &
DOVER RAILWAY
(LCDR) IN 1865.
CLOSED
THROUGHOUT BY
BRITISH RAIL IN 1954

LORDSHIP LANE
(1865-1954)

FOREST HILL
Forest Hill for Lordship Lane
Dartmouth Arms
(1839)

EAST LONDON LINE EXTENSIONS

PHASE 1 (2010): EXTENSION OVER
EXISTING RAILWAY SOUTH FROM NEW
CROSS GATE TO TERMINI AT CRYSTAL
PALACE AND WEST CROYDON,
SERVING INTERMEDIATE STATIONS

1857
1892

BELLINGHAM
(1892)

SYDENHAM HILL
(1863)

Crescent Wood Tunnel

UPPER
SYDENHAM
(1884-1954)

Penge Tunnel

1863

1865-1954

SYDENHAM
GASWORKS
(1878-1971)

1892

CARRIAGE
SIDINGS

LOWER SYDENHAM
(1857-1906)

LOWER SYDENHAM (1906)

BECKENHAM HILL
(1892)

GOODS
(1954)

Paxton
Tunnel

CRYSTAL PALACE
HIGH LEVEL
Crystal Palace & Upper Norwood
(1865-1954)

SYDENHAM (1839)

Sydenham
Up Jcn

- Sydenham Down Jcn

1857

1892

Crystal
Palace
Tunnel

Crystal Palace
Tunnel Jcn

1856

1854

CRYSTAL PALACE
Crystal Palace Low Level
(1854)

PENGE EAST
Penge Lane
Penge
(1863)

NEW BECKENHAM (1866)

New Beckenham Junction -

NEW BECKENHAM (1864-1866)

CURVE SINGLED 1987

1857

PENGE WEST
Penge Bridges
Penge
(1863)

1839

1863

KENT HOUSE (1884)

1864

1858

ANERLEY
Anerley Bridge
Anerley
(1839)

1863

1858

2000

Penge Jcn

2000

BECKENHAM JUNCTION
Beckenham
(1857)

1858

Bromley Up Jcn -

AVENUE ROAD
(2000)

BECKENHAM
ROAD
(2000)

CLOCK HOUSE
(1890)

GOODS (1964)

1857

* SPUR CLOSED IN 1966 BUT
NOT DISMANTLED UNTIL 1972

1858

2000

* CURVE AT KENT HOUSE:

EARTHWORKS COMPLETED BUT TRACK
WAS NEVER LAID FOR THROUGH
RUNNING. EMBANKMENT OCCUPIED BY A
SIDING FOR A TIME.

- Bromley Down Jcn

1857

1858

Spur Jcn

1858

BIRKBECK
(1930)

COUNCIL SIDING

1864

1839

1862-1966

2000

NORWOOD
(JOLLY SAILOR)
(1839-1859)

HARRINGTON ROAD
(2000)

GOODS (1964)

Elmers End Junction -

ELMERS END (1864)

NORWOOD JUNCTION
Norwood Junction & South
Norwood for Woodside
(1859)

WORKS

1882

- Norwood Fork Jcn

EDEN PARK (1882)

1841

2000

1864-1997

2000

ARENA (2000)

BRITISH RAIL ELMERS END TO
ADDISCOMBE:

BRITISH RAIL SERVICES ELMERS END TO
ADDISCOMBE VIA WOODSIDE WITHDRAWN
IN 1997 TO ALLOW PARTIAL CONVERSION
OF ROUTE TO CROYDON TRAMLINK. THE
ORIGINAL 1864 ADDISCOMBE STATION
REMAINS CLOSED

1882

GOODS
(1965)

WOODSIDE (2000)
WOODSIDE
Woodside & South Norwood
(1871-1997)
(On Same Site)

Woodside Junction -

ROYAL
BETHLEM
HOSPITAL
(1928-1930)

WEST WICKHAM (1882)

1864-1997

BLACKHORSE LANE (2000)

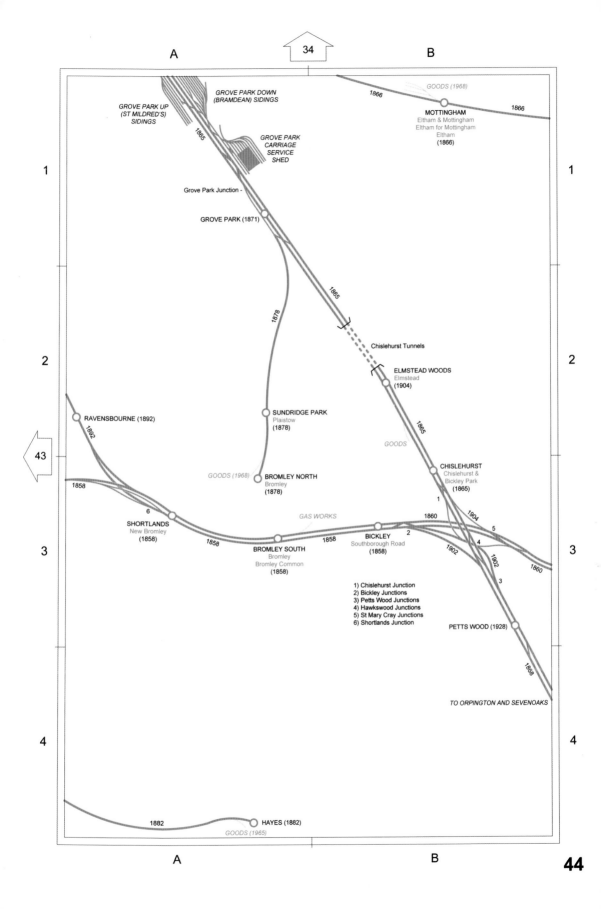

GROVE PARK UP
(ST MILDRED'S)
SIDINGS

GROVE PARK DOWN
(BRAMDEAN) SIDINGS

GROVE PARK
CARRIAGE
SERVICE
SHED

1865

Grove Park Junction -

GROVE PARK (1871)

1878

1865

1866

GOODS (1968)

MOTTINGHAM
Eltham & Mottingham
Eltham for Mottingham
Eltham
(1866)

1866

Chislehurst Tunnels

ELMSTEAD WOODS
Elmstead
(1904)

1865

SUNDRIDGE PARK
Plaistow
(1878)

RAVENSBOURNE (1892)

1892

GOODS

GOODS (1968)

BROMLEY NORTH
Bromley
(1878)

CHISLEHURST
Chislehurst &
Bickley Park
(1865)

1858

1

GAS WORKS

1860

1904

5

6

SHORTLANDS
New Bromley
(1858)

1858

BROMLEY SOUTH
Bromley
Bromley Common
(1858)

1858

BICKLEY
Southborough Road
(1858)

2

4

1902

1902

3

1860

1) Chislehurst Junction
2) Bickley Junctions
3) Petts Wood Junctions
4) Hawkswood Junctions
5) St Mary Cray Junctions
6) Shortlands Junction

PETTS WOOD (1928)

1868

TO ORPINGTON AND SEVENOAKS

1882

HAYES (1882)

GOODS (1965)

1
2
43
3
4

A B

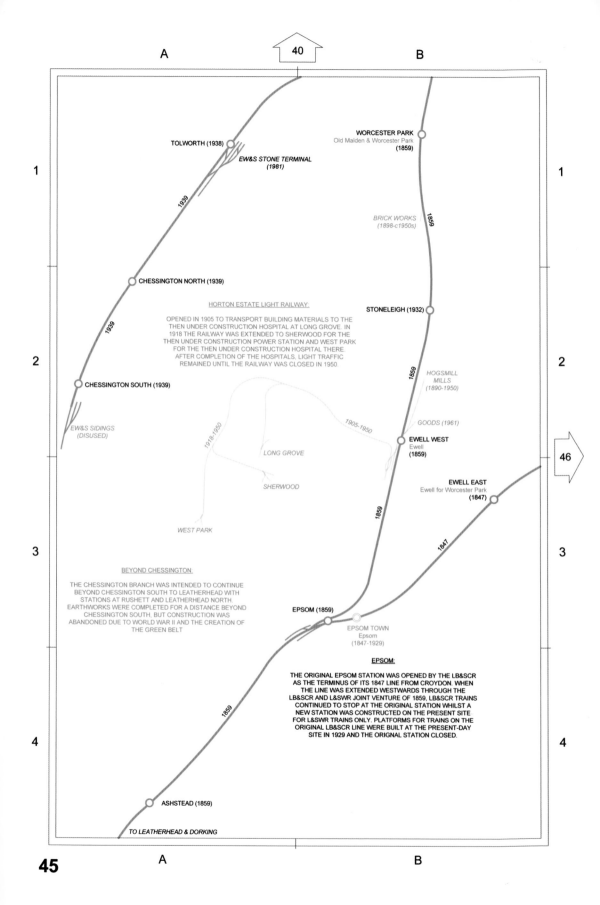

1

TOLWORTH (1938)

EW&S STONE TERMINAL
(1981)

WORCESTER PARK
Old Malden & Worcester Park
(1859)

1939

*BRICK WORKS
(1898-c1950s)*

1859

CHESSINGTON NORTH (1939)

HORTON ESTATE LIGHT RAILWAY:

OPENED IN 1905 TO TRANSPORT BUILDING MATERIALS TO THE
THEN UNDER CONSTRUCTION HOSPITAL AT LONG GROVE. IN
1918 THE RAILWAY WAS EXTENDED TO SHERWOOD FOR THE
THEN UNDER CONSTRUCTION POWER STATION AND WEST PARK
FOR THE THEN UNDER CONSTRUCTION HOSPITAL THERE.
AFTER COMPLETION OF THE HOSPITALS, LIGHT TRAFFIC
REMAINED UNTIL THE RAILWAY WAS CLOSED IN 1950.

STONELEIGH (1932)

1859

1939

2

CHESSINGTON SOUTH (1939)

*HOGSMILL
MILLS
(1890-1950)*

*EW&S SIDINGS
(DISUSED)*

1905-1950

GOODS (1961)

EWELL WEST
Ewell
(1859)

1918-1950

LONG GROVE

SHERWOOD

EWELL EAST
Ewell for Worcester Park
(1847)

46

WEST PARK

1859

1847

3

BEYOND CHESSINGTON:

THE CHESSINGTON BRANCH WAS INTENDED TO CONTINUE
BEYOND CHESSINGTON SOUTH TO LEATHERHEAD WITH
STATIONS AT RUSHETT AND LEATHERHEAD NORTH.
EARTHWORKS WERE COMPLETED FOR A DISTANCE BEYOND
CHESSINGTON SOUTH, BUT CONSTRUCTION WAS
ABANDONED DUE TO WORLD WAR II AND THE CREATION OF
THE GREEN BELT

EPSOM (1859)

*EPSOM TOWN
Epsom
(1847-1929)*

EPSOM:

THE ORIGINAL EPSOM STATION WAS OPENED BY THE LB&SCR
AS THE TERMINUS OF ITS 1847 LINE FROM CROYDON. WHEN
THE LINE WAS EXTENDED WESTWARDS THROUGH THE
LB&SCR AND L&SWR JOINT VENTURE OF 1859, LB&SCR TRAINS
CONTINUED TO STOP AT THE ORIGINAL STATION WHILST A
NEW STATION WAS CONSTRUCTED ON THE PRESENT SITE
FOR L&SWR TRAINS ONLY. PLATFORMS FOR TRAINS ON THE
ORIGINAL LB&SCR LINE WERE BUILT AT THE PRESENT-DAY
SITE IN 1929 AND THE ORIGNAL STATION CLOSED.

1859

4

ASHSTEAD (1859)

TO LEATHERHEAD & DORKING

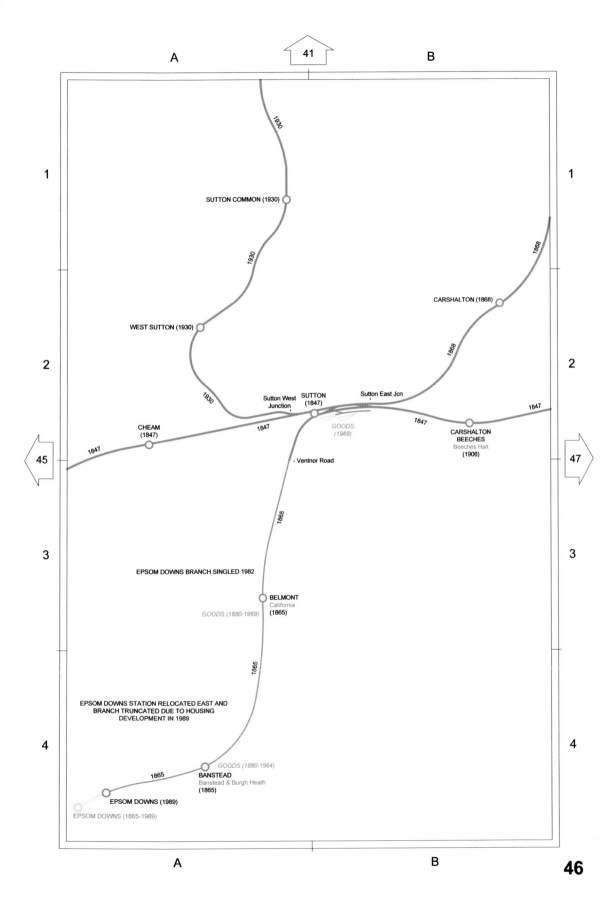

1

1930

SUTTON COMMON (1930)

1930

CARSHALTON (1868)

1868

WEST SUTTON (1930)

1868

2

1930

Sutton West Junction

SUTTON (1847)

Sutton East Jcn

1847

CHEAM (1847)

1847

GOODS (1968)

1847

CARSHALTON BEECHES
Beeches Halt
(1906)

1847

- Ventnor Road

45

47

1865

3

EPSOM DOWNS BRANCH SINGLED 1982

BELMONT
California
(1865)

GOODS (1880-1969)

1865

EPSOM DOWNS STATION RELOCATED EAST AND
BRANCH TRUNCATED DUE TO HOUSING
DEVELOPMENT IN 1989

4

GOODS (1880-1964)

1865

BANSTEAD
Banstead & Burgh Heath
(1865)

EPSOM DOWNS (1989)

EPSOM DOWNS (1865-1989)

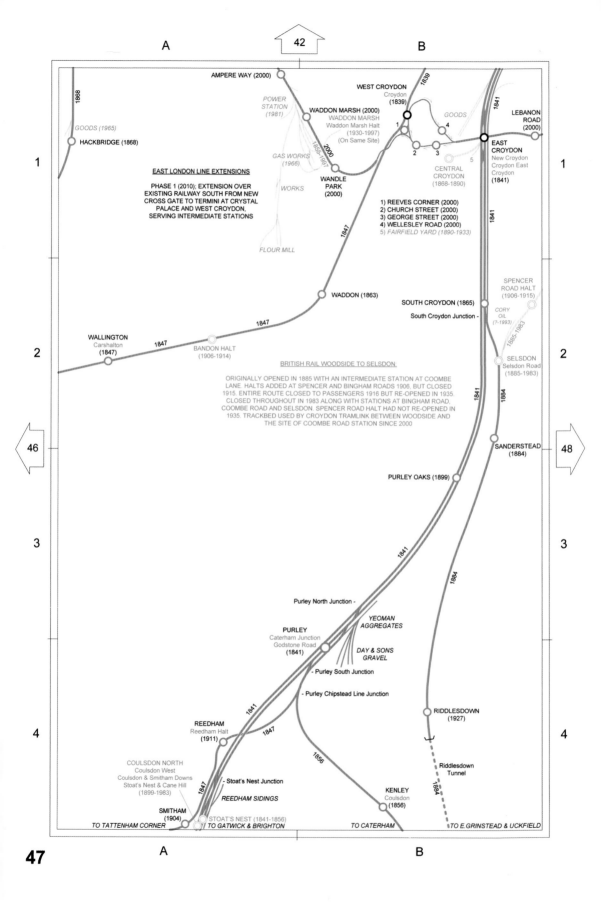

1868

GOODS *(1965)*

HACKBRIDGE (1868)

AMPERE WAY (2000)

POWER STATION (1981)

WADDON MARSH (2000)
WADDON MARSH
Waddon Marsh Halt
(1930-1997)
(On Same Site)

WEST CROYDON
Croydon
(1839)

1839

GOODS

LEBANON ROAD
(2000)

1841

1

GAS WORKS (1966)

2000
1855-1897

WORKS

WANDLE PARK
(2000)

1

FLOUR MILL

1847

1
EAST CROYDON

EAST LONDON LINE EXTENSIONS

PHASE 1 (2010); EXTENSION OVER
EXISTING RAILWAY SOUTH FROM NEW
CROSS GATE TO TERMINI AT CRYSTAL
PALACE AND WEST CROYDON,
SERVING INTERMEDIATE STATIONS

*CENTRAL CROYDON
(1868-1890)*

1
2
3
4

EAST CROYDON
New Croydon
Croydon East
Croydon
(1841)

5

1) REEVES CORNER (2000)
2) CHURCH STREET (2000)
3) GEORGE STREET (2000)
4) WELLESLEY ROAD (2000)
5) *FAIRFIELD YARD (1890-1933)*

1841

SPENCER ROAD HALT
(1906-1915)

*CORY OIL
(?-1993)*

WADDON (1863)

SOUTH CROYDON (1865)

South Croydon Junction -

1847

WALLINGTON
Carshalton
(1847)

1847

BANDON HALT
(1906-1914)

1847

1885-1983

SELSDON
Selsdon Road
(1885-1983)

BRITISH RAIL WOODSIDE TO SELSDON:

ORIGINALLY OPENED IN 1885 WITH AN INTERMEDIATE STATION AT COOMBE
LANE. HALTS ADDED AT SPENCER AND BINGHAM ROADS 1906, BUT CLOSED
1915. ENTIRE ROUTE CLOSED TO PASSENGERS 1916 BUT RE-OPENED IN 1935.
CLOSED THROUGHOUT IN 1983 ALONG WITH STATIONS AT BINGHAM ROAD,
COOMBE ROAD AND SELSDON. SPENCER ROAD HALT HAD NOT RE-OPENED IN
1935. TRACKBED USED BY CROYDON TRAMLINK BETWEEN WOODSIDE AND
THE SITE OF COOMBE ROAD STATION SINCE 2000

SANDERSTEAD
(1884)

PURLEY OAKS (1899)

1841

1841

1884

3

1841

1884

3

Purley North Junction -

*YEOMAN
AGGREGATES*

PURLEY
Caterham Junction
Godstone Road
(1841)

*DAY & SONS
GRAVEL*

- Purley South Junction

- Purley Chipstead Line Junction

RIDDLESDOWN
(1927)

1841

Riddlesdown
Tunnel

REEDHAM
Reedham Halt
(1911)

1847

1856

4

COULSDON NORTH
Coulsdon West
Coulsdon & Smitham Downs
Stoat's Nest & Cane Hill
(1899-1983)

1847

- Stoat's Nest Junction

REEDHAM SIDINGS

KENLEY
Coulsdon
(1856)

1884

SMITHAM
(1904)

STOAT'S NEST (1841-1856)

TO TATTENHAM CORNER *TO GATWICK & BRIGHTON* *TO CATERHAM* *TO E.GRINSTEAD & UCKFIELD*

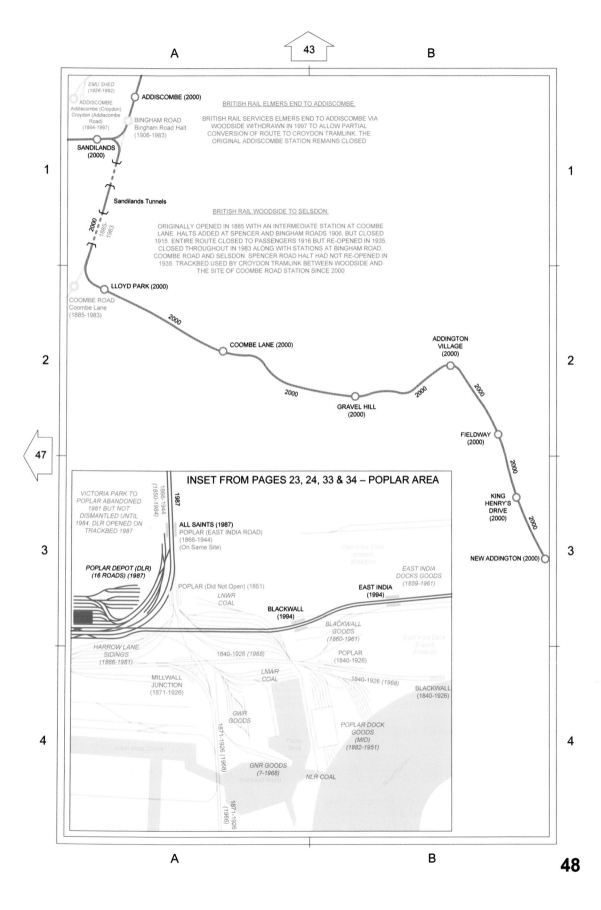

EMU SHED
(1926-1992)

ADDISCOMBE
Addiscombe (Croydon)
Croydon (Addiscombe
Road)
(1864-1997)

ADDISCOMBE (2000)

BINGHAM ROAD
Bingham Road Halt
(1906-1983)

SANDILANDS
(2000)

1

Sandilands Tunnels

2000
1885-1983

LLOYD PARK (2000)

COOMBE ROAD
Coombe Lane
(1885-1983)

BRITISH RAIL ELMERS END TO ADDISCOMBE:

BRITISH RAIL SERVICES ELMERS END TO ADDISCOMBE VIA
WOODSIDE WITHDRAWN IN 1997 TO ALLOW PARTIAL
CONVERSION OF ROUTE TO CROYDON TRAMLINK. THE
ORIGINAL ADDISCOMBE STATION REMAINS CLOSED

BRITISH RAIL WOODSIDE TO SELSDON:

ORIGINALLY OPENED IN 1885 WITH AN INTERMEDIATE STATION AT COOMBE
LANE. HALTS ADDED AT SPENCER AND BINGHAM ROADS 1906, BUT CLOSED
1915. ENTIRE ROUTE CLOSED TO PASSENGERS 1916 BUT RE-OPENED IN 1935.
CLOSED THROUGHOUT IN 1983 ALONG WITH STATIONS AT BINGHAM ROAD,
COOMBE ROAD AND SELSDON. SPENCER ROAD HALT HAD NOT RE-OPENED IN
1935. TRACKBED USED BY CROYDON TRAMLINK BETWEEN WOODSIDE AND
THE SITE OF COOMBE ROAD STATION SINCE 2000

ADDINGTON
VILLAGE
(2000)

2000

COOMBE LANE (2000)

2

2000

GRAVEL HILL
(2000)

2000

2000

FIELDWAY
(2000)

2

47

2000

KING
HENRY'S
DRIVE
(2000)

2000

NEW ADDINGTON (2000)

3

INSET FROM PAGES 23, 24, 33 & 34 – POPLAR AREA

VICTORIA PARK TO
POPLAR ABANDONED
1981 BUT NOT
DISMANTLED UNTIL
1984. DLR OPENED ON
TRACKBED 1987

1866-1944
(1850-1984)

1987

ALL SAINTS (1987)
POPLAR (EAST INDIA ROAD)
(1866-1944)
(On Same Site)

East India Dock
(Import)
(Filled In)

EAST INDIA
DOCKS GOODS
(1859-1961)

**POPLAR DEPOT (DLR)
(16 ROADS) (1987)**

POPLAR (Did Not Open) (1851)

LNWR
COAL

**EAST INDIA
(1994)**

BLACKWALL
(1994)

BLACKWALL
GOODS
(1860-1961)

East India Dock
(Export)
(Filled In)

HARROW LANE
SIDINGS
(1866-1981)

1840-1926 (1968)

POPLAR
(1840-1926)

MILLWALL
JUNCTION
(1871-1926)

LNWR
COAL

1840-1926 (1968)

BLACKWALL
(1840-1926)

GWR
GOODS

1871-1926 (1968)

West India Docks

Poplar
Dock

POPLAR DOCK
GOODS
(MID)
(1882-1951)

GNR GOODS
(?-1968)

NLR COAL

1871-1926
(1968)

Blackwall Basin

River Thames

3

4

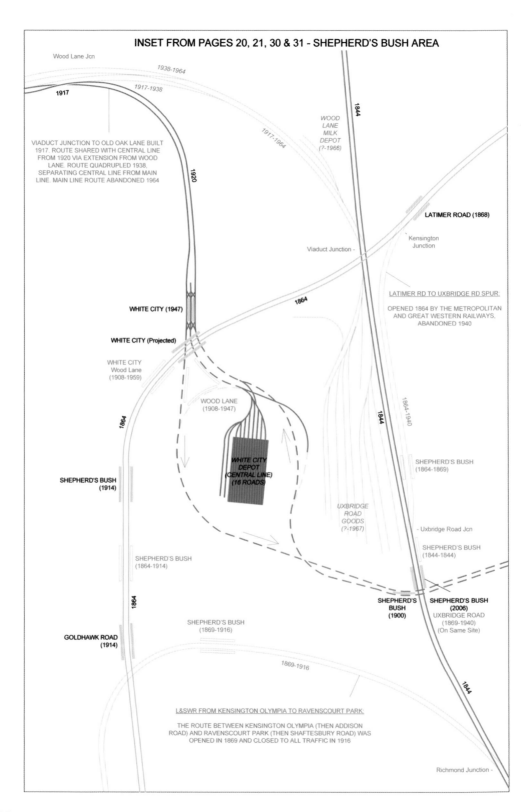

Wood Lane Jcn

1938-1964

1917-1938

1917

1917-1964

1844

WOOD
LANE
MILK
DEPOT
(?-1966)

VIADUCT JUNCTION TO OLD OAK LANE BUILT
1917. ROUTE SHARED WITH CENTRAL LINE
FROM 1920 VIA EXTENSION FROM WOOD
LANE. ROUTE QUADRUPLED 1938,
SEPARATING CENTRAL LINE FROM MAIN
LINE. MAIN LINE ROUTE ABANDONED 1964

1920

LATIMER ROAD (1868)

Kensington
Junction

Viaduct Junction -

LATIMER RD TO UXBRIDGE RD SPUR:

WHITE CITY (1947)

1864

OPENED 1864 BY THE METROPOLITAN
AND GREAT WESTERN RAILWAYS,
ABANDONED 1940

WHITE CITY (Projected)

WHITE CITY
Wood Lane
(1908-1959)

WOOD LANE
(1908-1947)

1864

1844

1864-1940

WHITE CITY
DEPOT
(CENTRAL LINE)
(16 ROADS)

SHEPHERD'S BUSH
(1864-1869)

SHEPHERD'S BUSH
(1914)

UXBRIDGE
ROAD
GOODS
(?-1967)

- Uxbridge Road Jcn

SHEPHERD'S BUSH
(1864-1914)

SHEPHERD'S BUSH
(1844-1844)

1864

SHEPHERD'S
BUSH
(1900)

SHEPHERD'S BUSH
(2006)
UXBRIDGE ROAD
(1869-1940)
(On Same Site)

GOLDHAWK ROAD
(1914)

SHEPHERD'S BUSH
(1869-1916)

1869-1916

1844

L&SWR FROM KENSINGTON OLYMPIA TO RAVENSCOURT PARK:

THE ROUTE BETWEEN KENSINGTON OLYMPIA (THEN ADDISON
ROAD) AND RAVENSCOURT PARK (THEN SHAFTESBURY ROAD) WAS
OPENED IN 1869 AND CLOSED TO ALL TRAFFIC IN 1916

Richmond Junction -

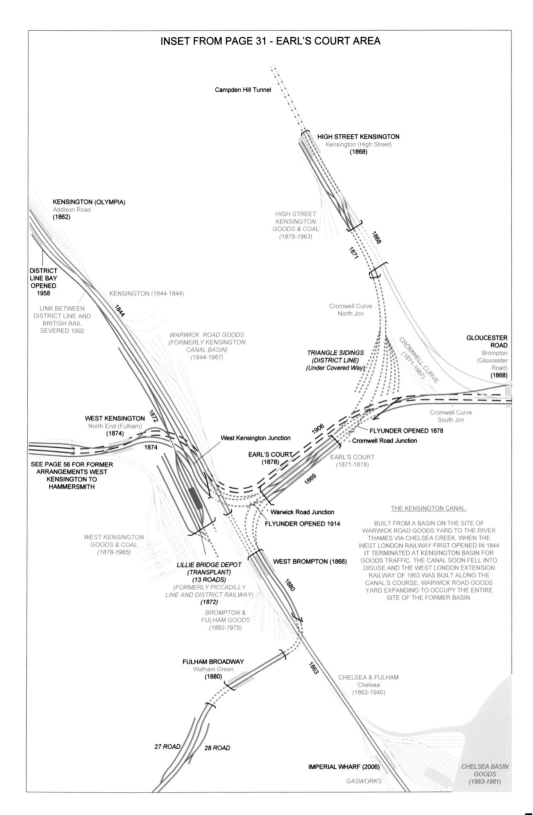

INSET FROM PAGE 31 - EARL'S COURT AREA

Campden Hill Tunnel

HIGH STREET KENSINGTON
Kensington (High Street)
(1868)

*HIGH STREET
KENSINGTON
GOODS & COAL
(1878-1963)*

KENSINGTON (OLYMPIA)
Addison Road
(1862)

1868

1871

**DISTRICT
LINE BAY
OPENED
1958**

LINK BETWEEN
DISTRICT LINE AND
BRITISH RAIL
SEVERED 1992

KENSINGTON (1844-1844)

1844

Cromwell Curve
North Jcn

**GLOUCESTER
ROAD**
Brompton
(Gloucester
Road)
(1868)

*WARWICK ROAD GOODS
(FORMERLY KENSINGTON
CANAL BASIN)
(1844-1967)*

*TRIANGLE SIDINGS
(DISTRICT LINE)
(Under Covered Way)*

*CROMWELL CURVE
(1871-1957)*

Cromwell Curve
South Jcn

WEST KENSINGTON
North End (Fulham)
(1874)

1872

West Kensington Junction

1906

FLYUNDER OPENED 1878

· Cromwell Road Junction

1874

**EARL'S COURT
(1878)**

*EARL'S COURT
(1871-1878)*

**SEE PAGE 56 FOR FORMER
ARRANGEMENTS WEST
KENSINGTON TO
HAMMERSMITH**

1869

Warwick Road Junction

FLYUNDER OPENED 1914

THE KENSINGTON CANAL:

BUILT FROM A BASIN ON THE SITE OF
WARWICK ROAD GOODS YARD TO THE RIVER
THAMES VIA CHELSEA CREEK. WHEN THE
WEST LONDON RAILWAY FIRST OPENED IN 1844
IT TERMINATED AT KENSINGTON BASIN FOR
GOODS TRAFFIC. THE CANAL SOON FELL INTO
DISUSE AND THE WEST LONDON EXTENSION
RAILWAY OF 1863 WAS BUILT ALONG THE
CANAL'S COURSE, WARWICK ROAD GOODS
YARD EXPANDING TO OCCUPY THE ENTIRE
SITE OF THE FORMER BASIN.

*WEST KENSINGTON
GOODS & COAL
(1878-1965)*

WEST BROMPTON (1866)

*LILLIE BRIDGE DEPOT
(TRANSPLANT)
(13 ROADS)*
*(FORMERLY PICCADILLY
LINE AND DISTRICT RAILWAY)
(1872)*

1880

*BROMPTON &
FULHAM GOODS
(1892-1975)*

FULHAM BROADWAY
Walham Green
(1880)

1863

*CHELSEA & FULHAM
Chelsea
(1863-1940)*

27 ROAD   28 ROAD

IMPERIAL WHARF (2006)

GASWORKS

*CHELSEA BASIN
GOODS
(1863-1981)*

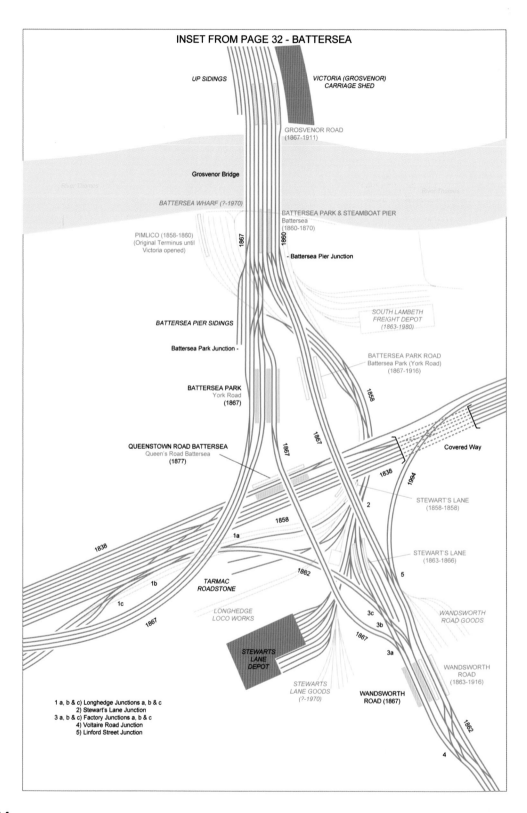

INSET FROM PAGE 32 - BATTERSEA

UP SIDINGS

VICTORIA (GROSVENOR)
CARRIAGE SHED

GROSVENOR ROAD
(1867-1911)

Grosvenor Bridge

River Thames

BATTERSEA WHARF (?-1970)

BATTERSEA PARK & STEAMBOAT PIER
Battersea
(1860-1870)

PIMLICO (1858-1860)
(Original Terminus until
Victoria opened)

- Battersea Pier Junction

SOUTH LAMBETH
FREIGHT DEPOT
(1863-1980)

BATTERSEA PIER SIDINGS

Battersea Park Junction -

BATTERSEA PARK ROAD
Battersea Park (York Road)
(1867-1916)

BATTERSEA PARK
York Road
(1867)

1858

QUEENSTOWN ROAD BATTERSEA
Queen's Road Battersea
(1877)

1867

1867

Covered Way

1838

1994

STEWART'S LANE
(1858-1858)

2

1858

STEWART'S LANE
(1863-1866)

1a

1838

1862

5

1b

TARMAC
ROADSTONE

WANDSWORTH
ROAD GOODS

1c

3c

1867

LONGHEDGE
LOCO WORKS

3b

3a

WANDSWORTH
ROAD
(1863-1916)

STEWARTS
LANE
DEPOT

1867

STEWARTS
LANE GOODS
(?-1970)

WANDSWORTH
ROAD (1867)

1862

1 a, b & c) Longhedge Junctions a, b & c
2) Stewart's Lane Junction
3 a, b & c) Factory Junctions a, b & c
4) Voltaire Road Junction
5) Linford Street Junction

4

51

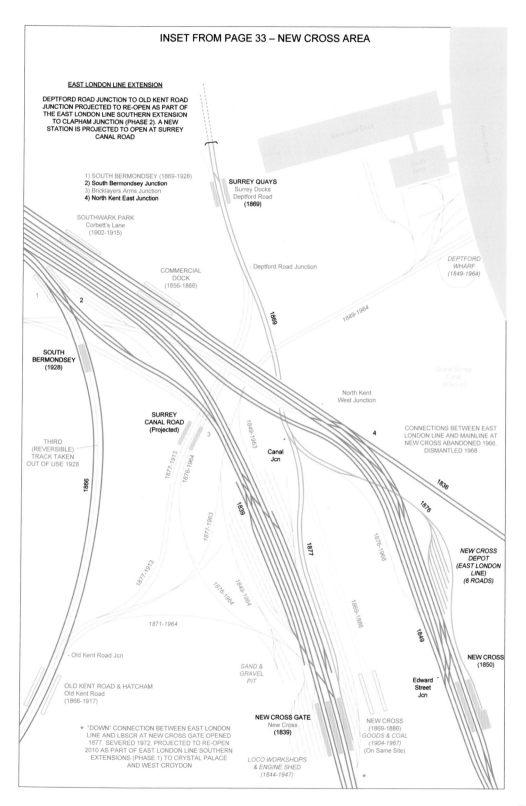

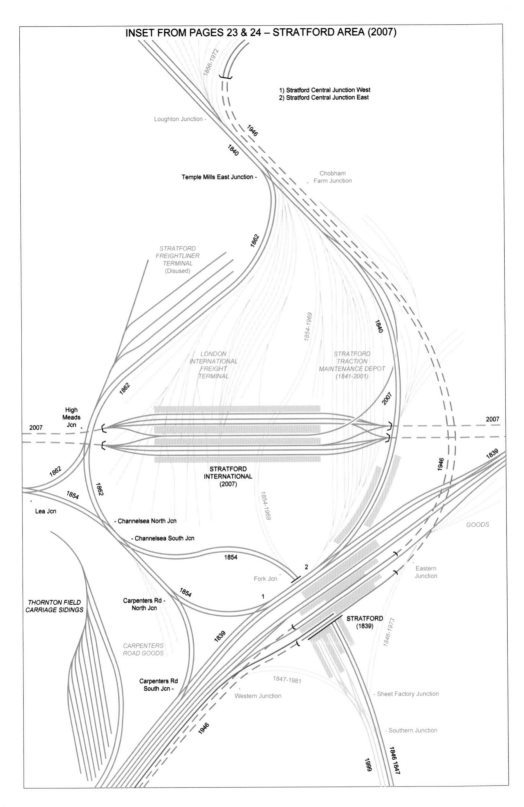

1) Stratford Central Junction West
2) Stratford Central Junction East

Loughton Junction -

1866-1972

1946

1940

Temple Mills East Junction -

Chobham
Farm Junction

1862

STRATFORD
FREIGHTLINER
TERMINAL
(Disused)

1854-1969

1840

LONDON
INTERNATIONAL
FREIGHT
TERMINAL

STRATFORD
TRACTION
MAINTENANCE DEPOT
(1841-2001)

2007

1862

High
Meads
Jcn

2007

2007

1946

1839

1862

1854

STRATFORD
INTERNATIONAL
(2007)

1854-1969

1862

Lea Jcn

- Channelsea North Jcn

- Channelsea South Jcn

GOODS

1854

Eastern
Junction

2

Fork Jcn

THORNTON FIELD
CARRIAGE SIDINGS

Carpenters Rd -
North Jcn

1854

1

STRATFORD
(1839)

1846-1973

CARPENTERS
ROAD GOODS

1839

Carpenters Rd
South Jcn -

1847-1981

- Sheet Factory Junction

Western Junction

1946

- Southern Junction

1846 1847

1999

53

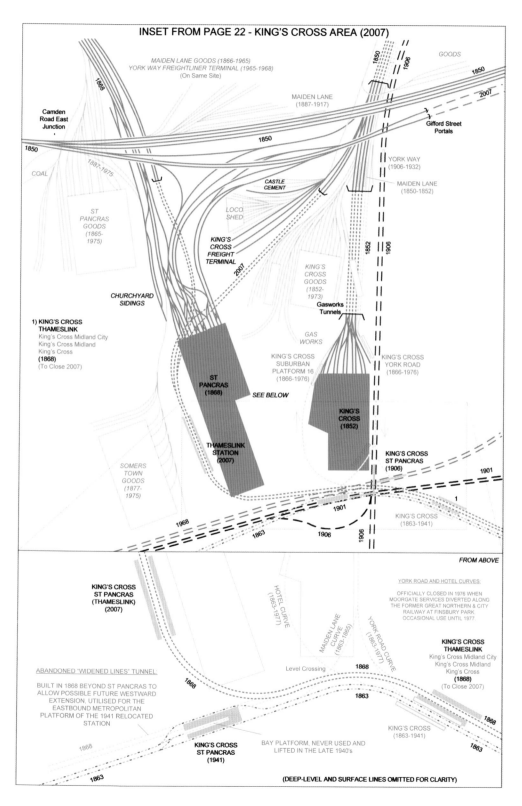

INSET FROM PAGE 22 - KING'S CROSS AREA (2007)

MAIDEN LANE GOODS *(1866-1965)*
YORK WAY FREIGHTLINER TERMINAL *(1965-1968)*
(On Same Site)

GOODS

1850

1906

1850

2007

1868

MAIDEN LANE
(1887-1917)

1850

Camden
Road East
Junction

Gifford Street
Portals

1850

1850

YORK WAY
(1906-1932)

1887-1975

COAL

MAIDEN LANE
(1850-1852)

CASTLE
CEMENT

*ST
PANCRAS
GOODS
(1865-
1975)*

LOCO
SHED

1852

1906

KING'S
CROSS
FREIGHT
TERMINAL

*KING'S
CROSS
GOODS
(1852-
1973)*

2007

CHURCHYARD
SIDINGS

Gasworks
Tunnels

1) KING'S CROSS
THAMESLINK
King's Cross Midland City
King's Cross Midland
King's Cross
(1868)
(To Close 2007)

*GAS
WORKS*

KING'S CROSS
SUBURBAN
PLATFORM 16
(1866-1976)

KING'S CROSS
YORK ROAD
(1866-1976)

**ST
PANCRAS
(1868)**

SEE BELOW

**KING'S
CROSS
(1852)**

**THAMESLINK
STATION
(2007)**

*SOMERS
TOWN
GOODS
(1877-
1975)*

**KING'S CROSS
ST PANCRAS
(1906)**

1901

1968

1901

1

1863

1906

1906

KING'S CROSS
(1863-1941)

FROM ABOVE

**KING'S CROSS
ST PANCRAS
(THAMESLINK)
(2007)**

HOTEL CURVE
(1863-1977)

MAIDEN LANE
CURVE
(1863-1865)

YORK ROAD CURVE
(1863-1977)

<u>YORK ROAD AND HOTEL CURVES:</u>

OFFICIALLY CLOSED IN 1976 WHEN
MOORGATE SERVICES DIVERTED ALONG
THE FORMER GREAT NORTHERN & CITY
RAILWAY AT FINSBURY PARK.
OCCASIONAL USE UNTIL 1977.

**KING'S CROSS
THAMESLINK**
King's Cross Midland City
King's Cross Midland
King's Cross
(1868)
(To Close 2007)

<u>ABANDONED "WIDENED LINES" TUNNEL:</u>

BUILT IN 1868 BEYOND ST PANCRAS TO
ALLOW POSSIBLE FUTURE WESTWARD
EXTENSION. UTILISED FOR THE
EASTBOUND METROPOLITAN
PLATFORM OF THE 1941 RELOCATED
STATION

Level Crossing

1868

1863

1868

KING'S CROSS
(1863-1941)

1868

1863

1868

**KING'S CROSS
ST PANCRAS
(1941)**

BAY PLATFORM, NEVER USED AND
LIFTED IN THE LATE 1940's

1863

(DEEP-LEVEL AND SURFACE LINES OMITTED FOR CLARITY)

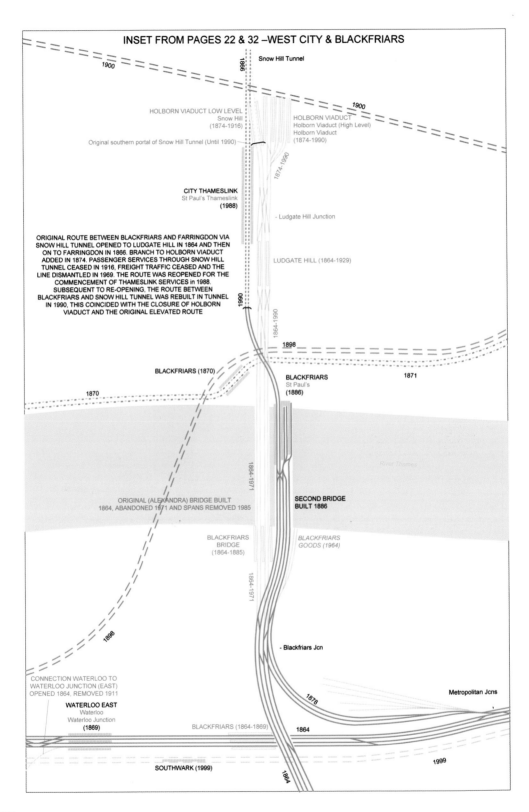

INSET FROM PAGES 22 & 32 –WEST CITY & BLACKFRIARS

Snow Hill Tunnel

1900

1866

1900

HOLBORN VIADUCT LOW LEVEL
Snow Hill
(1874-1916)

HOLBORN VIADUCT
Holborn Viaduct (High Level)
Holborn Viaduct
(1874-1990)

Original southern portal of Snow Hill Tunnel (Until 1990)

1874-1990

CITY THAMESLINK
St Paul's Thameslink
(1988)

- Ludgate Hill Junction

ORIGINAL ROUTE BETWEEN BLACKFRIARS AND FARRINGDON VIA
SNOW HILL TUNNEL OPENED TO LUDGATE HILL IN 1864 AND THEN
ON TO FARRINGDON IN 1866. BRANCH TO HOLBORN VIADUCT
ADDED IN 1874. PASSENGER SERVICES THROUGH SNOW HILL
TUNNEL CEASED IN 1916, FREIGHT TRAFFIC CEASED AND THE
LINE DISMANTLED IN 1969. THE ROUTE WAS REOPENED FOR THE
COMMENCEMENT OF THAMESLINK SERVICES in 1988.
SUBSEQUENT TO RE-OPENING, THE ROUTE BETWEEN
BLACKFRIARS AND SNOW HILL TUNNEL WAS REBUILT IN TUNNEL
IN 1990, THIS COINCIDED WITH THE CLOSURE OF HOLBORN
VIADUCT AND THE ORIGINAL ELEVATED ROUTE

LUDGATE HILL (1864-1929)

1960

1864-1990

1898

BLACKFRIARS (1870)

1870

BLACKFRIARS
St Paul's
(1886)

1871

1864-1971

ORIGINAL (ALEXANDRA) BRIDGE BUILT
1864, ABANDONED 1971 AND SPANS REMOVED 1985

SECOND BRIDGE
BUILT 1886

River Thames

BLACKFRIARS
BRIDGE
(1864-1885)

*BLACKFRIARS
GOODS (1964)*

1864-1971

- Blackfriars Jcn

1898

CONNECTION WATERLOO TO
WATERLOO JUNCTION (EAST)
OPENED 1864, REMOVED 1911

WATERLOO EAST
Waterloo
Waterloo Junction
(1869)

BLACKFRIARS (1864-1869)

1864

1878

Metropolitan Jcns

SOUTHWARK (1999)

1864

1999

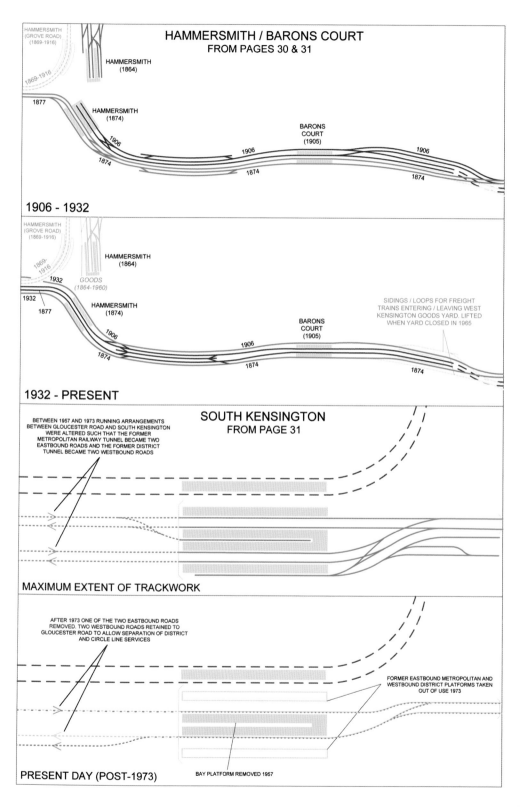

HAMMERSMITH / BARONS COURT
FROM PAGES 30 & 31

HAMMERSMITH
(GROVE ROAD)
(1869-1916)

HAMMERSMITH
(1864)

1869-1916

1877

HAMMERSMITH
(1874)

BARONS
COURT
(1905)

1906

1906

1906

1906

1874

1874

1874

1874

1906 - 1932

HAMMERSMITH
(GROVE ROAD)
(1869-1916)

HAMMERSMITH
(1864)

1869-1916

1932

GOODS
(1864-1960)

1932

1877

HAMMERSMITH
(1874)

BARONS
COURT
(1905)

SIDINGS / LOOPS FOR FREIGHT
TRAINS ENTERING / LEAVING WEST
KENSINGTON GOODS YARD. LIFTED
WHEN YARD CLOSED IN 1965

1906

1906

1874

1874

1874

1932 - PRESENT

BETWEEN 1957 AND 1973 RUNNING ARRANGEMENTS
BETWEEN GLOUCESTER ROAD AND SOUTH KENSINGTON
WERE ALTERED SUCH THAT THE FORMER
METROPOLITAN RAILWAY TUNNEL BECAME TWO
EASTBOUND ROADS AND THE FORMER DISTRICT
TUNNEL BECAME TWO WESTBOUND ROADS

SOUTH KENSINGTON
FROM PAGE 31

MAXIMUM EXTENT OF TRACKWORK

AFTER 1973 ONE OF THE TWO EASTBOUND ROADS
REMOVED. TWO WESTBOUND ROADS RETAINED TO
GLOUCESTER ROAD TO ALLOW SEPARATION OF DISTRICT
AND CIRCLE LINE SERVICES

FORMER EASTBOUND METROPOLITAN AND
WESTBOUND DISTRICT PLATFORMS TAKEN
OUT OF USE 1973

PRESENT DAY (POST-1973)

BAY PLATFORM REMOVED 1957

Index

Entries in Black Plain Capital Text denote open or projected Passenger Stations, Red closed. Previous names are listed in reverse chronological order in Red Lower-Case Text below. Entries in Black Italic Capital Text denote open Non-Passenger facilities, Red closed. Entries in Black Lower-Case Text denote in-use Railway features, e.g. Junctions or Tunnels, Red Text disused.

Although UERL was formed in 1902, the constituent four railways are referred to by their original names prior to 1910 to acknowledge the huge growth of Underground Electric Railways in the 1900s and the independent identities then retained in line nomenclature. Developments between 1910 and 1933 are referred to under the banner "UERL" whilst the Metropolitan and Central London Railways are referred to independently. After 1933 all developments to the Underground network are referred to under the banner "LT", then "LUL" post-1985.

NAME: (Previous Names Below)	PAGE / GRID:	YEAR OPENED:	YEAR CLOSED:	OPENED BY:	NOTES:
AA OIL SIDINGS (ANGERSTEIN WHARF)	34 / 1A	?	?	PRIV	
Abbey Mills Lower Junction	24 / 4A	1858	1958	LTSR	Abbey Mills Curve closed to Passengers 1940, Freight 1958
Abbey Mills Upper Junction	24 / 3A	1858	1958	LTSR	Abbey Mills Curve closed to Passengers 1940, Freight 1958
ABBEY WOOD	35 / 1B	1850	N/A	SER	
Acton Canal Wharf Junction	20 / 3B	1868	N/A	MID	
ACTON CENTRAL Acton	30 / 1A	1853	N/A	N&SWJ	"Central" suffix added 1925
ACTON COAL	30 / 1A	?	1965	N&SWJ	
Acton Curve	40 / 2A	1878	1965	LSWR	
Acton Gatehouse Junction	30 / 1A	1857	1965	N&SWJ	Hammersmith & Chiswick Branch closed 1965
ACTON LANE (WILLESDEN)	20 / 3A	1861	1866	LNWR	Adjacent to current Harlesden Station
Acton Lane East Junction	30 / 2A & 40 / 2A	1879	1965	LSWR	
Acton Lane West Junction	30 / 2A & 40 / 2A	1878	1965	LSWR	
ACTON MAIN LINE	20 / 4A	1868	N/A	GWR	
ACTON TOWN Mill Hill Park	30 / 1A	1879	N/A	MDR	Rebuilt and renamed 1910, further rebuilt 1933. First served by Piccadilly Line 1932. South Acton Shuttle served a bay platform until 1959.
Acton Town North Junction	30 / 1A	1883	N/A	MDR	Extensively remodelled 1932 during Turnham Green to Northfields quadrupling
Acton Town South Junction	30 / 1A & 40 / 1A	1899	1959	MDR	First passenger use 1905, last freight use 1914
Acton Wells Junction	20 / 4B	1877	N/A	N&SWJ	
ACTON WORKS (RAILWAY ENGINEERING WORKS)	30 / 1A	1923	N/A	UERL	Operated by Metronet Ltd
ACTON YARD (YEOMAN AGGREGATES)	20 / 4A	?	N/A	PRIV	
ADDINGTON VILLAGE	48 / 2B	2000	N/A	CTL	
ADDISCOMBE (SER) Addiscombe (Croydon)	48 / 1A	1864	1997	SER	Renamed "Addiscombe (Croydon)" 1925, "Croydon" suffix dropped 1955. Goods Yard closed 1968. Elmers End to Addiscombe closed 1997
ADDISCOMBE (CTL)	48 / 1A	2000	N/A	CTL	
ADDISCOMBE EMU SHED	48 / 1A	1926	1992	SR	On site of former Loco Shed
AEC MOTOR WORKS	29 / 1A	?	?	PRIV	
AGGREGATE INDUSTRIES LTD (ANGERSTEIN WHARF)	34 / 1A	?	N/A	PRIV	
AGGREGATE INDUSTRIES LTD (NEASDEN)	20 / 2B	?	N/A	PRIV	On site of former Loco Shed
AIRCRAFT SIDINGS Nos 1 & 2 (KIDBROOKE)	34 / 3A	?	?	PRIV	War Depot established at Kidbrooke during WWI
ALDERSBROOK (UP) CAR HOLDING SIDINGS	24 / 1B	?	N/A	BR	
ALDGATE	23 / 4A & 7 / 2A	1876	N/A	MET	
Aldgate Junction	23 / 4A & 7 / 2A	1884	N/A	MET	
ALDGATE EAST (1st)	23 / 4A & 7 / 2A	1884	1938	MDR & MET	Relocated East 1938 (Junction Remodelling)
ALDGATE EAST (2nd)	23 / 4A & 7 / 2A	1938	N/A	LT (DIS & MET)	
Aldgate East Junction	23 / 4A & 7 / 2A	1884	N/A	MDR & MET	Junction relocated East 1938
ALDWYCH Strand (Aldwych) Strand	22 / 4A	1907	1994	GNP&BR	Aldwych Branch closed to passengers 1994, but track and a train retained for filming work
Alexandra Bridge	55	1864	1971	LCDR	Spans removed 1985, piers remain
ALEXANDRA PALACE Alexandra Park (1891-1892 only) Alexandra Palace	12 / 3A	1873	1954	GNR	Nominally opened by Muswell Hill & Palace Railway, but operated by GNR from opening. Closed and re-opened several times during its existence, known as Alexandra Park 1891-1892. Closed when Alexandra Palace to Finsbury park service withdrawn 1954. Had been intended for electrification and transfer to LT Northern Line, but works abandoned post-WW2.
ALEXANDRA PALACE Wood Green Wood Green (Alexandra Park) Wood Green	12 / 3A	1859	N/A	GNR	Renamed "Wood Green (Alexandra Palace)" 1971, renamed "Alexandra Palace" 1982
ALL SAINTS	23 / 4B & 48 / 3A	1987	N/A	DLR	On Site of former NLR Poplar Station
ALPERTON Perivale & Alperton Perivale Alperton	19 / 3B	1903	N/A	MDR	Renamed "Alperton" 1910. First served Piccadilly Line 1932, last served District Line 1933
AMERSHAM Amersham & Chesham Bois Amersham	1 / 2A	1892	N/A	MET	"& Chesham Bois" 1922-1934. Metropolitan Line services beyond Amersham ceased 1961
AMEY ROADSTONE (WEST DRAYTON)	27 / 1B	?	N/A	PRIV	Gravel Terminal
AMPERE WAY	47 / 1A	2000	N/A	CTL	

NAME: (Previous Names Below)	PAGE / GRID:	YEAR OPENED:	YEAR CLOSED:	OPENED BY:	NOTES:
ANERLEY	43 / 2A	1839	N/A	LCR	East London Line projected to serve from 2010
Anerley Bridge					
Annerley					
ANGEL	22 / 3B	1901	N/A	C&SLR	Closed 1922-1924 (tunnel widening)
ANGEL ROAD	13 / 2A	1840	N/A	ECR	
Water Lane					
Edmonton					
Angerstein Junction	34 / 2A	1852	N/A	SER	
ANGERSTEIN WHARF	34 / 1A	1852	N/A	SER	
ARCHWAY	22 / 1A	1907	N/A	CCE&HR	Terminus 1907-1939, opened as "Highgate".
Highgate (Archway)					"Archway" prefix added 1939, reversed 1941,
Archway (Highgate)					"Highgate" prefix dropped 1947
Highgate					
ARENA	43 / 4A	2000	N/A	CTL	
ARNOS GROVE	12 / 2A	1932	N/A	UERL (PIC)	Terminus of extension from Finsbury Park
					1932-1933
ARNOS GROVE SIDINGS	12 / 2A	1932	N/A	UERL (PIC)	Stabling Sidings for Piccadilly Line
ARSENAL	22 / 1B	1906	N/A	GNP&BR	Opened as "Gillespie Road", renamed "Arsenal
Arsenal (for Highbury Hill)					(for Highbury Hill)" 1932, suffix gradually
Gillespie Road					dropped
ASCOT ROAD	2 / 4A	N/A	N/A	LUL (MET)	Projected; Station on Metropolitan Line Watford
					Junction Extension
ASHBURTON GROVE GOODS	22 / 2B & 15 / 4B	?	?	GNR	
ASHFORD (MIDDX.)	37 / 1B	1848	N/A	LSWR	
ASHSTEAD	45 / 4A	1859	N/A	LSWR & LBSCR	
AVENUE ROAD	43 / 3A	2000	N/A	CTL	
BAKER STREET	21 / 4B	1863	N/A	MET	Platforms to Swiss Cottage opened 1868 (Now
					Metropolitan Line Platforms). Baker Street &
					Waterloo Railway opened 1906, Jubilee Line
					opened 1979.
BALHAM	42 / 1A	1856	N/A	LBSCR	Opened by West End of London & Crystal
Balham & Upper Tooting					Palace Railway, but operated by LBSCR
Balham					from outset. Northern Line Station and
					interchange opened 1926. "& Upper Tooting"
					suffix dropped 1969
BANDON HALT	47 / 2A	1906	1914	LBSCR	
BANK	22 / 4B	1898	N/A	LSWR (W&C)	Opened by LSWR (Waterloo & City Line).
City (W&C only)					C&SLR and CLR platforms opened 1900,
					DLR platforms opened 1991. Waterloo & City
					platforms renamed from "City" to "Bank"
					1940
BANSTEAD	46 / 4A	1865	N/A	LBSCR	"& Burgh Heath" suffix 1898-1928. Goods Yard
Banstead & Burgh Heath					in use 1880-1964
BARBICAN	22 / 4B	1865	N/A	MET	Opened as "Aldersgate Street", City Widened
Aldersgate & Barbican					Lines platforms added 1868 (now
Aldersgate					Thameslink). "Street" suffix dropped 1910,
					"& Barbican" suffix added 1923, "Aldersgate"
					prefix dropped 1968
BARKING	25 / 2A	1854	N/A	LTSR	Served by District Railway since 1902 (no
					service 1905-1908), Served by Metropolitan
					Railway since 1936 ("Hammersmith & City
					Line" since 1990). Extensively rebuilt
					1959-1961
Barking East Junction	25 / 2B	1961	N/A	BR	All junctions in Barking area extensively
					remodelled 1959-1961
BARKING GOODS	25 / 1B	1854	1957	LTSR	
BARKING POWER STATION	25 / 4B	1925	1981	PRIV	
BARKINGSIDE (GER)	15 / 3A	1903	1947	GER	Closed 1916-1919. Fairlop Loop closed 1947
					to allow electrification and transfer to
					LT Central Line. Freight traffic remained
					until 1965
BARKINGSIDE (LT)	15 / 3A	1948	N/A	LT (CEN)	First served by LT Central Line Trains 1948.
					Goods yard closed 1965
BARKING SIDINGS	25 / 2A	1958	N/A	LT (DIS)	Stabling sidings for District and Hammersmith
					& City Line Trains
Barking Station Junction	25 / 1A	1961	N/A	BR	Junction for Bay Platform used by Gospel Oak
					(formerly Kentish Town) trains
Barking Tilbury Line Junction East	25 / 2A	1961	N/A	BR	All junctions in Barking area extensively
					remodelled 1959-1961
Barking Tilbury Line Junction West	25 / 1A	1961	N/A	BR	All junctions in Barking area extensively
					remodelled 1959-1961
Barking West Junction	25 / 1A	1961	N/A	BR	All junctions in Barking area extensively
					remodelled 1959-1961
BARNEHURST	36 / 3A	1895	N/A	SER	Goods Yard closed 1968
BARNES	30 / 3B	1846	N/A	LSWR	
BARNES BRIDGE	30 / 3B	1916	N/A	LSWR	
Barnes Bridge	30 / 3B	1849	N/A	LSWR	
Barnes Junction	30 / 3B	1849	N/A	LSWR	
Barnet Tunnels	11 / 1B	1850	N/A	GNR	
BARONS COURT	31 / 2A & 56	1905	N/A	MDR	GNP&BR platforms opened 1906
BATH ROAD	30 / 1B	1909	1917	N&SWJR	Passenger services withdrawn from
					Hammersmith & Chiswick Branch 1917

NAME: (Previous Names Below)	PAGE / GRID:	YEAR OPENED:	YEAR CLOSED:	OPENED BY:	NOTES:
BATTERSEA	31 / 3B	1863	1940	WLER	Passenger service withdrawn Willesden Jcn to Clapham Jcn 1940
BATTERSEA PARK & STEAMBOAT PIER	32 / 2A & 51	1860	1870	LBSCR	
Battersea					
BATTERSEA PARK (2nd)	32 / 3A & 51	1867	N/A	LBSCR	Renamed "Battersea Park" 1870
Battersea Park & York Road					
York Road & Battersea Park					
York Road					
Battersea Park Junction	51	1867	N/A	LBSCR	
BATTERSEA PARK ROAD	32 / 2A & 51	1867	1916	LCDR	Renamed 1877
Battersea Park (York Road)					
Battersea Pier Junction	32 / 2A & 51	1867	N/A	LCDR	
BATTERSEA PIER SIDINGS	51	?	N/A	LBSCR	
BATTERSEA WHARF	51	?	1970	LBSCR	
BAYSWATER	21 / 4A	1868	N/A	MET	Opened as "Bayswater", renamed "Bayswater (Queens Road) & Westbourne Grove" 1923, "- & Westbourne Grove" suffix dropped 1933, renamed "Bayswater (Queensway)" 1946, suffix gradually dropped
Bayswater (Queensway)					
Bayswater (Queens Road) & Westbourne Grove					
Bayswater					
BECKENHAM HILL	43 / 2B	1892	N/A	LCDR	
BECKENHAM HILL CARRIAGE SIDINGS	43 / 2B	?	N/A	SR	
BECKENHAM JUNCTION	43 / 3B	1857	N/A	SER	Built by the Mid Kent Railway, but operated by SER from opening
Beckenham					
BECKENHAM ROAD	43 / 3A	2000	N/A	CTL	
BECKTON (GER)	25 / 4A	1873	1940	GER	Passenger services withdrawn from Beckton and Gallions 1940
BECKTON (DLR)	24 / 4B	1994	N/A	DLR	
BECKTON DEPOT	25 / 4A	1994	N/A	DLR	DLR Depot
BECKTON GAS WORKS	25 / 4A	1872	1971	PRIV	
Beckton Junction	24 / 4B	1880	1940	GER	Divergence of Beckton and Gallions Branches
BECKTON PARK	24 / 4B	1994	N/A	DLR	
BECONTREE (LMS)	25 / 2B	1926	1962	LMS	Opened on existing LTSR Main Line. First served by District Line after quadrupling in 1932. Last served by British Rail 1962 and "Fast" Platforms abandoned. Owned by LT since 1970.
Gale Street Halt					
BECONTREE (LT)	25 / 2B	1932	N/A	LMS	Barking to Upminster quadrupled by LMS 1932, new platforms at Becontree served by District Line from opening. Ownership transferred to LT 1970.
BECONTREE ESTATE RAILWAY	25 / 1B	1921	1934	LCC	Transported building materials during construction of Becontree Estate. Extended to the Thames
BEDDINGTON LANE (WCR)	42 / 4A	1855	1997	WCR	Opened as "Beddington", "Lane" suffix added 1887 Wimbledon to West Croydon closed 1997 prior to conversion to Tramlink
Beddington Lane Halt					
Beddington					
BEDDINGTON LANE (CTL)	42 / 4A	2000	N/A	CTL	On site of former Beddington Lane Station
BELGRAVE WALK	41 / 3B	2000	N/A	CTL	
BELLINGHAM	43 / 1B	1892	N/A	LCDR	
BELMONT (MIDDX.)	9 / 3B	1932	1964	LNWR	Belmont to Harrow & Wealdstone withdrawn 1964 and entire branch closed to freight
BELMONT (SURREY)	46 / 3A	1865	N/A	LBSCR	Renamed 1875. Goods Yard in use 1880-1969
California					
BELSIZE PARK	21 / 2B	1907	N/A	CCE&HR	
Belsize Tunnels	21 / 2B	1868	N/A	MID	
BELVEDERE	36 / 1A	1859	N/A	SER	
BERMONDSEY	33 / 1A	1999	N/A	LUL (JUB)	
BERRYLANDS	40 / 4A	1933	N/A	SR	
BETHNAL GREEN (GER)	23 / 3A	1872	N/A	GER	
Bethnal Green Junction					
BETHNAL GREEN (LT)	23 / 3A	1946	N/A	LT (CEN)	
BEXLEY	36 / 4A	1866	N/A	SER	Goods Yard closed 1963
BEXLEYHEATH	35 / 3B	1895	N/A	SER	Goods Yard situated ¼ Mile West of passenger station, closed 1968
Bexley Heath					
BICKLEY	44 / 3B	1858	N/A	LCDR	
Southborough Road					
Bickley Junctions	44 / 3B	1902	N/A	SECR	
BINGHAM ROAD	48 / 1A	1906	1983	SER	Closed 1915-1935, finally closed 1983
BIRKBECK	43 / 3A	1930	N/A	SR	Croydon Tramlink opened 2000
BISHOPSGATE (HIGH LEVEL)	23 / 4A	1840 (1882)	1874 (1964)	ECR	Terminus for Eastern Counties (later Great Eastern) Railway 1840-1874 Goods traffic commenced 1882 and remained until 1964
Bishopsgate					
Shoreditch					
BISHOPSGATE (LOW LEVEL)	23 / 4A	1872	1916	GER	
BLACKFRIARS (SER)	32 / 1B & 55	1864	1869	SER	Replaced by Waterloo Junction (=East) to West
Great Surrey Street					
BLACKFRIARS (MDR)	22 / 4B	1870	N/A	MDR	Main Line station opened by LCDR 1886 as "St Paul's", renamed "Blackfriars" 1937
St Paul's					
BLACKFRIARS BRIDGE	32 / 1B & 55	1864	1885	LCDR	Replaced by St Paul's (=Blackfriars) on North bank of Thames
BLACKFRIARS GOODS	55	?	1964	LCDR	
Blackfriars Junction	32 / 1B & 55	1878	N/A	LCDR	
BLACKHEATH	34 / 3A	1849	N/A	SER	
BLACKHEATH HILL	33 / 3B	1871	1917	LCDR	Terminus 1871-1888. Passenger service withdrawn Nunhead to Greenwich Park 1917

NAME: (Previous Names Below)	PAGE / GRID:	YEAR OPENED:	YEAR CLOSED:	OPENED BY:	NOTES:
Blackheath Junction	34 / 3A	1895	N/A	SER	
Blackheath Tunnel	34 / 2A	1849	N/A	SER	
BLACKHORSE LANE	43 / 4A	2000	N/A	CTL	
BLACKHORSE ROAD	13 / 4A	1894	N/A	T&FG	Victoria Line station opened 1968
Black Horse Road					
BLACKWALL (LBR)	24 / 4A & 48 / 4B	1840	1926	LBR	Passenger service to Blackwall withdrawn 1926
BLACKWALL (DLR)	23 / 4B & 48 / 3A	1994	N/A	DLR	
BLACKWALL GOODS	48 / 3B	1860	1961	GNR	
BLAKE HALL	6 / 2B	1865	1981	GER	Epping to Ongar transferred to LT 1949, Electrified 1956, Blake Hall closed 1981
Bollo Lane Junction	30 / 2A & 40 / 2A	1878	1965	LSWR	Acton Curve dismantled 1965
BOND STREET	22 / 4A	1900	N/A	CLR	Jubilee Line platforms opened 1979
BOROUGH	32 / 1B	1890	N/A	C&SLR	Closed 1922-1925
Great Dover Street					
Borough Market Junction	32 / 1B	1866	N/A	SER	
BOROUGH ROAD	32 / 1B	1864	1907	LCDR	
BOSTON MANOR	29 / 1B	1883	N/A	MDR	Renamed 1911. First served by Piccadilly Line 1933. Last served by District Line 1964
Boston Road					
BOUNDS GREEN	12 / 2A	1932	N/A	UERL (PIC)	
BOUNDS GREEN DEPOT	12 / 3A	1929	N/A	LNER	
BOW	23 / 3B	1850	1944	NLR	Passenger service Dalston Junction to Poplar withdrawn 1944
BOW & BROMLEY	23 / 3B	1849	1850	LBR	Blackwall Extension Railway (London & Blackwall Rly) opened to passengers 1849, closed 1850
BOW CHURCH	23 / 3B	1987	N/A	DLR	On site of former NLR Bow Station
BOW GOODS	23 / 3B	?	N/A	GER	Plasmor, Aggregate Industries & Midland Waste
BOW GOODS	23 / 3B	?	?	NLR	
BOWES PARK	12 / 2A	1880	N/A	GNR	
Bow Junction	23 / 3B	1849	N/A	LBR & ECR	Junction between Eastern Counties Railway and Blackwall Extension Railway (LBR)
BOW ROAD (GER)	23 / 3B	1876	1949	GER	Closed 1941-1946. Passenger services Fenchurch Street to Stratford withdrawn 1949
BOW ROAD (MDR)	23 / 3B	1902	N/A	MDR & LTSR	Served by Metropolitan Line since 1936 ("Hammersmith & City Line" since 1990)
BOW ROAD GOODS	23 / 3B	1885	1964	GER	
BOW WORKS	23 / 4B	1863	1960	NLR	North London Railway Loco Works
BOYERS SIDING (FELTHAM)	38 / 1A	?	?	PRIV	
BRENT CROSS	11 / 4A	1923	N/A	UERL (CCE&HR)	Renamed 1976
Brent					
Brent Curve Junction	20 / 1B	1868	N/A	MID	
BRENTFORD (GWR)	29 / 2B	1860	1942	GWR	Closed 1915-1920. Passenger service on GWR Brentford Branch withdrawn 1942
BRENTFORD (LSWR)	29 / 2B	1849	N/A	LSWR	"Brentford Central" 1950-1980. Goods yard closed 1965
Brentford Central					
Brentford					
BRENTFORD DOCK	29 / 2B	1859	1964	GWR	
BRENTFORD GOODS	29 / 2B	1930	N/A	GWR	
BRENTFORD STONE TERMINAL	29 / 2B	?	N/A	PRIV	Aggregate Industries
BRENTFORD WASTE TERMINAL	29 / 2B	1977	N/A	PRIV	West London Waste
BRENTHAM (FOR NORTH EALING)	19 / 3B	1911	1947	GWR	Replaced Twyford Abbey Halt. Closed 1915-1920
Brentham					
BRENT WASTE TERMINAL	21 / 1A	?	N/A	PRIV	Shanks & McEwan Ltd
BREWERY SIDINGS (ROMFORD)	16 / 4B	1853	1963	PRIV	
BRICKLAYERS ARMS	32 / 1B	1844	1852 (1983)	LGR & LCR	Closed to passengers 1852, remained in use for Goods until 1983
Bricklayers Arms Junction	52	1844	1983	LGR & LCR	
BRIMSDOWN	5 / 3B	1884	N/A	GER	
BRITISH MUSEUM	22 / 4A	1900	1933	CLR	Closed when Central Line platforms opened at Holborn (Kingsway) 1933
BRIXTON (LCDR)	32 / 3B	1862	N/A	LCDR	
Brixton & South Stockwell					
Brixton					
BRIXTON (LT)	32 / 3B	1971	N/A	LT (VIC)	Southern terminus of Victoria Line
Brixton Junction	32 / 3B	1864	N/A	LCDR	
BROAD STREET	22 / 4B	1865	1985	NLR	
BROAD STREET GOODS	22 / 4B	1868	1969	LNWR	
BROAD STREET (TEMPORARY)	22 / 4B	1985	1986	BR	Opened due to demolition of Broad Street, prior to diversion of trains to Liverpool Street
BROCKLEY	33 / 3B	1871	N/A	LBSCR	East London Line projected to serve from 2010
BROCKLEY HILL	10 / 1A	N/A	N/A	LT (NOR)	On Northern Line extension to Bushey Heath from Edgware. Construction abandoned 1940
BROCKLEY LANE	33 / 3B	1872	1917	LCDR	Passenger service withdrawn Nunhead to Greenwich Park 1917
BROCKLEY LANE DEPOT	33 / 3A	1883	1970	GNR & LNWR	"Martins Siding" on Down Side LNWR Coal Yard 1885-1970
BROMLEY	23 / 4B	1858	1962	LTSR	Damaged by fire 1892, rebuilt to West 1894. Main Line services non-stopped since 1962 and Fast Platforms abandoned
BROMLEY-BY-BOW	23 / 4B	1902	N/A	MDR	First served by District Railway 1902, line quadrupled 1908, District Trains using Slow Lines. Served by Metropolitan Line since
Bromley					

NAME: (Previous Names Below)	PAGE / GRID:	YEAR OPENED:	YEAR CLOSED:	OPENED BY:	NOTES:
					1936 ("Hammersmith & City Line" since 1990), renamed 1967
Bromley Down Junction	43 / 3A	1857	N/A	LBSCR	
Bromley Junction	23 / 4B	1869	1959	LTSR	Resited to the West with Bromley Station 1894
BROMLEY GOODS	24 / 4A	1898	?	LTSR	
BROMLEY NORTH Bromley	44 / 3A	1878	N/A	SER	Renamed 1899. Goods yard closed 1968
BROMLEY SOUTH Bromley Bromley Common	44 / 3A	1858	N/A	LCDR	Renamed "Bromley South" 1899
Bromley Up Junction	43 / 3A	1857	N/A	LBSCR	
BROMPTON & FULHAM GOODS	31 / 2A & 50	1892	1975	LNWR	
BROMPTON ROAD	31 / 1B	1906	1934	GNP&BR	
BRONDESBURY Brondesbury (Edgware Road) Edgware Road & Brondesbury Edgware Road Edgware Road (Kilburn)	21 / 2A	1860	N/A	HJR	Opened as "Edgware Road (Kilburn)", "& Brondesbury" suffix added 1872, renamed "Brondesbury (Edgware Road)" 1873, renamed "Brondesbury" 1883. Closed 1995-1996
BRONDESBURY PARK	21 / 3A	1908	N/A	LNWR	Closed 1995-1996
BRUCE GROVE	13 / 3A	1872	N/A	GER	
BUCKHURST HILL (ECR)	14 / 1B	1856	1970	ECR	Majority of Passenger services transferred to LT in 1948. First Trains in the morning remained British Rail services until 1970
BUCKHURST HILL (LT)	14 / 1B	1948	N/A	LT (CEN)	First served by Central Line Trains 1948. Goods Yard closed 1964
BURDETT ROAD	23 / 4B	1871	1941	GER	
BURNT OAK Burnt Oak (Watling) Burnt Oak	10 / 3A	1924	N/A	UERL (CCE&HR)	"Watling" suffix introduced 1928, gradually dropped
Burroughs Tunnels	10 / 4B	1924	N/A	UERL (CCE&HR)	
Bury Street Junction	5 / 4A	1891	N/A	GER	
BUSHEY Bushey & Oxhey Bushey	2 / 4B	1841	N/A	L&B	Served by London Underground Bakerloo Line Trains 1917-1982. "& Oxhey" dropped 1974 Goods Yard closed 1969
BUSHEY HEATH	9 / 1B	N/A	N/A	LT (NOR)	Intended terminus of Northern Line extension from Edgware. Construction abandoned 1940
BUSH HILL PARK	5 / 4A	1880	N/A	GER	
CALEDONIAN ROAD (NLR)	22 / 2A	1852	1870	NLR	Original station, resited West and renamed "Barnsbury" 1870
CALEDONIAN ROAD (GNP&BR)	22 / 2A	1906	N/A	GNP&BR	
CALEDONIAN ROAD & BARNSBURY Barnsbury	22 / 2A	1870	N/A	NLR	Replaced original Caledonian Road Station to East. Renamed "Caledonian Road & Barnsbury" in 1893
CALEDONIAN ROAD GOODS	22 / 2A & 54	?	?	GNR	
CAMBERWELL Camberwell New Road Camberwell	32 / 3B	1862	1916	LCDR	Opened as "Camberwell", "New Road" suffix added 1863, dropped 1908
CAMBERWELL GOODS & COAL	32 / 2B	?	1964	LCDR	
Cambria Junction	32 / 3B	1872	N/A	LCDR	
CAMBRIDGE HEATH	23 / 3A	1884	N/A	GER	Closed during World War I, re-opening 1919
CAMDEN CARRIAGE SIDINGS	21 / 3B	?	N/A	LNWR	
Camden Junctions	21 / 2B	1851	N/A	LNWR	
CAMDEN ROAD (NLR) (1st)	22 / 2A	1850	1870	NLR	Original station on St Pancras Way. Replaced by Camden Town Station to West
CAMDEN ROAD (MID)	22 / 2A	1868	1916	MID	
CAMDEN ROAD (NLR) (2nd) Camden Town	22 / 2A	1870	N/A	NLR	Replaced first station to East. Renamed Camden Road 1950
Camden Road East Junctions	54	1850	N/A	NLR	
CAMDEN TOWN	22 / 2A	1907	N/A	CCE&HR	
Camden Town Junctions	22 / 3A	1907	N/A	CCE&HR	Extensively remodelled 1924 due to extension of Bank Branch from Euston
Campbell Road Junction	23 / 4B	1902	1959	LTSR & MDR	Junction between LTSR and District Railway, connection removed 1959
Campden Hill Tunnel	31 / 1A	1868	N/A	MET	
CANADA WATER	33 / 1A	1999	N/A	LUL (ELL)	Jubilee Line platforms opened 1 month after East London Line in 1999
Canal Junction	52	1876	N/A	ELR	
CANARY WHARF (DLR)	33 / 1B	1987	N/A	DLR	
CANARY WHARF (LUL)	33 / 1B	1999	N/A	LUL (JUB)	
CANNING TOWN (1st) Barking Road	24 / 4A	1847	1999	ECR	Renamed 1873. Relocated to the South in connection with Jubilee Line Extension
CANNING TOWN (2nd)	24 / 4A	1999	N/A	RT / DLR / LUL (JUB)	Combined North London Line / DLR / Jubilee Line Station. Replaced former NLL station to North
CANNING TOWN GOODS	24 / 4A	1880	1967	LNWR	
CANNON STREET	22 / 4B	1866	N/A	SER	District Railway station opened 1884
CANNON STREET ROAD	23 / 4A & 7 / 3B	1842	1848	LBR	
Cannon Street South Junction	32 / 1B	1866	N/A	SER	
CANONBURY	22 / 2B	1870	N/A	NLR	
Canonbury West Junction	22 / 2B	1874	N/A	NLR & GNR	
CANONS PARK	9 / 2B	1932	N/A	MET	Opened by Metropolitan Railway. "Edgware"

NAME: (Previous Names Below)	PAGE / GRID:	YEAR OPENED:	YEAR CLOSED:	OPENED BY:	NOTES:
Canons Park (Edgware)					suffix dropped 1933. Transferred to Bakerloo Line 1939, Jubilee Line 1979
Canterbury Road Junction	32 / 3B	1865	N/A	LCDR	
Carlton Road Junction	21 / 2B & 11 / 4A	1868	N/A	MID	
CARPENDERS PARK (1st)	8 / 1B	1914	1952	LNWR	Served by London Underground Bakerloo Line Trains 1917-1952
CARPENDERS PARK (2nd)	8 / 1B	1952	N/A	BR	Served by London Underground Bakerloo Line Trains 1952-1982
CARPENTERS ROAD GOODS	53	?	?	GER	
Carpenters Road North Junction	53	1854	N/A	ECR	
Carpenters Road South Junction	53	1854	N/A	ECR	
CARSHALTON	46 / 2B	1868	N/A	LBSCR	
CARSHALTON BEECHES	46 / 2B	1906	N/A	LBSCR	Renamed 1925
Beeches Halt					
CARTERHATCH LANE	5 / 3A	1916	1919	GER	
CASTLE BAR PARK	19 / 4A	1904	N/A	GWR	"Halt" suffix dropped 1969
Castle Bar Park Halt					
CASTLE CEMENT (KINGS CROSS)	54	?	N/A	PRIV	
CATFORD	33 / 4B	1892	N/A	LCDR	
CATFORD BRIDGE	33 / 4B	1857	N/A	SER	Built by the Mid Kent Railway, but operated by SER from opening. Goods yard closed 1968
CENTRAL	24 / 4B	1880	1940	PLA	Passenger services withdrawn from Gallions Branch 1940
CENTRAL CROYDON	47 / 1B	1868	1890	LBSCR	Closed 1871-1886
CHADWELL HEATH	25 / 1B	1864	N/A	GER	
Chadwell Heath for Becontree					
Chadwell Heath					
CHAFFORD HUNDRED	16 / 3B	1993	N/A	BR	
CHALFONT & LATIMER	1 / 2A	1889	N/A	MET	Renamed 1915. Goods yard closed 1966
Chalfont Road					
CHALK FARM (CCE&HR)	21 / 2B	1907	N/A	CCE&HR	
CHALK FARM (LNWR)	21 / 2B	1851	1915	LNWR	
Camden					
CHANCERY LANE	22 / 4B	1900	N/A	CLR	"Gray's Inn" suffix introduced 1934, gradually dropped
Chancery Lane (Gray's Inn)					
Chancery Lane					
Channelsea North Junction	23 / 2B & 53	1862	N/A	GER	
Channelsea South Junction	53	1854	N/A	ECR	
CHARING CROSS (SER)	22 / 4A	1864	N/A	SER	
CHARING CROSS (LT-JUB)	22 / 4A & 28 / 2A	1979	1999	LT (JUB)	Station closed when Jubilee Line extension opened 1999. Retained for emergencies.
CHARING CROSS (CCE&HR)	22 / 4A & 28 / 2A	1907	N/A	CCE&HR	Opened as Charing Cross. Renamed Charing Cross (Strand) 1914. Renamed Strand 1915. Closed 1973-1979 in connection with Jubilee Line construction, re-opened as Charing Cross 1979 with interchange with Bakerloo and Jubilee Lines.
Strand					
Charing Cross (Strand)					
Charing Cross					
CHARING CROSS (BS&WR)	22 / 4A & 28 / 2A	1906	N/A	BS&WR	Station renamed and interchange with Jubilee and Northern Lines provided 1979
Trafalgar Square					
CHARLTON	34 / 2B	1849	N/A	SER	
Charlton Junction	34 / 2A	1873	N/A	SER	
Charlton Tunnel	34 / 1B	1849	N/A	SER	
CHEAM	46 / 2A	1847	N/A	LBSCR	
CHELSEA BASIN GOODS	31 / 3B & 50	1863	1981	LNWR & GWR	
CHELSEA & FULHAM	31 / 2A & 50	1863	1940	WLER	"& Fulham" after 1902. Passenger service withdrawn Willesden Jcn to Clapham Jcn 1940
Chelsea					
CHERTSEY	37 / 4A	1848	N/A	LSWR	
CHESHAM	1 / 1A	1889	N/A	MET & GCR	Goods yard closed 1966
CHESHUNT	5 / 1B	1846	N/A	GER	
Cheshunt Junction	5 / 1B	1891	N/A	GER	
CHESSINGTON NORTH	45 / 2A	1939	N/A	SR	
CHESSINGTON SOUTH	45 / 2A	1939	N/A	SR	
CHESSINGTON SOUTH SIDINGS	45 / 2A	1939	N/A	SR	Formerly Goods Yard (closed 1963), then Coal Depot (closed 1988)
CHIGWELL (GER)	14 / 1B	1903	1947	GER	Fairlop Loop closed 1947 to allow electrification and transfer to LT Central Line. Freight traffic remained until 1965
CHIGWELL (LT)	14 / 1B	1948	N/A	LT (CEN)	First served by LT Central Line Trains 1948
CHINGFORD	14 / 1A	1878	N/A	GER	Good Yard closed 1965
CHINGFORD (BULL LANE)	14 / 1A	1873	1878	GER	Original terminus of extension from Walthamstow. Closed when Chingford relocated
CHISLEHURST	44 / 3B	1865	N/A	SER	
Chislehurst & Bickley Park					
Chislehurst Junction	44 / 3B	1904	N/A	SECR	
Chislehurst Tunnels	44 / 2B	1865	N/A	SER	
CHISWICK	30 / 2A	1849	N/A	LSWR	Renamed 1948. Goods Yard closed 1958
Chiswick & Grove Park					
Chiswick					
Chiswick Junction (1)	30 / 2A	1869	1932	LSWR	Chiswick Curve dismantled 1932
Chiswick Junction (2)	30 / 3B	1862	1881	LSWR	Barnes Curve disused since 1869 but not dismantled until 1881

NAME: (Previous Names Below)	PAGE / GRID:	YEAR OPENED:	YEAR CLOSED:	OPENED BY:	NOTES:
CHISWICK PARK	30 / 2A & 40 / 1A	1879	N/A	MDR	Opened as Acton Green, renamed Chiswick
Chiswick Park & Acton Green					Park & Acton Green 1887, renamed Chiswick
Acton Green					Park 1910. Completely rebuilt 1933 due to
					quadrupling works
Chobham Farm Junction	53	1854	1969	GER	
CHORLEYWOOD	1 / 3B	1889	N/A	MET	Opened as "Chorley Wood", "& Chenies" suffix
Chorley Wood					in use 1915-1934, became "Chorleywood"
Chorley Wood & Chenies					1964
Chorley Wood					Goods yard closed 1966
Christian Street Junction	23 / 4A & 7 / 3B	1886	N/A	LTSR	Originally Junction for Commercial Road
					Goods, Now point where 4 tracks become 2
CHRISTIE'S SIDING	34 / 2A	?	?	PRIV	
CHURCHBURY	5 / 4A	1891	1919	GER	Closed 1909-1915. Site now occupied by
					Southbury Station
CHURCH MANOR WAY HALT	35 / 1B	1917	1919	SECR	Provided for munitions workers
CHURCH STREET	47 / 1B	2000	N/A	CTL	
CHURCHYARD SIDINGS	54	1868	N/A	MID	
CITY GOODS	23 / 4A & 7 / 3A	1862	1949	MID	
CITY ROAD	22 / 3B	1901	1922	C&SLR	
CITY THAMESLINK	22 / 4B & 55	1990	N/A	BR	Renamed 1991
St Paul's Thameslink					
CLAPHAM COMMON (LSWR)	31 / 4B	1838	1863	LSWR	Replaced by Clapham Junction Station to North
Wandsworth					
CLAPHAM COMMON (C&SLR)	32 / 3A	1900	N/A	C&SLR	Terminus of City & South London Railway
					1900-1926. Closed 1923-1924
CLAPHAM GOODS	32 / 3A	?	?	LCDR	
CLAPHAM HIGH STREET	32 / 3A	1862	N/A	LCDR	LBSCR platforms opened 1867, LCDR
Clapham					platforms closed 1916.
Clapham & North Stockwell					Renamed "Clapham High Street" 1989
Clapham Road & North Stockwell					
Clapham & North Stockwell					
Clapham					
CLAPHAM JUNCTION	31 / 3B	1863	N/A	LSWR	
CLAPHAM NORTH	32 / 3A	1900	N/A	C&SLR	Closed 1923-1924, Renamed 1926
Clapham Road					
CLAPHAM SOUTH	32 / 4A	1926	N/A	UERL (NOR)	
CLAPHAM YARD	31 / 4B	?	N/A	LSWR	
CLAPTON	23 / 1A	1872	N/A	GER	
CLAPTON GOODS	23 / 1A	1900	1964	GER	
Clapton Junction	23 / 1A	1872	N/A	GER	
CLARENCE YARD GOODS	22 / 1B & 15 / 3B	?	1960	GNR	
CLOCK HOUSE	43 / 3B	1890	N/A	SER	Goods Yard closed 1964
COBORN ROAD FOR OLD FORD	23 / 3B	1865	1946	GER	
Coborn Road					
Old Ford					
COCKFOSTERS	3 / 3B	1933	N/A	LT (PIC)	
COCKFOSTERS DEPOT	4 / 4A	1933	N/A	LT (PIC)	
COLINDALE	10 / 3B	1924	N/A	UERL (CCE&HR)	
COLLIERS WOOD	41 / 2B	1926	N/A	UERL (NOR)	
COLNBROOK	27 / 2A	1884	1965	GWR	Terminus of branch from West Drayton
					1884-1885. Passenger service withdrawn
					between West Drayton and Staines West
					1965
COLNBROOK ESTATE HALT	27 / 2A	1961	1965	BR	Passenger service West Drayton to Staines
					West withdrawn 1965
COLNBROOK GOODS	27 / 2A	1884	1966	GWR	
COLNBROOK OIL TERMINAL (ELF)	27 / 2A	1990	N/A	PRIV	Aviation Fuel terminal for Heathrow Airport
COMMERCIAL DOCK	33 / 1A & 52	1856	1866	SER	
COMMERCIAL ROAD GOODS	23 / 4A & 7 / 2B	1886	1967	LTSR	
Connaught Bridge	34 / 1B	1855	1967	GER	
CONNAUGHT ROAD	24 / 4B	1880	1940	PLA	Passenger services withdrawn from Gallions
					Branch 1940
Connaught Tunnel	24 / 4B	1876	N/A	GER	North Woolwich Branch diverted underground
					due to construction of Royal Albert Dock
COOMBE LANE	48 / 2A	2000	N/A	CTL	
COOMBE ROAD	48 / 2A	1885	1983	SER	Closed 1916-1935, Renamed upon re-opening,
Coombe Lane					finally closed 1983
Copenhagen Tunnels	22 / 2A	1850	N/A	GNR	
Coppermill North Junction	13 / 4A	1872	N/A	GER	Junction between Lea Valley Line and 1872
					route from Hackney Downs
Coppermill South Junction	13 / 4A	1885	1960	GER	Junction between Lea Valley Line and 1885
					curve to Chingford
CORY OIL (SELSDON)	47 / 2B	c.1960s	1993	PRIV	Originally Selsdon Goods Yard
Cottage Junction	42 / 4B	1983	N/A	BR	
COULSDON NORTH	47 / 4A	1899	1983	LBSCR	Renamed "Coulsdon & Smitham Downs" 1911,
Coulsdon West					renamed "Coulsdon West" 1923 for 3 weeks,
Coulsdon & Smitham Downs					then finally renamed "Coulsdon North"
Stoat's Nest & Cane Hill					
Courthill Loop North Junction	33 / 3B	1929	N/A	SR	
Courthill Loop South Junction	33 / 3B	1929	N/A	SR	
COVENT GARDEN	22 / 4A	1907	N/A	GNP&BR	
COWLEY	17 / 4B	1904	1962	GWR	Passenger services withdrawn from Uxbridge
					Vine Street Branch 1962, freight in 1964
CRANLEY GARDENS	12 / 3A	1902 (1897)	1954 (1957)	GNR	Closed when Alexandra Palace to Finsbury park

NAME: (Previous Names Below)	PAGE / GRID:	YEAR OPENED:	YEAR CLOSED:	OPENED BY:	NOTES:
					service withdrawn 1954. Had been intended for electrification and transfer to LT Northern Line, but works abandoned post-WW2. Also closed to passengers 1951-1952. Goods yard in operation 1897-1957.
CRAYFORD	36 / 4B	1866	N/A	SER	Goods Yard closed 1965
Crayford Creek Junction	36 / 3B	1895	N/A	SER	
Crayford Spur "A" Junction	36 / 3B	1942	N/A	SER	
Crayford Spur "B" Junction	36 / 4B	1942	N/A	SER	
Cremorne Bridge	31 / 3B	1863	N/A	WLER	
Crescent Wood Tunnel	43 / 1A	1865	1954	LCDR	Closed 1917-1919. Nunhead to Crystal Palace (High Level) closed 1954 (Passengers and Goods)
CREWS HILL	4 / 1A	1910	N/A	GNR	
CRICKLEWOOD Childs Hill & Cricklewood	21 / 1A	1870	N/A	MID	
Cricklewood Curve Junction	21 / 1A	1870	N/A	MID	
CRICKLEWOOD ENGINE SHEDS	20 / 1B	1882	1964	MID	1st shed 1882, 2nd added 1893
CRICKLEWOOD RECESS SIDINGS	20 / 1B	?	N/A	?	
CROFTON PARK	33 / 4B	1892	N/A	LCDR	
Crofton Road Junction	32 / 3B	?	N/A	LCDR & LBSCR	
Cromwell Curve North Junction	31 / 2A & 50	1871	1957	MDR	Cromwell Curve lifted 1957. Area rafted over and Traingle Sidings built on site.
Cromwell Curve South Junction	31 / 2B & 50	1871	1957	MDR	Cromwell Curve lifted 1957. Area rafted over and Traingle Sidings built on site.
Cromwell Road Junction	50	1871	N/A	MDR	
CROSSHARBOUR & LONDON ARENA Crossharbour	33 / 1B	1987	N/A	DLR	On site of former Millwall Docks Station
Cross Street Tunnel	35 / 1A	1849	N/A	SER	
CROUCH END	12 / 4A	1867	1954	GNR	Nominally opened by Edgware, Highgate & London Railway, but operated by GNR from opening. Closed when Alexandra Palace to Finsbury park service withdrawn 1954. Had been intended for electrification and transfer to LT Northern Line, but works abandoned post-WW2
CROUCH HILL	12 / 4A	1868	N/A	T&HJ	
CROXLEY Croxley Green	1 / 4B	1925	N/A	MET & LNER	"Green" suffix dropped 1949. Goods Yard closed 1966
CROXLEY GREEN	2 / 4A	1912	1996	LNWR	Croxley Green Branch service suspended 1996
CROXLEY TIP	1 / 4B	1902	N/A	MET	Not in Regular Use. Formerly Gravel Pit

CRYSTAL PALACE
  Crystal Palace Low Level
  Crystal Palace
	43 / 2A	1854	N/A	LBCSR	"Low Level" 1923-1955. East London Line projected to serve from 2010

CRYSTAL PALACE HIGH LEVEL
  Crystal Palace & Upper Norwood
  Crystal Palace High Level & Upper Norwood
  Crystal Palace High Level
	43 / 2A	1865	1954	LCDR	"& Upper Norwood" added 1898. Closed 1917-1919 and 1944-1946. Nunhead to Crystal Palace (High Level) closed 1954 (Passengers and Goods)

Crytsal Palace Tunnel	43 / 2A	1856	N/A	LBSCR	
Crystal Palace Tunnel Junction	43 / 2A	1856	N/A	LBSCR	

CUSTOM HOUSE
  Custom House Victoria Dock
  Custom House
	24 / 4A	1855	N/A	ECR	DLR Platforms opened 1994

CUTTY SARK	33 / 2B	1999	N/A	DLR	
CYPRUS	24 / 4B	1994	N/A	DLR	
DAGENHAM DOCK	26 / 3A	1908	N/A	LTSR	
DAGENHAM DOCK	26 / 4A	1887	?	PRIV	
DAGENHAM EAST (LTSR) Dagenham	26 / 2A	1885	1962	LTSR	Served by District Railway trains 1902-1905. British Rail services withdrawn 1962 and "Fast" platforms abandoned
DAGENHAM EAST (MDR) Dagenham	26 / 2A	1902	N/A	MDR	1902 date denotes first time District railway served original LTSR platforms at Dagenham. District trains withdrawn East Ham to Upminster 1905, reinstated Barking to Upminster 1932. Current District platforms constructed 1932 during LMS quadrupling of route. Renamed 1949, ownership of "Slow" platforms transferred to LT 1970. Goods Yard closed 1968
DAGENHAM HEATHWAY Heathway	26 / 2A	1932	N/A	LMS	Barking to Upminster quadrupled by the LMS in 1932 and 4 new stations opened. Served by District Line from opening. Renamed 1949, ownership transferred to LT in 1970
DALSTON	23 / 2A & 18 / 4B	2010	N/A	LUL (ELL)	Projected northern terminus of East London Line Extension Phase 1. On site of former Dalston Junction Station
Dalston Eastern Junction	23 / 2A & 18 / 3B	1865	1965	NLR	Dalston Eastern Curve closed to passengers 1944, freight 1965
DALSTON JUNCTION	23 / 2A & 18 / 4B	1865	1986	NLR	Platforms 5 & 6 closed 1944, 3 & 4 closed 1976. To re-open 2010 as "Dalston"
Dalston Junction	23 / 2A & 18 / 4B	1865	1965	NLR	Dalston Eastern Curve closed to passengers 1944, freight 1965

NAME: (Previous Names Below)	PAGE / GRID:	YEAR OPENED:	YEAR CLOSED:	OPENED BY:	NOTES:
DALSTON KINGSLAND	23 / 2A & 18 / 3A	1983	N/A	BR	On site of former Kingsland Station
Dalston Western Junction	23 / 2A & 18 / 3A	1865	1986	NLR	
Dartford Junction	36 / 4B	1866	N/A	SER	
DAY & SONS GRAVEL (PURLEY)	47 / 4B	?	N/A	PRIV	
DEBDEN (GER)	6 / 3A	1865	1970	GER	Majority of Passenger services transferred to LT
Chigwell Lane					and station became "Debden" in 1949
Chigwell Road					First Trains in the morning remained British
					Rail services until 1970
DEBDEN (LT)	6 / 3A	1949	N/A	LT (CEN)	First served by Central Line Trains 1949.
					Goods yard closed 1966
DENHAM	7 / 4A	1906	N/A	GCR & GWR	Projected terminus of Central Line extension
Denham For Harefield					from West Ruislip, but works cancelled
					post-WW2
Denham East Junction	17 / 1B	1907	1916	GCR & GWR	
Denham South Junction	17 / 1A	1907	1916	GCR & GWR	
Denham West Junction	17 / 1A	1907	1962	GCR & GWR	
DENMARK HILL	32 / 3B	1865	N/A	LCDR	
DEPTFORD	33 / 2B	1836	N/A	LGR	Terminus 1836-1838, closed 1915-1926
DEPTFORD BRIDGE	33 / 3B	1999	N/A	DLR	
Deptford Road Junction	33 / 2A & 52	1871	1964	ELR	Projected to re-open as part of East London
					Line Extension Phase 2
DEPTFORD WHARF	33 / 1B & 52	1849	1964	LBSCR	
DEVONSHIRE STREET (MILE END)	23 / 3A	1839	1843	ECR	London Terminus of ECR 1839-1840.
					Replaced by Mile End to West
DEVONS ROAD	23 / 4B	1987	N/A	DLR	
DEVONS ROAD DEPOT	23 / 4B	1882	1964	NLR	Locomotive Depot
District Junction (South Acton)	40 / 1A	1899	1932	MDR	"Clipped" out of use since 1914, not physically
					removed until 1932
Dockyard Tunnel	34 / 1B	1849	N/A	SER	
DOLLIS HILL	20 / 2B	1909	N/A	MET	Last served Metropolitan Line 1940. Served by
Dollis Hill & Gladstone Park					Bakerloo Line 1939-1979, Jubilee thereafter
Dollis Hill					
DOWN SIDINGS (PLUMSTEAD)	35 / 1A	?	N/A	?	
DOWN SIDINGS (WIMBLEDON)	41 / 2A	?	N/A	LSWR	
DOWN STREET	32 / 1A	1907	1932	GNP&BR	
Down Street, Mayfair					
DOWN YARD (SOUTHALL)	28 / 1B	1859	N/A	GWR	
DRAYTON GREEN	19 / 4A	1905	N/A	GWR	
Drayton Green Ealing Halt					
Drayton Green Junction	19 / 4A	1903	N/A	GWR	
Drayton Green Tunnel	19 / 4A	1974	N/A	BR	Covered Way over line in connection with
					housing development
DRAYTON PARK	22 / 2B	1904	N/A	GN&CR	Opened by GN&CR, bought by Metropolitan
					Railway 1913, transferred to Northern Line
					1939, closed by London Underground 1975,
					re-opened by British Rail 1976
DRAYTON PARK DEPOT	22 / 2B	1904	1975	GN&CR	
DUDDING HILL FOR WILLESDEN & NEASDEN	20 / 2B	1875	1902	MID	Closed 1888-1893
Dudding Hill					
Dudding Hill for Church End Willesden					
Willesden & Dudden Hill					
Dudding Hill Junction	20 / 1B	1870	N/A	MID	
DUNDONALD ROAD	41 / 2A	2000	N/A	CTL	
DURNSFORD ROAD SIDINGS	41 / 1A	1916	N/A	LSWR	Part of Wimbledon Traincare Depot (SWT)
EAGLE LANE GOODS	14 / 3A	1899	1966	GER	
EALING BROADWAY	19 / 4B	1838	N/A	GWR	Served by District Railway since 1879. Served
Ealing					by Central London Railway since 1920.
EALING COMMON	30 / 1A	1879	N/A	MDR	"& West Acton" 1886-1910. Served by Piccadilly
Ealing Common & West Acton					Line since 1932
Ealing Common					
EALING COMMON DEPOT	30 / 1A	1905	N/A	MDR	District Line Depot. Used also for Piccadilly Line
					1932-1964.
EARDLEY CARRIAGE SIDINGS	42 / 2A	?	1960	LBSCR	
EARL'S COURT (1st)	31 / 2A & 50	1871	1878	MDR	Resited West 1878
EARL'S COURT (2nd)	31 / 2A & 50	1878	N/A	MDR	GNP&BR platforms opened 1906.
					Closed 1997-1998 (Piccadilly Line only)
EARLSFIELD	41 / 1B	1884	N/A	LSWR	Renamed 1902
Earlsfield & Summerstown					
Earlsfield					
EAST ACTON	20 / 4B	1920	N/A	CLR	Viaduct Junction to North Acton built by GWR
					1917
EAST BRIXTON	32 / 3B	1866	1976	LBSCR	Renamed "Loughborough Park & Brixton" 1870,
Loughborough Park & Brixton					then "East Brixton" 1894
Loughborough Park					
EASTCOTE	8 / 4B	1906	N/A	MET	Served by District Line Trains 1910-1933,
					Piccadilly Line thereafter. Goods Yard closed
					1964
EAST CROYDON	47 / 1B	1841	N/A	L&BR	East Croydon and New Croydon nominally 2
New Croydon					separate stations, combined 1909
Croydon East					Croydon Tramlink opened 2000
Croydon					
EAST DULWICH	32 / 4B	1868	N/A	LBSCR	Renamed 1888
Champion Hill					

NAME: (Previous Names Below)	PAGE / GRID:	YEAR OPENED:	YEAR CLOSED:	OPENED BY:	NOTES:
Eastern Junction (Stratford)	53	1846	1973	ECR	Eastern Curve at Stratford dismantled 1973
EAST FINCHLEY (GNR) East End Finchley	11 / 3B	1867	1941	GNR	Nominally opened by Edgware, Highgate & London Railway, but operated by GNR from opening. Became terminus of LNER service from Finsbury Park 1939, withdrawn 1941
EAST FINCHLEY (LT)	11 / 3B	1939	N/A	LT (NOR)	Terminus of LT Northern Line extension from Archway 1939-1940. Goods yard closed 1962
East Finchley Junction	11 / 3B	1939	N/A	LT (NOR) & LNER	Junction of Northern Line with former LNER route to Finsbury Park (now depot access)
EAST GOODS YARD (FINSBURY PARK)	15 / 3B	?	1960	GNR	
EAST HAM (LTSR)	24 / 2B	1858	1962	LTSR	Main Line services non-stopped since 1962, and Fast Platforms abandoned
EAST HAM (MDR)	24 / 2B	1902	N/A	MDR	First served by District Railway 1902, line quadrupled 1908, District Trains using Slow Lines. Served by Metropolitan Line since 1936 ("Hammersmith & City Line" since 1990) Bay Platform for Kentish Town via T&FG and T&H abandoned 1958. Goods Yard closed 1962
EAST HAM DEPOT	24 / 2B	1961	N/A	BR	On Site of former District Line Little Ilford Depot
East Ham Loop North Junction	24 / 2B	1894	1958	T&FG	East Ham Loop dismantled when services diverted to Barking
East Ham Loop South Junction	24 / 2B	1894	1958	T&FG	East Ham Loop dismantled when services diverted to Barking
EAST INDIA	24 / 4A & 48 / 3B	1994	N/A	DLR	
EAST INDIA DOCKS GOODS	24 / 4A & 48 / 3B	1859	1961	GER	
EAST PUTNEY (MDR)	31 / 4A	1889	N/A	LSWR	Putney Bridge to Wimbldeon built by LSWR but operated by District Railway from opening
EAST PUTNEY (LSWR)	31 / 4A	1889	1941	LSWR	Last regular passenger service withdrawn 1941, although Main Line services called on occasions until 1969. Point Pleasant Jcn to Wimbledon still used for empty stock working and diversions.
East Putney Junction	31 / 4A	1889	N/A	LSWR	
East Putney Tunnel	31 / 4A	1889	N/A	LSWR	
EAST SIDINGS (ACTON TOWN)	30 / 1A & 40 / 1A	1932	N/A	UERL (DIS & PIC)	Current layout since 1932
EAST SIDINGS (SOUTHALL)	28 / 1B	1884	N/A	GWR	Originally Engine Shed, expanded 1954, later became DMU Shed until 1986. Used by railway preservation societies since 1988
EAST SMITHFIELD / LONDON DOCKS GOODS	23 / 4A & 7 / 3A	1864	1966	GER	
EAST YARD (TEMPLE MILLS)	23 / 1B	1959	N/A	BR	
EDEN PARK	43 / 4B	1882	N/A	SER	
EDGWARE (GNR)	10 / 2A	1867	1939 (1964)	GNR	Nominally opened by Edgware, Highgate & London Railway, but operated by GNR from opening. Closed to passengers 1939 and freight 1964
EDGWARE (UERL)	10 / 2A	1924	N/A	UERL (CCE&HR)	Built for through running to Bushey Heath, but extension abandoned 1940
EDGWARE ROAD (MET)	21 / 4B	1863	N/A	MET	Rebuilt 1926
EDGWARE ROAD (BS&WR)	21 / 4B	1907	N/A	BS&WR	
EDGWARE SIDINGS	10 / 2A	1924	N/A	UERL (CCE&HR)	Northern Line stabling sidings. Southern fan on site of intended curve to GNR branch
EDMONTON GREEN Lower Edmonton Lower Edmonton (High Level) Edmonton (High Level)	13 / 1A	1872	N/A	GER	
Edward Street Junction	52	?	N/A	SER	
ELEPHANT & CASTLE	32 / 1B	1862	N/A	LCDR	C&SLR Station opened 1890 (closed 1923-1924), BS&WR Station opened 1906 (closed 1996-1997)
ELMERS END	43 / 3A	1864	N/A	SER	Goods Yard closed 1964. Croydon Tramlink opened 2000
Elmers End Junction	43 / 3A	1882	1997	SER	Elmers End to Addiscombe closed 1997 prior to opening of Croydon Tramlink
ELM PARK	26 / 2B	1935	N/A	LMS	Opened on 1932 "Slow" lines built by the LMS. Served by District Line from opening
ELMSTEAD WOODS Elmstead	44 / 2B	1904	N/A	SECR	Renamed 1908
ELSTREE SOUTH	9 / 1B	N/A	N/A	LT (NOR)	On Northern Line extension to Bushey Heath from Edgware. Construction abandoned 1940
ELTHAM	34 / 3B	1985	N/A	BR	Replaced Eltham Well Hall and Eltham Park Stations (road scheme)
ELTHAM PARK Shooters Hill & Eltham Park	34 / 3B	1908	1985	SECR	Renamed 1927. Replaced by Eltham Station 1985
ELTHAM WELL HALL Well Hall & North Eltham Well Hall	34 / 3B	1895	1985	SER	Renamed 1927. Goods Yard expanded 1915, closed 1968. Replaced by Eltham Station 1985
ELVERSON ROAD	33 / 3B	1999	N/A	DLR	
EMBANKMENT	32 / 1A & 28 / 2A	1870	N/A	MDR	Baker Street & Waterloo platforms added 1906.

NAME: (Previous Names Below)	PAGE / GRID:	YEAR OPENED:	YEAR CLOSED:	OPENED BY:	NOTES:
Charing Cross Embankment Charing Cross					CCE&HR Loop platform added 1914, southbound platform on Kennington extension opened 1926. Renamed Charing Cross Embankment 1974, shortened to Embankment 1976.
EMERSON PARK Emerson Park & Great Nelmes	16 / 2A	1909	N/A	GER	
Engine Shed Junction	22 / 2A & 11 / 4A	1868	1981	MID	Eliminated when curve used by Barking Trains abandoned
ENFIELD	4 / 3B	1871	1910	GNR	Original terminus of GNR Enfield Branch from Alexandra Palace
ENFIELD CHASE	4 / 3B	1910	N/A	GNR	
ENFIELD GOODS	4 / 3B	1910	1974	BR	Goods station on site of original GNR Enfield terminus. Carriage Sidings in use until 1979
ENFIELD LOCK Ordnance Factory	5 / 2B	1855	N/A	GER	
ENFIELD TOWN Enfield	4 / 3B	1849	N/A	GER	Goods Yard closed 1959
EPPING (GER)	6 / 2A	1865	1970	GER	Majority of Passenger services transferred to LT in 1949. First Trains in the morning remained British Rail services until 1970
EPPING (LT)	6 / 2A	1949	N/A	LT (CEN)	First served by Central Line Trains 1949. Goods yard closed 1966
EPSOM	45 / 3B	1859	N/A	LSWR	Originally LSWR only, platforms opened on former LBSCR line 1929
EPSOM DOWNS (1st)	46 / 4A	1865	1989	LBSCR	Resited East and land sold for housing development
EPSOM DOWNS (2nd)	46 / 4A	1989	N/A	BR	Replaced original station to West
EPSOM TOWN Epsom	45 / 3B	1847	N/A	LBSCR	Terminus 1847-1859. Became "Epsom Town" 1923. Closed when platforms opened at Epsom on former LBSCR line 1929
ERITH	36 / 2B	1849	N/A	SER	
ERITH WHARF	36 / 2B	?	?	SER	
ESSEX ROAD Canonbury & Essex Road Essex Road	22 / 2B	1904	N/A	GN&CR	Opened by GN&CR, bought by Metropolitan Railway 1913, transferred to Northern Line 1939, closed by London Underground 1975, re-opened by British Rail 1976. Renamed 1948
EUSTON	22 / 3A	1837	N/A	L&B	C&SLR platforms opened 1901 (closed 1922-1924), CCE&HR platforms 1907, Victoria Line platforms 1968
EUSTON SQUARE Gower Street	22 / 3A	1863	N/A	MET	Renamed 1909
EWELL EAST Ewell for Worcester Park	45 / 3B	1847	N/A	LBSCR	Renamed 1923
EWELL WEST Ewell	45 / 2B	1859	N/A	LSWR	Goods yard closed 1961
EW&S STONE TERMINAL (TOLWORTH)	45 / 1A	1981	N/A	BR	Former Goods Yard (open 1939-1965), then Coal Terminal (open 1965-1989)
EXPRESS DAIRY (MORDEN)	41 / 4A	1954	1978	PRIV	
Factory Junctions	32 / 3A & 51	1862	N/A	LCDR	
FAIRFIELD YARD	47 / 1B	1890	1933	LBSCR	Permanent Way Yard on truncated Croydon Central Branch
FAIRLOP (GER)	15 / 3A	1903	1947	GER	Fairlop Loop closed 1947 to allow electrification and transfer to LT Central Line. Freight traffic remained until 1965
FAIRLOP (LT)	15 / 3A	1948	N/A	LT (CEN)	First served by LT Central Line Trains 1948. Goods yard closed 1965
Falcon Junction	31 / 4B	1863	N/A	LBSCR & WLER	
FALCON LANE GOODS	31 / 3B	1869	1968	LNWR	
FALCONWOOD	35 / 3A	1936	N/A	SR	
FARRINGDON Farringdon & High Holborn Farringdon Street	22 / 4B	1865	N/A	MET	City Widened Lines platforms added 1868 (now Thameslink). "Farringdon Street" became "Farringdon & High Holborn" 1922, suffix dropped 1936
FARRINGDON GOODS	22 / 4B	1909	1952	MID	
FARRINGDON STREET	22 / 4B	1863	1865	MET	Original City terminus of Metropolitan Railway, abandoned when line extended to Moorgate
FELTHAM	38 / 1A	1848	N/A	LSWR	
Feltham Junction	28 / 4B	1850	N/A	LSWR	
FELTHAM LOCO SHED	28 / 4B	1922	1967	LSWR	
FELTHAM MARSHALLING YARD	28 / 4B	1922	1968	LSWR	
FENCHURCH STREET	22 / 4B & 7 / 3A	1841	N/A	LBR	
FERME PARK DOWN SIDINGS	12 / 4B	1888	N/A	GNR	Former Ferme Park Yard, opened 1888
FIELDWAY	48 / 2B	2000	N/A	CTL	
FINCHLEY (CHURCH END) Finchley Finchley & Hendon	11 / 3A	1867	1939	GNR	Nominally opened by Edgware, Highgate & London Railway, but operated by GNR from opening. Opened as "Finchley & Hendon", "& Hendon" suffix dropped 1872, "Church End" added 1896. Closed in 1939 to enable electrification and transfer to LT Northern Line, re-opened as "Central"

NAME: (Previous Names Below)	PAGE / GRID:	YEAR OPENED:	YEAR CLOSED:	OPENED BY:	NOTES:
FINCHLEY CENTRAL	11 / 3A	1940	N/A	LT (NOR)	On site of former GNR "Church End" station. Goods / Coal yard closed 1962
Finchley Central Junction	11 / 3A	1872	N/A	GNR	Divergence of High Barnet Branch from original Edgware Line (now Mill Hill East Branch)
FINCHLEY ROAD (MID) Finchley Road & St John's Wood	21 / 2B	1868	1927	MID	
FINCHLEY ROAD (MET) Finchley Road (South Hampstead) Finchley Road	21 / 2B	1879	N/A	MET	"South Hampstead" suffix 1885-1914. Served by Bakerloo Line 1939-1979, Jubilee Line thereafter. Goods yard opened 1894, closed 1941
FINCHLEY ROAD & FROGNAL Finchley Road St John's Wood	21 / 2B	1860	N/A	HJR	Renamed 1880. Goods Yard open 1870-1967. Closed 1995-1996
FINSBURY PARK Seven Sisters Road	22 / 1B & 15 / 3B	1861	N/A	GNR	Opened as "Seven Sisters Road", renamed "Finsbury Park" 1869. Great Northern & City Line opened 1904 (Closed 1964), Piccadilly Line opened 1906, Victoria Line opened 1968. Southbound Victoria & Piccadilly Lines use former GN&C tunnel
FINSBURY PARK GOODS & COAL	22 / 1B & 15 / 2B	?	?	GNR	
Finsbury Park Junction	22 / 1B & 15 / 3B	1976	N/A	BR	Junction of Great Northern main Line with Great Northern & City route ex-Moorgate
FIRESTONE TYRES (BRENTFORD)	29 / 2B	1928	1964	PRIV	
FORD FREIGHTLINER DEPOT (DAGENHAM)	26 / 3A	?	N/A	PRIV	
FORD MOTOR WORKS (DAGENHAM)	26 / 3A	1932	N/A	PRIV	
FOREST GATE	24 / 2A	1840	N/A	ECR	
Forest Gate Junction	24 / 2B	1854	N/A	ECR	
FOREST HILL Forest Hill for Lordship lane Dartmouth Arms	43 / 1A	1839	N/A	LCR	East London Line projected to serve from 2010
FORTY HILL	5 / 2A	1891	1919	GER	Closed 1909-1915. Site now occupied by Turkey Street Station
Fulham Bridge	31 / 3A	1889	N/A	LSWR	Built by London & South-Western Railway but only ever used by District Railway trains
FULHAM BROADWAY Walham Green	31 / 2A & 50	1880	N/A	MDR	Renamed 1952
FULWELL Fulwell for Hampton Hill Fulwell & Hampton Hill Fulwell & New Hampton Fulwell	39 / 2A	1864	N/A	LSWR	
Fulwell Junction	39 / 2A	1894	N/A	LSWR	
FULWELL LOCO DEPOT	39 / 2A	1897	1916	LSWR	Replaced by Strawberry Hill EMU Depot
GALLIONS	25 / 4A	1880	1940	PLA	Passenger services withdrawn from Gallions Branch 1940
GALLIONS REACH	25 / 4A	1994	N/A	DLR	
GANTS HILL	14 / 4B	1947	N/A	LT (CEN)	
GARSTON	2 / 2B	1966	N/A	BR	
Gas Factory Junction	23 / 4B	1850	N/A	LTSR & NLR	Access to Bow Road Goods elimiated 1964, Curve to NLR eliminated 1968
George IV Tunnel	34 / 1B	1849	N/A	SER	
GEORGE LANE (WOODFORD)	14 / 3A	1856	1970	ECR	Majority of Passenger services transferred to LT in 1947 (station later became South Woodford). First Trains in the morning remained British Rail services until 1970
GEORGE STREET	47 / 1B	2000	N/A	CTL	
GIDEA PARK Gidea Park & Squirrels Heath Squirrels Heath & Gidea Park	16 / 4B	1910	N/A	GER	Renamed "Gidea Park & Squirrels Heath" 1913, "& Squirrels Heath" dropped 1969
Gifford Street Portals	54	2007	N/A	L&CR	
GIPSY HILL Gipsy Hill for Upper Norwood	42 / 2B	1856	N/A	LBSCR	Opened by West End of London & Crystal Palace Railway, but operated by LBSCR from outset. Goods Yard closed 1969
GLOBE ROAD	23 / 3A	1884	1916	GER	
GLOUCESTER ROAD Brompton (Gloucester Road)	31 / 2B & 50	1868	N/A	MET	District Railway platforms opened 1869. GNP&BR platforms opened 1906 as Gloucester Road. Entire station renamed Gloucester Road 1907. Piccadilly Line platforms closed 1987-1989
Gloucester Road Junction	42 / 4B	1983	N/A	BR	
GOLDERS GREEN	11 / 4A	1907	N/A	CCE&HR	Northern Terminus of Charing Cross, Euston and Hampstead Railway when opened
GOLDERS GREEN DEPOT	11 / 4A	1907	N/A	CCE&HR	Northern Line Depot
GOLDHAWK ROAD	30 / 1B & 49	1914	N/A	MET & GWR	Replaced Shepherd's Bush Station to North
GOODGE STREET Tottenham Court Road	22 / 4A	1907	N/A	CCE&HR	Renamed 1908
GOODMANS YARD GOODS	23 / 4A & 7 / 3A	1861	1951	LBR	
GOODMAYES	25 / 1B	1901	N/A	GER	
GOODMAYES FREIGHT YARDS	25 / 1B	1901	1962	GER	
GORDON HILL	4 / 3B	1910	N/A	GNR	
GOSPEL OAK Kentish Town	21 / 1B & 11 / 4A	1860	N/A	HJR	Renamed 1867. Bay Platform for Barking Trains since 1981
Gospel Oak Junction	21 / 1B & 11 / 4A	1914	N/A	T&HJ	Junction established 1914, eliminated 1920. Re-established 1940

NAME: (Previous Names Below)	PAGE / GRID:	YEAR OPENED:	YEAR CLOSED:	OPENED BY:	NOTES:
GRAHAM ROAD GOODS	23 / 2A	1894	1965	GER	
GRANGE HILL (GER)	15 / 2A	1903	1947	GER	Fairlop Loop closed 1947 to allow electrification
Grange Hill Hill for Chigwell Row					and transfer to LT Central Line. Freight traffic
					remained until 1965
GRANGE HILL (LT)	15 / 2A	1948	N/A	LT (CEN)	First served by LT Central Line Trains 1948.
					Goods yard closed 1965
Grange Hill Tunnel	15 / 2A	1903	N/A	GER	
GRANGE PARK	4 / 4B	1910	N/A	GNR	
GRAVEL HILL	48 / 2B	2000	N/A	CTL	
GRAYS	16 / 3B	1854	N/A	LTSR	
GREAT PORTLAND STREET	22 / 3A	1863	N/A	MET	Opened as "Portland Road", renamed "Great
Great Portland Street & Regent's Park					Portland Street" 1917, "& Regent's Park"
Great Portland Street					suffix added 1923, dropped 1933
Portland Road					
GREENFORD (GWR)	19 / 2A	1904	1963	GWR	Station on GWR Birmingham Line. Bay Platform
					between Central Line Platforms still open
GREENFORD (LT)	19 / 2A	1947	N/A	LT (CEN) & BR	Terminus of Central Line extension from North
					Acton 1947-48
Greenford East Junction	19 / 3A	1903	N/A	GWR	
GREENFORD GOODS	19 / 2A	1932	1980	GWR	
GREENFORD S & T	19 / 2A	?	N/A	BR	
Greenford South Junction	19 / 2A	1904	N/A	GWR	
Greenford West Junction	19 / 3A	1904	N/A	GWR	
GREEN PARK	32 / 1A	1906	N/A	GNP&BR	Renamed 1933. Victoria Line platforms opened
Dover Street					1969, Jubilee Line 1979
GREENWICH	33 / 2B	1838	N/A	LGR	Terminus 1838-1878. DLR Platforms opened
					1999
GREENWICH PARK	33 / 2B	1888	1917	LCDR	Renamed 1900. Passenger service withdrawn
Greenwich					Nunhead to Greenwich Park 1917
Grosvenor Bridge	32 / 2A & 51	1860	N/A	LBSCR	
GROSVENOR DEPOT	32 / 2A & 51	1862	N/A	LCDR	
GROSVENOR ROAD	32 / 2A & 51	1867	1911	LCDR	LBSCR Platforms opened 1870, closed 1907
GROVE PARK	44 / 1A	1871	N/A	SER	
GROVE PARK CARRIAGE SERVICE SHED	44 / 1A	?	N/A	SER	
GROVE PARK DOWN (BRAMDEAN) SIDINGS	44 / 1A	1900	N/A	SECR	
Grove Park Junction	44 / 1A	1878	N/A	SER	
GROVE PARK UP (ST MILDRED'S) SIDINGS	44 / 1A	1900	N/A	SECR	
GUINNESS (PARK ROYAL)	20 / 3A	1933	N/A	PRIV	Brewery, Disused
GUNNERSBURY	30 / 2A & 40 / 2A	1869	N/A	LSWR	First served District & Metropolitan Railways
Brentford Road					1877. Last served Metropolitan railway 1906.
					Originally had 5 platforms, 3 of which were
					abandoned in 1930. Remodelled 1932.
Gunnersbury Junction	30 / 2A & 40 / 2A	1869	N/A	LSWR	
Gunnersbury East Junction					
Gunnersbury West Junction	30 / 2A	1869	1932	LSWR	Chiswick Curve dismantled 1932
HACKBRIDGE	47 / 1A	1868	N/A	LBSCR	
HACKNEY (1st)	23 / 2A	1850	1870	NLR	Resited to West 1870
HACKNEY (2nd)	23 / 2A	1870	1944	NLR	Replaced original station to East. Passenger
					service Dalston Junction to Poplar withdrawn
					1944
HACKNEY CENTRAL	23 / 2A	1980	N/A	BR	On site of former NLR Hackney Station (2nd)
HACKNEY COAL	23 / 2A	?	?	NLR	
HACKNEY DOWNS	23 / 2A	1872	N/A	GER	
Hackney Downs Junction					
Hackney Downs Junctions	23 / 2A	1872	N/A	GER	
HACKNEY WICK	23 / 2B	1980	N/A	BR	
HACKNEY WICK GOODS	23 / 2B	1877	1967	GNR	
HADLEY WOOD	3 / 3B	1885	N/A	GNR	
Hadley Wood North Tunnel	3 / 2B	1850	N/A	GNR	
Hadley Wood South Tunnel	3 / 3B	1850	N/A	GNR	
HAGGERSTON (NLR)	23 / 3A	1867	1940	NLR	To re-open 2010 (East London Line Extension)
HAGGERSTON (LUL)	23 / 3A	2010	N/A	LUL (ELL)	Projected to re-open 2010 as part of East
					London Line Extension Phase 1
HAINAULT (GER)	15 / 2A	1903	1947	GER	Closed 1908-1930. Fairlop Loop closed 1947 to
					allow electrification and transfer to LT
					Central Line. Freight traffic remained until
					1965.
HAINAULT (LT)	15 / 2A	1948	N/A	LT (CEN)	First served by LT Central Line Trains 1948
HAINAULT DEPOT	15 / 2A	1943	N/A	LT (CEN)	Opened 1943-1945 for temporary wartime use,
					Central Line Depot since 1948
Hall Farm North Junction	13 / 4A	1872	1967	GER	Junction between original Walthamstow Branch
					and 1872 line to Hackney Downs
Hall Farm South Junction	13 / 4A	1885	1960	GER	Junction between Chingford Branch and curve
					to Lea Valley Line
HAMMERSMITH (District & Piccadilly Lines)	30 / 2B & 56	1874	N/A	MDR	GNP&BR terminus 1906-1932
HAMMERSMITH (Hammersmith & City Line)	30 / 2B & 56	1864	N/A	MET & GWR	Relocated south 1868. Goods Yard closed 1960
HAMMERSMITH & CHISWICK	30 / 2B	1858 (1857)	1917 (1965)	N&SWJR	Opened to freight traffic 1857, passenger traffic
Hammersmith					1858. "& Chiswick" suffix added 1880
					Passenger traffic withdrawn 1917, freight
					remaining until 1965
HAMMERSMITH DEPOT	30 / 1B	1864	N/A	MET	Hammersmith & City Line Depot
HAMMERSMITH (GROVE ROAD)	30 / 2B & 56	1869	1916	LSWR	Served by Metropolitan Railway 1877-1906.

NAME: (Previous Names Below)	PAGE / GRID:	YEAR OPENED:	YEAR CLOSED:	OPENED BY:	NOTES:
					Addison Road to Studland Road Jcn closed 1916.
HAMPSTEAD	21 / 1B	1907	N/A	CCE&HR	
Hampstead (Heath Street)					
HAMPSTEAD HEATH	21 / 1B	1860	N/A	HJR	Closed 1995-1996
HAMPSTEAD HEATH GOODS	21 / 1B	1860	1972	HJR	
Hampstead Heath Tunnel	21 / 2B	1860	N/A	HJR	
HAMPTON	38 / 2B	1864	N/A	LSWR	
HAMPTON COURT	39 / 3A	1849	N/A	LSWR	"Moulsey" also spelt "Molesey" at times.
Hampton Court for Moulsey					Goods yard closed 1965
Hampton Court & East Moulsey					
Hampton Court					
Hampton Court Junction	39 / 4B	1849	N/A	LSWR	
HAMPTON WICK	39 / 3B	1863	N/A	LSWR	
HANGER LANE	19 / 3B	1947	N/A	LT (CEN)	
Hanger Lane Junction	20 / 4A	1903	N/A	MDR	Divergence of District Railway South Harrow Branch from line to Ealing Broadway
HANWELL	19 / 4A	1838	N/A	GWR	Served by District Railway Trains 1883-1885
Hanwell & Elthorne					
Hanwell					
Hanwell Junction	19 / 4A	1903	N/A	GWR	
HARLESDEN	20 / 3A	1912	N/A	LNWR	Served by Bakerloo Line Trains since 1917
HARLESDEN (FOR WEST WILLESDEN & STONEBRIDGE PARK)	20 / 3B	1875	1902	MID	Closed 1888-1893
Stonebridge Park for West Willesden & Harlesden					
Harrow Road for Stonebridge Park & Harlesden					
Harrow Road for Stonebridge & Harlesden					
Harrow Road					
Harrow Road for Stonebridge Park & Harlesden					
Harrow Road for Stonebridge Park & West Willesden					
HARLESDEN GOODS	20 / 3A	?	?	MID	
Harlesden Junction	20 / 3B	1868	N/A	MID & LNWR	
HAROLD WOOD	16 / 1A	1868	N/A	GER	
HARRINGAY	12 / 4B	1885	N/A	GNR	
Harringay West					
Harringay					
HARRINGAY GREEN LANES	12 / 4B	1880	N/A	T&HJ	
Harringay East					
Harringay Stadium					
Harringay Park					
Harringay Park, Green Lanes					
Green Lanes					
Harringay Junction	12 / 4B	1864	N/A	GNR	Junction with curve to Tottenham & Hampstead Junction Railway
Harringay Park Junction	12 / 4B	1864	N/A	T&HJ	Junction with curve to GNR Main Line
HARRINGTON ROAD	43 / 3A	2000	N/A	CTL	
HARROW LANE SIDINGS	48 / 4A	1866	1981	NLR & LBR	
Harrow North Junction	9 / 4A	1904	N/A	MET	
HARROW-ON-THE-HILL	9 / 4A	1880	N/A	MET	Country terminus of Metropolitan Railway 1880-1885. Renamed 1894. Served by GCR since 1899. Goods Yard closed 1967
Harrow					
HARROW-ON-THE-HILL GOODS	9 / 4A	1880	1967	MET	
HARROW & WEALDSTONE	9 / 3A	1837	N/A	L&B	Renamed 1897. Terminus for London Underground Bakerloo Line Trains since 1984. Goods Yard closed 1967
Harrow					
Harrow Weald					
HARVEY'S SIDING	34 / 2A	?	?	PRIV	
HATCH END	8 / 2B	1844	N/A	LNWR	Served by London Underground Bakeloo Line Trains 1917-1982. "Pinner & Hatch End" became "Hatch End (for Pinner)" 1920, suffix dropped 1956
Hatch End (For Pinner)					
Pinner & Hatch End					
Pinner					
HATCH END GOODS	8 / 3B	?	1966	LNWR	
HATTON CROSS	28 / 4A	1975	N/A	LT (PIC)	Terminus 1975-1977
HAVERSTOCK HILL	21 / 2B	1868	1916	MID	
Hawkswood Junctions	44 / 3B	1904	N/A	SECR	
HAYDON SQUARE GOODS	23 / 4A & 7 / 2A	1853	1962	LNWR	
Haydon Square Junction	23 / 4A & 7 / 3A	1853	1962	LNWR	
HAYDONS ROAD	41 / 2B	1868	N/A	LSWR & LBSCR	Closed 1917-1923
Haydens Lane					
HAYES	44 / 4A	1882	N/A	SER	Goods Yard closed 1965
HAYES & HARLINGTON	28 / 1A	1864	N/A	GWR	Served by District Railway Trains 1883-1885
Hayes					
HAYS DISTRIBUTION DEPOT (RIPPLE LANE)	25 / 3B	?	N/A	PRIV	
HEADSTONE LANE	9 / 3A	1913	N/A	LNWR	Served by London Underground Bakeloo Line Trains 1917-1982. Goods Yard closed 1966
Heathrow Airport Junction	28 / 1A	1998	N/A	RT (HEX)	
HEATHROW EXPRESS DEPOT	20 / 4B	1998	N/A	HEX	
HEATHROW TERMINALS 1, 2 & 3	27 / 3B	1977	N/A	LT (PIC)	Terminus 1977-1986. Heathrow Express platforms opened 1998
Heathrow Central					
HEATHROW TERMINAL 4	27 / 4B	1986	N/A	LUL (PIC)	Heathrow Express opened 1998. Closed 2005-2006 in connection with Terminal 5 Extension
HEATHROW TERMINAL 5	27 / 3A	2008	N/A	LUL (PIC) & NR (HEX)	Under construction, To open 2008
Heathrow Tunnel Junction	27 / 1B	1998	N/A	RT (HEX)	

NAME: (Previous Names Below)	PAGE / GRID:	YEAR OPENED:	YEAR CLOSED:	OPENED BY:	NOTES:
HENDON	10 / 4B	1868	N/A	MID	
HENDON CENTRAL	10 / 4B	1923	N/A	UERL (CCE&HR)	Terminus of extension from Golders Green 1923-1924
HERNE HILL	32 / 4B	1862	N/A	LCDR	
HERNE HILL GOODS	32 / 4B	1855	?	LCDR	
Herne Hill North Junction	32 / 4B	1862	N/A	LCDR	
Herne Hill South Junction	32 / 4B	1869	N/A	LCDR	
HERON QUAYS	33 / 1B	1987	N/A	DLR	Closed 2001-2002
HIGHAMS PARK	14 / 2A	1873	N/A	GER	Renamed from "Hale End" to "Highams Park (Hale End)" 1894. Goods Yard closed 1965
Highams Park & Hale End					
Highams Park (Hale End)					
Hale End					
HIGH BARNET (LT)	3 / 4A	1940	N/A	LT (NOR)	Original GNR branch re-opened by LT after electrification. Goods yard closed 1962
HIGH BARNET (GNR)	3 / 4A	1872	1939	GNR	Former GNR High Barnet Branch closed 1939 for transfer to LT
HIGH BARNET SIDINGS	3 / 4A	1941	N/A	LT (NOR)	Stabling Sidings for Northern Line
HIGHBURY GOODS & COAL	22 / 2B	?	1969	NLR	
HIGHBURY & ISLINGTON	22 / 2B	1850	N/A	NLR	Opened as "Islington", renamed "Highbury or Islington" 1864, "Highbury & Islington" 1872 GN&CR station opened 1904 (=Highbury), Victoria Line platforms opened 1968
Highbury (Great Northern & City Railway)					
Highbury or Islington (North London Railway)					
Islington (North London Railway)					
Highbury Vale Junction	22 / 2A	1904	N/A	GN&CR	
HIGHBURY VALE GOODS	22 / 2B & 15 / 3B	?	1971	GNR	
HIGHGATE	12 / 4A	1941	N/A	LT (NOR)	Line through station opened 1939, but station did not open until 1941
Highgate East Tunnel	12 / 4A	1867	1970	GNR	Remained open for Northern Line Stock transfer until 1970
HIGHGATE HIGH LEVEL	12 / 4A	1867	1954	GNR	Nominally opened by Edgware, Highgate & London Railway, but operated by GNR from opening Closed when Alexandra Palace to Finsbury park service withdrawn 1954. Had been intended for electrification and transfer to LT Northern Line, but works abandoned post-WW2
Highgate					
HIGHGATE ROAD HIGH LEVEL	22 / 1A & 11 / 3A	1868	1915	T&HJ	
Highgate Road for Parliament Hill					
Highgate Road					
Highgate Road Junction	22 / 1A & 11 / 3A	1888	1964	T&HJ	Junction between Tottenham & Hampstead Junction Railway and curve to Kentish Town
HIGHGATE ROAD LOW LEVEL	22 / 1A & 11 / 4A	1900	1918	MID	
Highgate West Tunnel	12 / 4A	1867	1970	GNR	Remained open for Northern Line Stock transfer until 1970
HIGHGATE WOOD DEPOT	11 / 4B	1962	N/A	LT (NOR)	On site of GNR Wellington Sidings. Remodelled 1970, closed 1984-1989
High Meadows Junction	23 / 2B & 53	1862	N/A	GER	
HIGH STREET KENSINGTON	31 / 1A & 50	1868	N/A	MET	Metropolitan District Railway platforms opened 1871. Renamed gradually by 1880
Kensington (High Street)					
HIGH STREET KENSINGTON GOODS & COAL	31 / 1A & 50	1878	1963	MID	
HILLINGDON (1st)	17 / 2B	1923	1992	MET	Served by District Line Trains 1923-1933, Piccadilly Line trains thereafter "Swakeleys" suffix after 1934, gradually dropped. Goods Yard closed 1964
Hillingdon (Swakeleys)					
Hillingdon					
HILLINGDON (2nd)	17 / 2B	1992	N/A	LUL (MET)	Relocated due to road scheme
HITHER GREEN	34 / 4A	1895	N/A	SER	
Hither Green Junction	34 / 4A	1866	N/A	SER	
HOGSMILL MILLS	45 / 2B	1890	1950	PRIV	Siding serving Mills on Hogsmill River
HOLBORN	22 / 4A	1906	N/A	GNP&BR	Central Line platforms opened and "Kingsway" suffix added 1933, suffix gradually dropped
Holborn (Kingsway)					
Holborn					
HOLBORN VIADUCT	22 / 4B & 55	1874	1990	LCDR	"High Level" 1912-1916
Holborn Viaduct (High Level)					
Holborn Viaduct					
HOLBORN VIADUCT (LOW LEVEL)	22 / 4B & 55	1874	1916	LCDR	Renamed 1912
Snow Hill					
HOLLAND PARK	31 / 1A	1900	N/A	CLR	
HOLLOWAY & CALEDONIAN ROAD	22 / 2A	1852	1915	GNR	
Holloway					
HOLLOWAY CATTLE	22 / 2A	?	?	GNR	
HOLLOWAY ROAD	22 / 2A	1906	N/A	GNP&BR	
HOMERTON (1st)	23 / 2A	1868	1944	NLR	Passenger service Dalston Junction to Poplar withdrawn 1944
HOMERTON (2nd)	23 / 2A	1985	N/A	BR	On site of former NLR Homerton Station
HONOR OAK	33 / 4A	1865	1954	LCDR	Closed 1917-1919 and 1944-1946. Nunhead to Crystal Palace (High Level) closed 1954
HONOR OAK PARK	33 / 4A	1886	N/A	LBSCR	East London Line projected to serve from 2010
HORNCHURCH (LTSR)	16 / 2A	1885	1962	LTSR	Served by District Railway trains 1902-1905. British Rail services withdrawn 1962 and "Fast" platforms abandoned
HORNCHURCH (MDR)	16 / 2A	1902	N/A	DIS	1902 date denotes first time District railway served original LTSR platforms at Hornchurch. District trains withdrawn East Ham to Upminster 1905, reinstated Barking

NAME: (Previous Names Below)	PAGE / GRID:	YEAR OPENED:	YEAR CLOSED:	OPENED BY:	NOTES:
					to Upminster 1932. Current District platforms constructed 1932 during LMS quadrupling of route. Ownership of "Slow" platforms transferred to LT 1970. Goods Yard closed 1982
HORNSEY	12 / 3A	1850	N/A	GNR	
HORNSEY EMU DEPOT	12 / 4B	1976	N/A	BR	On site of Ferme Park "Up" Yard, opened 1888
HORNSEY ROAD (FOR HORNSEY RISE)	22 / 1A	1872	1943	T&HJ	
Hornsey Road					
HORNSEY STEAM SHED	12 / 4B	?	1961	GNR	
HORNSEY UP CARRIAGE SIDINGS	12 / 3A	?	N/A	GNR	
Hotel Curve	54	1863	1977	GNR	Last regular service 1976
HOUNSLOW	29 / 4A	1850	N/A	LSWR	Goods Yard closed 1967
Hounslow & Whitton					
Hounslow					
HOUNSLOW CENTRAL	29 / 3A	1886	N/A	MDR	Opened by District Railway. Renamed Hounslow Central 1925. First served by Piccadilly Line 1933. Last served by District Line 1964
Heston-Hounslow					
HOUNSLOW EAST	29 / 3A	1909	N/A	MDR	Opened to replace Hounslow Town terminal station 1909. Renamed Hounslow East 1925. First served by Piccadilly Line 1933. Last served by District Line 1964
Hounslow Town					
Hounslow Junction	28 / 4B	1883	N/A	LSWR	
HOUNSLOW TOWN	29 / 3A	1883	1909	MDR	Original terminus of District Railway Hounslow Branch. Renamed "Town" 1884. Closed 1886 but re-opened 1905, closed for good 1909 and branch dismantled.
Hounslow					
HOUNSLOW WEST	28 / 3B	1884	N/A	MDR	Opened by District Railway. First served by Piccadilly Line 1933. Last served by District Line 1964. Terminus 1884-1975; station reconstructed on a lower level 1975 due to extension. Renamed Hounslow West 1925.
Hounslow Barracks					
HOXTON	23 / 3A	2010	N/A	LUL (ELL)	Projected to open 2010 as part of East London Line Extension Phase 1
HYDE PARK CORNER	31 / 1B	1906	N/A	GNP&BR	
ICKENHAM	17 / 2B	1905	N/A	MET	Served by District Line Trains 1910-1933, Piccadilly Line trains thereafter
ILFORD	24 / 1B	1839	N/A	ECR	
ILFORD DEPOT	25 / 1A	1949	N/A	BR	"New Shed" opened 1959 on site of West Curve to Newbury Park
ILFORD GOODS & COAL	25 / 1A	?	1968	GER	
Ilford Carriage Sidings Junction	25 / 1A	1903	1948	GER	Western Curve dismantled 1948 and Ilford Depot built on route
IMPERIAL WHARF	31 / 3B & 50	2006	N/A	NR	New Network Rail station, projected opening 2006
International Junction	32 / 1B	1994	N/A	RT	Divergence of lines into Waterloo International platforms
ISLAND GARDENS (1st)	33 / 2B	1987	1999	DLR	Closed and re-opened in tunnel due to Lewisham Extension
ISLAND GARDENS (2nd)	33 / 2B	1999	N/A	DLR	Replaced original station
ISLEWORTH	29 / 3A	1850	N/A	LSWR	Replaced Smallberry Green to East. "Spring Grove & Isleworth" 1855-1911
Spring Grove & Isleworth					
Isleworth					
IVER	27 / 1A	1924	N/A	GWR	
JUNCTION ROAD	22 / 1A & 11 / 3B	1872	1943	T&HJ	
Junction Road for Tufnell Park					
Junction Road Junction	22 / 1A & 11 / 3B	1888	N/A	T&HJ	Junction between Tottenham & Hampstead Junction and Midland Railways
KEMPTON PARK	38 / 2B	1878	N/A	LSWR	Race Days only
KENLEY	47 / 4B	1856	N/A	LBSCR	Renamed 1856
Coulsdon					
KENNINGTON	32 / 2B	1890	N/A	C&SLR	Closed 1923-1925
Kennington New Street					
Kennington					
KENSAL GREEN	20 / 3B	1916	N/A	LNWR	Served by Bakerloo Line Trains since 1917
KENSAL GREEN & HARLESDEN	20 / 3B	1861	1873	HJR	
Kensal Green Junction	20 / 3B	1860	N/A	HJR	
KENSAL RISE	20 / 3B	1873	N/A	LNWR	Renamed 1890. Closed 1995-1996
Kensal Green					
KENSINGTON	31 / 1A & 50	1844	1844	WLR	Original WLR Station, open for 6 months. Passenger service withdrawn from WLR 1844 to 1862
Kensington Junction	49	1864	1940	MET & GWR	Metropolitan Line services between Latimer Road and Addison Road withdrawn 1940
KENSINGTON (OLYMPIA)	31 / 1A & 50	1862	N/A	WLR	WLR re-opened to passengers from Willesden Junction to Addison Road 1862. First served by Metropolitan Railway 1864, rebuilt and
Addison Road					

NAME: (Previous Names Below)	PAGE / GRID:	YEAR OPENED:	YEAR CLOSED:	OPENED BY:	NOTES:
					renamed Addison Road 1868. District Railway services commenced 1872. All services withdrawn and station closed 1940. Station re-opened 1946 for shuttle service to Clapham Junction and exhibition traffic to Earl's Court station. Regular District Line service provided since 1986. Through Mainline service re-introduced 1994.
KENSINGTON OLYMPIA MOTORAIL TERMINAL	31 / 1A	1965	1982	BR	
KENSINGTON SIDINGS	31 / 3B	1863	N/A	LSWR	
KENT HOUSE	43 / 3A	1884	N/A	LCDR	
KENTISH TOWN	22 / 2A & 11 / 4B	1868	N/A	MID	CCE&HR station opened 1907
Kentish Town Junction	22 / 2A & 11 / 4A	1888	1964	MID	Junction between Midland main Line and curve to Highagte Road High Level
KENTISH TOWN WEST	22 / 2A	1867	N/A	HJR	"West" suffix added 1924. Closed 1971-1981
Kentish Town					(arson) and again 1995-1996 (engineering works)
KENTON	9 / 4B	1912	N/A	LNWR	Served by London Underground Bakeloo Line
Kenton (for Northwick Park)					Trains 1917-1982. Goods Yard opened
Kenton					1911, closed 1965
KEW	30 / 2A	1853	1862	N&SWJR	Closed when services diverted along 1862 Kew Curve to new Kew station
KEW BRIDGE	30 / 2A	1849	N/A	LSWR	
Kew					
KEW BRIDGE	30 / 2A	1862	1940	N&SWJR	Passenger services between South Acton and
Kew					Kew Bridge withdrawn 1940
Kew East Junction	30 / 2A	1862	N/A	N&SWJR	
KEW GARDENS	30 / 3A	1869	N/A	LSWR	First served District & Metropolitan Railways 1877. Last served Metropolitan Railway 1906. Sidings and Bay Platform in use until 1931
KEW GOODS (LSWR)	30 / 2A	1849	1964	LSWR	
KEW GOODS (MID)	30 / 2A	?	1977	MID	
KEW GOODS (SR)	30 / 2A	1929	1967	SR	
KIDBROOKE	34 / 3A	1895	N/A	SER	Goods Yard closed 1968
Kidbrooke Tunnel	34 / 3A	1895	N/A	SER	
KILBURN	21 / 2A	1879	N/A	MET	"& Brondesbury" until 1950. Served by Bakerloo
Kilburn & Brondesbury					Line 1939-1979, Jubilee thereafter Last served Metropolitan Line 1940
KILBURN HIGH ROAD	21 / 3A	1851	N/A	LNWR	Closed 1917, re-opened and renamed "Kilburn
Kilburn & Maida Vale					High Road" 1922
Kilburn					
KILBURN PARK	21 / 3A	1915	N/A	UERL (BAK)	
KING GEORGE V	34 / 1B	2005	N/A	DLR	Terminus of DLR extension 2005-2009
KING HENRY'S DRIVE	48 / 3B	2000	N/A	CTL	
KINGSBURY	10 / 4A	1932	N/A	MET	Opened by Metropolitan Railway. Transferred to Bakerloo Line 1939, Jubilee Line 1979
KINGS CROSS	22 / 3A & 54	1852	N/A	GNR	
KINGS CROSS GOODS	22 / 3A & 54	1852	1973	GNR	
KINGS CROSS FREIGHT TERMINAL	54	?	N/A	BR	
KINGS CROSS ST PANCRAS (MET)	22 / 3A & 54	1863	1941	MET	Original Metropolitan Railway station. "& St
Kings Cross & St Pancras					Pancras" after 1925, "&" dropped 1933
Kings Cross					Closed when new station opened to the West in 1941
KINGS CROSS ST PANCRAS (LT)	22 / 3A & 54	1901	N/A	C&SLR	GNP&BR (Piccadilly) Platforms opened 1906 as
Kings Cross for St Pancras					"King's Cross", "for St Pancras" added 1927
King's Cross					C&SLR (later Northern Line) Platforms opened 1907 as "King's Cross for St Pancras", closed 1922-1924, 1987-1989 and 1995-1996. Both lines renamed "King's Cross St Pancras" 1933. Relocated Metropolitan Line platforms opened 1941, Victoria Line platforms opened 1968
KINGS CROSS SUBURBAN PLATFORM 16	22 / 3A & 54	1866	1976	GNR	Northbound only. Service withdrawn when trains diverted along Great Northern & City Line
KINGS CROSS THAMESLINK	22 / 3A & 54	1868	N/A	MET	Anticipated to close 2007 when St Pancras
Kings Cross Midland City					Thameslink Station opened "Thameslink"
Kings Cross Midland					after 1988
Kings Cross					
KINGS CROSS YORK ROAD	22 / 3A & 54	1866	1976	GNR	Southbound only. Service withdrawn when trains diverted along Great Northern & City Line
KINGSLAND	23 / 2A & 18 / 3A	1850	1865	NLR	Re-opened 1983 as Dalston Kingsland
KINGSLAND GOODS	23 / 2A & 18 / 3B	?	?	NLR	
Kingsley Road Junction	29 / 3A	1905	1909	MDR	
KINGSTON	39 / 4B	1869	N/A	LSWR	Rebuilt and expanded 1935. Goods Yard closed
Kingston High Level					1966
KINGSTON LOW LEVEL	39 / 4B	1863	1935	LSWR	Original terminus 1863-1869. Closed when High
Kingston					Level Station rebuilt 1935
KING WILLIAM STREET	22 / 4B	1890	1900	C&SLR	Original terminus of C&SLR from Stockwell. Abandoned when line extended to Moorgate
KNIGHTSBRIDGE	31 / 1B	1906	N/A	GNP&BR	
KNIGHTS HILL GOODS	32 / 4B	1892	1968	LNWR	

NAME: (Previous Names Below)	PAGE / GRID:	YEAR OPENED:	YEAR CLOSED:	OPENED BY:	NOTES:
LADBROKE GROVE	21 / 4A	1864	N/A	MET & GWR	Opened as "Notting Hill", "& Ladbroke Road"
Ladbroke Grove (North Kensington)					suffix added 1880, renamed "Ladbroke
Notting Hill & Ladbroke Grove					Grove (North Kensington)" 1919, suffix
Notting Hill					dropped 1938
LADYWELL	33 / 4B	1857	N/A	SER	Built by the Mid Kent Railway, but operated by
Lady Well					SER from opening
Ladywell Junction	33 / 4B	1866	N/A	SER	
LAMBETH NORTH	32 / 1B	1906	N/A	BS&WR	Opened as Kennington Road, renamed
Lambeth (North)					Westminster Bridge Road 1906, renamed
Westminster Bridge Road					Lambeth (North) 1917, renamed Lambeth
Kennington Road					North c.1928, closed 1996-1997,
Lampton Junction	29 / 3A	1884	1909	MDR	
LANCASTER GATE	21 / 4B	1900	N/A	CLR	
Latchmere Junctions Nos. 1, 2 & 3	31 / 3B	1863	N/A	WLER	
LATIMER ROAD	21 / 4A & 49	1868	N/A	MET & GWR	
LEA BRIDGE	23 / 1B	1840	1985	ECR	Closed when Tottenham Hale to North
Lea Bridge Road					Woolwich service withdrawn
Lea Bridge Junction	23 / 1B	1870	1967	GER	Southern Junction of Hall Farm Curve
Lea Junction	23 / 2B & 53	1862	N/A	GER	
LEBANON ROAD	47 / 1B	2000	N/A	CTL	
LEE	34 / 4A	1866	N/A	SER	Goods Yard closed 1968
Lee Loop Junction	34 / 4A	1900	N/A	SER	
Lee Spur Junction	34 / 4A	1900	N/A	SER	
LEICESTER SQUARE	22 / 4A	1906	N/A	GNP&BR	CCE&HR platforms opened 1907
Leigham Court Tunnel	42 / 1A	1856	N/A	LBSCR	Opened by West End of London & Crystal
					Palace Railway, but operated by LBSCR
					from outset
Leigham Junction	42 / 1B	1868	N/A	LBSCR	
Leigham Tunnel	42 / 1A	1868	N/A	LBSCR	
LEMAN STREET	23 / 4A & 7 / 3B	1877	1941	LTSR	Closed 1916-1919
LEWISHAM	33 / 3B	1849	N/A	SER	Renamed 1929
Lewisham Junction					
Lewisham					
LEWISHAM	33 / 3B	1999	N/A	DLR	
Lewisham Crossover	33 / 3B	1929	N/A	SR	
LEWISHAM ROAD	33 / 3B	1871	1917	LCDR	Passenger service withdrawn Nunhead to
					Greenwich Park 1917
Lewisham Vale Junction	33 / 3B	1976	N/A	BR	
LEY STREET YARD SIDINGS	25 / 1A	?	N/A	GER	
LEYTON (ECR)	23 / 1B	1856	1970	ECR	"Low" prefix dropped 1867. Majority of
Low Leyton					Passenger services transferred to LT in
					1947. First Trains in the morning remained
					British Rail services until 1970
LEYTON (LT)	23 / 1B	1947	N/A	LT (CEN)	First served by LT Central Line trains in 1947.
					Goods Yard closed 1968
LEYTON MIDLAND ROAD	13 / 4B	1894	N/A	T&FG	Renamed 1949
Leyton					
LEYTONSTONE (ECR)	24 / 1A	1856	1970	ECR	Majority of Passenger services transferred to LT
					in 1947. First Trains in the morning remained
					British Rail services until 1970
LEYTONSTONE (LT)	24 / 1A	1947	N/A	LT (CEN)	First served by LT Central Line trains in 1947.
					Goods Yard closed 1955
LEYTONSTONE HIGH ROAD	24 / 1A	1894	N/A	T&FG	Renamed 1949
Leytonstone					
Leytonstone Junction	14 / 4A	1947	N/A	LT (CEN)	Divergence of 1947 route to Newbury Park from
					Epping Line
LILLIE BRIDGE DEPOT	31 / 2A & 50	1872	N/A	MDR	Originally built by District Railway. Used by
					GNP&BR (Piccadilly Line) 1906-1932.
					Used for engineering purposes (now
					"Transplant") since 1932
LIMEHOUSE (1st)	23 / 4B	1840	1926	LBR	Passenger service to Blackwall and North
					Greenwich withdrawn 1926
LIMEHOUSE (2nd)	23 / 4B	1840	N/A	LBR	Opened as Stepney, renamed Stepney East in
Stepney East					1923. DLR platforms opened and Main Line
Stepney					station further renamed to Limehouse in
					1987
Limehouse Junction	23 / 4B	1880	1951	LBR	
Linford Street Junction	32 / 3A & 51	1994	N/A	RT	
LITTLE ILFORD DEPOT	24 / 2B	1905	1958	MDR	District Railway Depot. Closed when Upminster
					Depot opened, replaced by East Ham BR
					Depot
LIVERPOOL STREET	22 / 4B	1874	N/A	GER	First served by Metropolitan Railway February
Bishopsgate (Metropolitan Railway only)					1875 (direct into GER station). Separate
					Metropolitan Railway platforms opened as
					"Bishopsgate" July 1875, CLR platforms
					opened 1912
LLOYD PARK	48 / 2A	2000	N/A	CTL	
LONDON BRIDGE	32 / 1B	1836	N/A	LGR	C&SLR Platforms opened 1900 (closed
					1923-1924), Jubilee Line 1999
LONDON CITY AIRPORT	34 / 1B	2005	N/A	DLR	
LONDON FIELDS	23 / 2A	1872	N/A	GER	Closed during World War I, re-opening 1919
LONDON INTERNATIONAL FREIGHT TERMINAL	53	?	?	BR	
LONDON ROAD DEPOT	32 / 1B	1906	N/A	BS&WR	Bakerloo Line Depot
LONG GROVE HOSPITAL	45 / 2A	1905	1950	PRIV	Horton Estate Light Railway opened to supply
					building materials, later fuel, to hospitals

NAME: (Previous Names Below)	PAGE / GRID:	YEAR OPENED:	YEAR CLOSED:	OPENED BY:	NOTES:
Longhedge Junctions	32 / 3A & 51	1862	N/A	LCDR	
LONGHEDGE LOCO WORKS	51	1862	?	LCDR	
LORD'S	21 / 3B	1868	1939	MET	Opened as "St John's Wood Road", "Road"
St John's Wood Road					suffix dropped 1925, renamed "Lord's" June
					1939, closed November 1939
LORDSHIP LANE	43 / 1A	1865	1954	LCDR	Closed 1917-1919 and 1944-1946. Nunhead to
					Crystal Palace (High Level) closed 1954
LOUGHBOROUGH JUNCTION (1st)	32 / 3B	1864	1916	LCDR	Renamed "Loughborough Road" July 1872,
Loughborough Road					then "Junction" December 1872
Brixton Junction					
LOUGHBOROUGH JUNCTION (2nd)	32 / 3B	1872	N/A	LCDR	Opened July 1872, renamed December 1872.
Loughborough Road					Platforms on curve to Denmark Hill closed
					1925
LOUGHTON (ECR)	6 / 3B	1856	1865	ECR	Original terminus of branch from Stratford.
					Closed when line extended to Ongar.
LOUGHTON (GER)	6 / 4B	1865	1970	GER	Relocated East 1940. Majority of Passenger
					services transferred to LT in 1948
					First Trains in the morning remained British
					Rail services until 1970
LOUGHTON (LT)	6 / 4B	1948	N/A	LT (CEN)	First served by Central Line Trains 1948
LOUGHTON GOODS	6 / 3B	1858	1966	GER	On site of original ECR Loughton Station
Loughton Junction	23 / 1B	1856	1972	ECR	Divergence of ECR Loughton Branch. Last
					passenger train 1970, lifted 1972
LOUGHTON SIDINGS	6 / 4B	1948	N/A	LT (CEN)	Stabling Sidings for Central Line
LOWER EDMONTON (LOW LEVEL)	13 / 1A	1872	1939	GER	Station on original GER Enfield Branch from
					Angel Road. Closed to passengers 1939 .
					Angel Road to Lower Edmonton Junction
					remained open for freight, closing in 1964
					Goods Yard in use 1900-1965
Lower Edmonton Junction	13 / 1A	1872	1964	GER	Angel Road to Lower Edmonton Junction
					closed in 1964
LOWER SYDENHAM (1st)	43 / 2B	1857	1906	SER	Built by the Mid Kent Railway, but operated by
					SER from opening. Resited South 1906
LOWER SYDENHAM (2nd)	43 / 2B	1906	N/A	SECR	Goods Yard closed 1966
LOWER SYDENHAM GASWORKS	43 / 1A	1878	1971	PRIV	
LUDGATE HILL	22 / 4B & 55	1864	1929	LCDR	Terminus 1864-1866
Ludgate Hill Junction	55	1874	1969	LCDR	
Ludgate Junction	31 / 3B	1862	N/A	LCDR & LSWR	
MAIDA VALE	21 / 3B	1915	N/A	UERL (BAK)	
MAIDEN LANE	22 / 2A & 54	1887	1917	NLR	
Maiden Lane Curve	54	1863	1865	GNR	Possibly never used
MAIDEN LANE GOODS	54	1866	1965	NLR	
MALDEN MANOR	40 / 4B	1938	N/A	SR	
MANOR HOUSE	12 / 4B	1932	N/A	UERL (PIC)	
MANOR PARK	24 / 2B	1873	N/A	GER	
Manor Park & Little Ilford					
MANOR ROAD GOODS	22 / 1B	1872	1965	GER	
MANOR WAY	25 / 4A	1880	1940	PLA	Passenger services withdrawn from Gallions
Royal Albert Dock Manor Way					Branch 1940
Royal Albert Dock Manor Road					
MANSION HOUSE	22 / 4B	1871	N/A	MDR	Terminus of District Railway 1871-1884.
					Closed 1989-1991
MARBLE ARCH	21 / 4B	1900	N/A	CLR	
MARCON STONE TERMINAL (ANGERSTEIN WHARF)	34 / 1A	?	N/A	PRIV	
MARCON STONE TERMINAL (PADDINGTON)	21 / 4A	?	N/A	PRIV	
MARCON STONE TERMINAL (PARK ROYAL)	20 / 3A	?	N/A	PRIV	
MARLBOROUGH ROAD	21 / 3B	1868	1939	MET	
MARYLAND	24 / 2A	1873	N/A	GER	
Maryland Point					
MARYLEBONE	21 / 4B	1899	N/A	GCR	Terminus of Great Central Railway. Served by
Great Central					Bakerloo Line since 1907
MARYLEBONE CARRIAGE SIDINGS	21 / 3B	1899	N/A	GCR	
MARYLEBONE GOODS & COAL	21 / 3B	1898	1967	GCR	
MAYER-PARRY SCRAP (WILLESDEN)	20 / 3B	?	N/A	PRIV	Car-crushing plant. Opened in 1960's on site of
					former carriage sidings
MAZE HILL	34 / 2A	1873	N/A	SER	
Maze Hill (for National Maritime Museum)					
Maze Hill (East Greenwich) for National Maritime Museum					
Maze Hill & East Greenwich					
Maze Hill & Greenwich Park					
Maze Hill & East Greenwich					
Greenwich (Maze Hill)					
Maze Hill Tunnel	34 / 2A	1878	N/A	SER	
MCVITIE & PRICE'S SIDING	20 / 3A	1902	?	PRIV	Later United Biscuits
MERTON ABBEY	41 / 3B	1868	1929 *(1975)*	LSWR & LBSCR	Closed 1917-1923. Merton Park to Tooting
					Junction closed to passengers 1929
					Junction at Tooting severed 1934 with freight
					traffic accessing from the Merton Park end
					Freight ceased 1968 (Tooting) and 1975
					(Merton Abbey)
MERTON PARK (LBSCR & LSWR)	41 / 3A	1868	1997	LSWR & LBSCR	Platform for Wimbledon to Croydon trains not
Lower Merton					opened until 1870. Renamed 1887.

NAME: (Previous Names Below)	PAGE / GRID:	YEAR OPENED:	YEAR CLOSED:	OPENED BY:	NOTES:
					Wimbledon to West Croydon closed 1997 prior to conversion to Tramlink
MERTON PARK (CTL)	41 / 3A	2000	N/A	CTL	On site of former Merton Park Station
Metropolitan Junctions	32 / 1B & 55	1866	N/A	SER	
METROPOLITAN WATER BOARD RAILWAY (HAMPTON)	38 / 2B & 3B	1915	1947	PRIV	A self-contained Narrow Gauge (2 foot) Railway supplying Pumping Stations with Coal
MG GAS PRODUCTS (WILLESDEN)	20 / 3B	?	N/A	PRIV	
MIDDLESEX OIL & CHEMICAL WORKS	17 / 4A	1966	1979	PRIV	Last section of GWR Uxbridge (Vine Street) Branch to close
MILDMAY PARK	22 / 2B	1880	1934	NLR	
MILEAGE YARD (GOODS & COAL)	21 / 4A	?	?	GWR	
MILE END (ECR)	23 / 3A	1843	1872	ECR	Replaced by Bethnal Green Junction to West
MILE END (MDR)	23 / 4B	1902	N/A	MDR & LTSR	Served by Metropolitan Line since 1936. Central Line platforms opened 1946
MILE END COAL	23 / 3A	?	?	GER	
MILE END GOODS	23 / 3A	?	?	GER	
MILITARY SIDING (FELTHAM)	38 / 1A	?	?	PRIV	
MILL HILL BROADWAY Mill Hill	10 / 2A	1868	N/A	MID	Renamed 1950
MILL HILL EAST (GNR) Mill Hill East for Mill Hill Barracks	11 / 2A	1867	1939	GNR	Nominally opened by Edgware, Highgate & London Railway, but operated by GNR from opening. Closed in 1939 to enable doubling and electrification of Finchley Central to Edgware prior to transfer to LT Northern Line. Doubling abandoned and Mill Hill East became terminus
MILL HILL EAST (LT)	11 / 2A	1941	N/A	LT (NOR)	On site of former GNR station. Goods Yard closed 1962
MILL HILL (THE HALE) The Hale Halt	10 / 2A	1906	1939	GNR	Originally opened as "The Hale Halt", renamed "Mill Hill (The Hale)" 1928 Closed in 1939 to enable doubling and electrification of Finchley Central to Edgware prior to transfer to LT Northern Line. Works abandoned and station did not re-open. Goods yard closed 1964
MILLWALL DOCKS	33 / 1B	1871	1926	LBR	Terminus 1871-1872. Passenger service to Blackwall and North Greenwich withdrawn 1926
MILLWALL GOODS	33 / 2B	1872	1925	LBR	
MILLWALL JUNCTION	23 / 4B & 48 / 4A	1871	1926	LBR	Rebuilt & resited 1888. Passenger service to Blackwall and North Greenwich withdrawn 1926
MINORIES	23 / 4A & 7 / 3A	1840	1853	LBR	
Minories Junction	23 / 4A & 7 / 2A	1884	N/A	MDR	
MITCHAM (WCR)	41 / 4B	1855	1997	WCR	Wimbledon to West Croydon closed 1997 prior to conversion to Tramlink
MITCHAM (CTL)	41 / 4B	2000	N/A	CTL	On site of former Mitcham Station
MITCHAM JUNCTION	41 / 4B	1868	N/A	LBSCR	Croydon Tramlink platforms opened 2000
MITRE BRIDGE GOODS	20 / 4B	?	?	LNWR	
Mitre Bridge Junction	20 / 4B	1860	N/A	HJR	
MONUMENT Eastcheap	22 / 4B	1884	N/A	MDR & MET	Opened as "Eastcheap" October 1884, renamed "The Monument" November 1884, "The" prefix gradually dropped
MOORGATE Moorgate Street	22 / 4B	1865	N/A	MET	City Widened Lines platforms opened 1868, C&SLR platforms opened 1900, GN&C (later Northern Line, then British Rail) platforms opened 1904. Renamed 1924
MOOR PARK Moor Park & Sandy Lodge Sandy Lodge	8 / 2A	1910	N/A	MET	Opened as "Sandy Lodge", "Moor Park" prefix after 1923, "Sandy Lodge" suffix dropped 1950. Goods Yard closed 1938
MORDEN	41 / 3A	1926	N/A	UERL (NOR)	
MORDEN DEPOT	41 / 3A	1926	N/A	UERL (NOR)	
MORDEN ROAD (WCR) Morden Road Halt Morden Halt Morden	41 / 3A	1857	1997	WCR	"Road" suffix added 1951 Wimbledon to West Croydon closed 1997 prior to conversion to Tramlink
MORDEN ROAD (CTL)	41 / 3A	2000	N/A	CTL	On site of former Morden Road Station
MORDEN SOUTH	41 / 4A	1930	N/A	SR	
MORNINGTON CRESCENT	22 / 3A	1907	N/A	CCE&HR	Closed 1992-1998 for lift replacement works
Mortimer Street Junction	22 / 1A & 11 / 4A	1868	1981	MID	Junction of curve to Kentish Town, abandoned 1981 after diversion of Barking Trains
MORTLAKE Mortlake & East Sheen Mortlake	30 / 3A	1846	N/A	LSWR	Renamed 1948
Mortlake Junction	30 / 3B	1862	1881	LSWR	Barnes Curve disused since 1869 but not dismantled until 1881
MOTSPUR PARK	40 / 4B	1925	N/A	SR	
Motspur Park Junction	40 / 4B	1938	N/A	SR	
MOTTINGHAM Eltham & Mottingham Eltham for Mottingham Eltham & Mottingham Eltham	44 / 1B	1866	N/A	SER	Renamed "Mottingham" 1927. Goods Yard used by United Dairies after 1948, closed 1968
Mount Street Tunnel	34 / 1B	1849	N/A	SER	

NAME: (Previous Names Below)	PAGE / GRID:	YEAR OPENED:	YEAR CLOSED:	OPENED BY:	NOTES:
MUDCHUTE (1st)	33 / 2B	1987	1999	DLR	Closed and re-opened at lower level due to Lewisham Extension
MUDCHUTE (2nd)	33 / 2B	1999	N/A	DLR	Replaced original station
MUSWELL HILL Alexandra Park (Muswell Hill)	12 / 3A	1873	1954 *(1956)*	GNR	Nominally opened by Edgware, Highgate & London Railway, but operated by GNR from opening. Closed to passengers 1873-1875 and again 1951-1952 along with entire branch, finally closed when Alexandra Palace to Finsbury Park service withdrawn 1954. Had been intended for electrification and transfer to LT Northern Line, but works abandoned post-WW2. Remained open for freight traffic until 1956
Navarino Road Junction	23 / 2A	1986	N/A	BR	Curve opened due to closure of Broad Street. Passenger service withdrawn 1992
NEASDEN Neasden & Kingsbury Kingsbury & Neasden	20 / 2B	1880	N/A	MET	Opened as "Kingsbury & Neasden", renamed "Neasden & Kingsbury" 1910, suffix dropped 1932. Goods yard opened 1894, closed 1958. Served by Bakerloo Line 1939-1979, Jubilee thereafter. Last served Metropolitan Line 1940.
NEASDEN DEPOT	20 / 1B	1880	N/A	MET	Originally Metropolitan Railway Works & Power Station. Substantially rebuilt in 1930s. Stabled Bakerloo Line Trains 1939-1979, Jubilee Line Trains 1979-present
NEASDEN FREIGHT TERMINAL	20 / 2A	?	N/A	PRIV	Tibbett & Britten
Neasden Junction	20 / 2B	1906	N/A	GCR	
NEASDEN POWER STATION	20 / 1A	1905	1968	MET	Metropolitan Railway Power Station
Neasden South Junction	20 / 2B	1906	N/A	GCR	
NEASDEN SOUTH SIDINGS	20 / 2A	?	N/A	GCR	
NECROPOLIS	32 / 1B	1854	1941	LSWR	Station for funeral traffic to Brookwood Cemetary. Resited south 1902
NEW ADDINGTON	48 / 3B	2000	N/A	CTL	
NEW BARNET Barnet	3 / 4B	1850	N/A	GNR	
NEW BECKENHAM (1st)	43 / 2B	1864	1866	SER	Built by the Mid Kent Railway, but operated by SER from opening
NEW BECKENHAM (2nd)	43 / 2B	1866	N/A	SER	
New Beckenham Junction	43 / 2B	1864	N/A	SER	
NEWBURY PARK (GER)	15 / 4A	1903	1947	GER	Fairlop Loop closed 1947 to allow electrification and transfer to LT Central Line. Freight traffic remained until 1965
NEWBURY PARK (LT)	15 / 4A	1948	N/A	LT (CEN)	First served by LT Central Line Trains 1947 via branch from Leytonstone. Goods yard closed 1965
Newbury Park Junction	25 / 1A	1903	1948	GER	Western Curve dismantled 1948 and Ilford Depot built on route
NEWBURY PARK SIDINGS	15 / 4A	?	?	GER	Electrified 1947 for Central Line use, but lightly used after Hainault Depot's opening
NEW CROSS (SER)	33 / 2B & 52	1850	N/A	SER	First served by Metropolitan Railway 1884 (no service 1906-1913), became "East London Line" during 1980's, no service 1995-1998
NEW CROSS (ELR)	33 / 2B & 52	1869	1886	ELR	Original East London Railway terminus. Closed 1876-1884
NEW CROSS DEPOT	52	?	N/A	ELR	East London Line stabling sidings
NEW CROSS GATE New Cross	33 / 2A & 52	1839	N/A	LCR	First served District and Metropolitan Railways 1884, last served District 1905. No service Metropolitan Railway 1906-1913. "Gate" suffix added 1923. East London Line closed 1995-1998
NEW CROSS GOODS & COAL	52	1904	1967	GER	On site of original ELR terminus
NEW CROSS LOCO WORKSHOPS	52	1844	1947	LBSCR	
New Guildford Line Junction	39 / 4B	1885	N/A	LSWR	
NEWINGTON ROAD & BALLS POND	22 / 2B	1858	1870	NLR	
New Kew Junction	30 / 2A	1862	N/A	N&SWJR	
NEW MALDEN Malden Malden for Coombe Coombe & Malden New Malden & Coombe Malden	40 / 3B	1846	N/A	LSWR	Renamed "Malden for Coombe" 1955, then "New Malden" from 1957
NEW MALDEN GOODS	40 / 3A	1869	1964	LSWR	
New Malden Junction	40 / 3B	1869	N/A	LSWR	
NEW SOUTHGATE New Southgate & Friern Barnet New Southgate for Colney Hatch New Southgate & Colney Hatch Southgate & Colney Hatch Colney Hatch & Southgate	12 / 2A	1850	N/A	GNR	Suffix dropped 1871
NEW WANDSWORTH	31 / 4B	1858	1867	LBSCR	
NEW WANDSWORTH GOODS & COAL	31 / 4B	1858	?	LBSCR	
NINE ELMS	32 / 2A	1838	1848 *(1968)*	LSWR	LSWR London terminus until Waterloo opened 1848. Used for Goods traffic until 1968

NAME: (Previous Names Below)	PAGE / GRID:	YEAR OPENED:	YEAR CLOSED:	OPENED BY:	NOTES:
Nine Elms Junction	32 / 2A	1994	N/A	RT	
NINE ELMS SOUTH GOODS	32 / 2A	?	1968	LSWR	
NOEL PARK & WOOD GREEN	12 / 3B	1878	1963	GER	Renamed "Green Lanes & Noel Park" 1884,
Green Lanes & Noel Park					renamed "Noel Park & Wood Green" 1902
Green Lanes					Palace Gates Branch closed to passengers
					1963, freight remaining until 1965.
					Goods Yard in use 1883-1964
NORBITON	40 / 3A	1869	N/A	LSWR	Goods yard closed 1965
Nortbiton for Kingtson Hill					
NORBURY	42 / 3A	1878	N/A	LBSCR	
NORTH ACTON (CLR)	20 / 4A	1923	N/A	CLR	North Acton to Ealing Broadway opened by
					Great Western Railway 1920
NORTH ACTON (GWR)	20 / 4A	1904	1913	GWR	
North Acton Junction (1)	20 / 4A	1947	N/A	LT (CEN)	Junction between Central Line and extension to
					Greenford (later West Ruislip)
North Acton Junction (2)	20 / 4A	1917	1964	GWR	Junction between GWR Birmingham Main Line
					and route ex-Viaduct Junction
NORTH DULWICH	32 / 4B	1868	N/A	LBSCR	
NORTH EALING	20 / 4A	1903	N/A	MDR	First served Piccadilly Line 1932, last served
					District Line 1933
NORTH END (or BULL & BUSH)	21 / 1B	N/A	N/A	CCE&HR	Platforms built but station buildings and platform
					access never completed
NORTHFIELDS	29 / 1B	1932	N/A	UERL (DIS)	Replaced Northfields & Little Ealing due to
					construction of Northfields Depot
					Goods Yard closed 1932. First served by
					Piccadilly Line 1933. Last served by District
					Line 1964
NORTHFIELDS DEPOT	29 / 1B	1932	N/A	UERL (DIS & PIC)	Ceased to be regularly used by District Line
					Trains after 1964.
NORTHFIELDS & LITTLE EALING	29 / 1B	1908	1932	MDR	Renamed 1911, replaced by Northfields Station
Northfield (Ealing)					1932
NORTH GREENWICH & CUBITT TOWN	33 / 2B	1872	1926	LBR	Passenger service to Blackwall and North
North Greenwich					Greenwich withdrawn 1926
NORTH GREENWICH	34 / 1A	1999	N/A	LUL (JUB)	
NORTH HARROW	9 / 4A	1915	N/A	MET	
North Junction (Mitcham)	41 / 4B	1868	1997	LBSCR & WCR	Junction eliminated when Wimbldeon to
					Croydon line closed 1997
North Kent East Junction	33 / 2B & 52	1849	N/A	SER	
North Kent West Junction	52	1844	1983	LGR & LCR	
NORTH MIDDLESEX GASWORKS	10 / 2A	1886	1956	PRIV	
NORTHOLT (GWR)	18 / 2B	1907	1948	GWR	
Northolt (for West End) Halt					
Northolt Halt					
NORTHOLT (LT)	18 / 2B	1948	N/A	LT (CEN)	
Northolt Junction	18 / 2B	1906	N/A	GCR & GWR	
NORTHOLT PARK	19 / 2A	1906	N/A	GCR	Opened as "South Harrow & Roxeth", renamed
Northolt Park for Northolt Village					"Northolt Park for Northolt Village" 1929
South Harrow & Roxeth					"for Northolt Village" suffix dropped 1955
NORTH POLE DEPOT	20 / 4B	1994	2007 (?)	ES	Eurostar Depot. Projected to close when
					Temple Mills Depot opens, possible Crossrail
					Depot
North Pole Junction	20 / 4B	1844	N/A	WLR	Formerly provided connection to GWR Main
					Line, now only North Pole Depot
NORTHUMBERLAND PARK	13 / 3A	1840	N/A	ECR	
Marsh Lane					
NORTHUMBERLAND PARK DEPOT	13 / 3A	1968	N/A	LT (VIC)	Sole Depot for Victoria Line
NORTH SHED (QUEENS PARK)	21 / 3A	1915	N/A	UERL (BAK)	Stabling Shed for Bakerloo Line
NORTH SHEEN	30 / 3A	1930	N/A	SR	
NORTH WEALD	6 / 2A	1865	1994	GER	Epping to Ongar transferred to LT 1949,
					Electrified 1956, Closed 1994. Goods yard
					closed 1964
NORTH WEMBLEY	19 / 2B	1912	N/A	LNWR	Served by Bakerloo Line Trains 1917-1982,
					1984-Present
NORTHWICK PARK	9 / 4B	1923	N/A	MET	Renamed 1937
Northwick Park & Kenton					
NORTHWOOD	8 / 2A	1887	N/A	MET	Goods Yard closed 1966
NORTHWOOD HILLS	8 / 3A	1933	N/A	MET	
NORTH WOOLWICH	34 / 1B	1847	N/A	ECR	Goods Yard closed 1970
Norwood Fork Junction	43 / 4A	1862	N/A	LBSCR	
NORWOOD (JOLLY SAILOR)	43 / 3A	1839	1859	LCR	Resited South 1859 (Norwood Junction)
NORWOOD JUNCTION	43 / 3A	1859	N/A	LBSCR	Renamed 1955. East London Line projected to
Norwood Junction & South Norwood for Woodside					serve from 2010
Norwood Junction					
NOTTING HILL GATE	31 / 1A	1868	N/A	MET	Central London Railway platforms opened
					1900. Served by District Line since 1926
					Interchange facilites between Central and
					Circle / District Lines not provided until 1959
NUNHEAD (1st)	33 / 3A	1871	1925	LCDR	Relocated West 1925
NUNHEAD (2nd)	33 / 3A	1925	N/A	SR	Replaced original station to East
Nunhead Junction	33 / 3A	1892	N/A	LCDR	Crystal Palace (High Level) branch eliminated
					1954
OAKLEIGH PARK	3 / 4B	1873	N/A	GNR	

NAME: (Previous Names Below)	PAGE / GRID:	YEAR OPENED:	YEAR CLOSED:	OPENED BY:	NOTES:

OAKWOOD
   Enfield West (Oakwood)
   Enfield West
	4 / 4A	1933	N/A	LT (PIC)	Opened as "Enfield West", "Oakwood" suffix
					added 1934, renamed "Oakwood" 1946

OCKENDON	16 / 2B	1892	N/A	LTSR	Goods Yard closed 1968
OLD FORD	23 / 3B	1867	1944	NLR	Passenger service Dalston Junction to Poplar withdrawn 1944
OLD FORD GOODS	23 / 3B	1868	1967	NLR	
OLD KENT ROAD & HATCHAM Old Kent Road	33 / 2A & 52	1866	1917	LBSCR	Renamed 1870
Old Kent Road Junction	52	1871	1964	LBSCR	Projected to re-open as part of East London Line Extension Phase 2
Old Kew Junction	30 / 2A	1853	N/A	N&SWJR	
OLD OAK COMMON LOCO SHED	30 / 4B	1906	1964	GWR	Steam Depot closed 1965
OLD OAK COMMON SIDINGS	20 / 4B	?	N/A	GWR	
Old Oak Common West Junction	20 / 4B	1903	N/A	GWR	
OLD OAK LANE HALT	20 / 4B	1906	1947	GWR	
OLD OAK SIDINGS	20 / 3B	?	N/A	N&SWJR	
OLD STREET	22/ 3B	1901	N/A	C&SLR	GN&C (later Northern Line, later British Rail) platforms opened 1904
ONGAR	6 / 2B	1865	1994	GER	Epping to Ongar transferred to LT 1949, Electrified 1956, Closed 1994 Goods yard closed 1966
OSTERLEY	29 / 2A	1934	N/A	LT (DIS & PIC)	Replaced Osterley & Spring Grove Station. Last served by District Line 1964.
OSTERLEY & SPRING GROVE	29 / 2A	1883	1934	MDR	Served by Piccadilly Line after 1933. Replaced by Osterley Station.

OVAL
   The Oval
   Kennington Oval
	32 / 2B	1890	N/A	C&SLR	Renamed c.1894. Closed 1923-1924

OXFORD CIRCUS	22 / 4A	1900	N/A	CLR	BS&WR platforms opened 1906, Victoria Line platforms opened 1969
PADDINGTON (1st)	21 / 4B	1838	1854	GWR	Original terminus 1838-1854. Became Paddington Goods Station after 1854
PADDINGTON (2nd) Bishops Road (Metropolitan Railway only)	21 / 4B	1854	N/A	GWR	Metropolitan Railway Platforms opened 1863 (=Bishops Road), renamed "Paddington" 1933
PADDINGTON (MET) Paddington (Praed Street)	21 / 4B	1868	N/A	MET	Platforms on District / Circle Lines. Bakerloo Line platforms added 1913. Renamed 1948
PADDINGTON GOODS	21 / 4B	1854	1975	GWR	On site of original Paddington Station
PALACE GATES	12 / 3A	1878	1963	GER	Palace Gates Branch closed to passengers 1963, freight remaining until 1965
PALACE GATES COAL CONCENTRATION DEPOT	12 / 3A	1954	1984	PRIV	Charringtons Ltd. On site of former Goods Yard at Palace Gates
PALACE OF ENGINEERING	20 / 2A	1924	1925	PRIV	Goods station remained open until 1965

PALMERS GREEN
   Palmers Green & Southgate
   Palmer's Green
	12 / 2A	1871	N/A	GNR	Suffix dropped 1971. Goods Yard closed 1962

Park Junction	11 / 4B	1873	1957	GNR	Junction between GNR Alexandra Palace Branch and line to Edgware. All traffic ceased on Alexandra Palace Branch 1957 and junction eliminated.
PARK ROYAL (GWR)	20 / 4A	1903	1937	GWR	

PARK ROYAL (MDR)
   Park Royal (Hanger Hill)
   Park Royal
	20 / 4A	1931	N/A	LT (DIS)	Served by District Line 1931-1933, Piccadilly
					Line from 1932 onwards. "Hanger Hill" suffix
					in use 1936-1947

PARK ROYAL GOODS	20 / 3A	1903	1982	GWR	
PARK ROYAL & TWYFORD ABBEY Park Royal	20 / 3A	1903	1931	MDR	
PARK ROYAL WEST HALT	20 / 3A	1932	1948	GWR	
Parks Bridge Junction	33 / 3B	1866	N/A	SER	
PARSONS GREEN	31 / 3A	1880	N/A	MDR	
PARSONS GREEN SIDINGS	31 / 3A	1880	N/A	MDR	District Line stabling sidings
Paxton Tunnel	43 / 2A	1865	1954	LCDR	Closed 1917-1919. Nunhead to Crystal Palace (High Level) closed 1954 (Passengers and Goods)
PECKHAM COAL	33 / 3A	1891	1958	LNWR & MID	
PECKHAM RYE	33 / 3A	1865	N/A	LCDR	
PECKHAM RYE DEPOT	33 / 3A	1909	1961	LBSCR	Originally built to accommodate stock for LBSCR South London Line overhead electrification
Peckham Rye Junction	33 / 3A	1868	N/A	LBSCR	

PENGE EAST
   Penge Lane
   Penge
	43 / 2A	1863	N/A	LCDR	Renamed "Penge East" 1923

Penge Junction	43 / 3B	1863	N/A	LCDR	
Penge Tunnel	43 / 2A	1863	N/A	LCDR	

PENGE WEST
   Penge Bridges
   Penge
	43 / 2A	1863	N/A	LBSCR	Renamed "Penge West" 1879. East London
					Line projected to serve from 2010

PERIVALE HALT	19 / 3B	1904	1947	GWR	Closed 1915-1920
PERIVALE	19 / 3B	1947	N/A	LT (CEN)	
PERRY METALS (BRENTFORD)	29 / 2B	?	?	PRIV	Scrapyard

NAME: (Previous Names Below)	PAGE / GRID:	YEAR OPENED:	YEAR CLOSED:	OPENED BY:	NOTES:
Perry Street Fork Junction	36 / 3B	1895	N/A	SER	
PETTS WOOD	44 / 3B	1928	N/A	SR	
Petts Wood Junctions	44 / 3B	1902	N/A	SECR	
PHIPPS BRIDGE	41 / 3B	2000	N/A	CTL	
PICCADILLY CIRCUS	22 / 4A	1906	N/A	BS&WR	GNP&BR platforms opened December 1906
PIG HILL SIDINGS	31 / 3B	1863	N/A	WLER	
PIMLICO (LBSCR)	32 / 2A & 51	1858	1860	LBSCR	Opened by West End of London & Crystal Palace Railway, but operated by LBSCR from outset
PIMLICO (LT)	32 / 2A	1972	N/A	LT (VIC)	
PINNER	8 / 4B	1885	N/A	MET	Goods Yard closed 1967
PLAISTOW (LTSR)	24 / 3A	1858	1962	LTSR	Main Line services non-stopped since 1962, and Fast Platforms abandoned
PLAISTOW (MDR)	24 / 3A	1902	N/A	MDR	First served by District Railway 1902, line quadrupled 1908, District Trains using Slow Lines. Served by Metropolitan Line since 1936 ("Hammersmith & City Line" since 1990)
PLAISTOW DEPOT	24 / 3A	1911	1962	LTSR	
PLAISTOW LOCO WORKS	24 / 3A	1858	1925	LTSR	
PLAISTOW & WEST HAM GOODS	24 / 4A	1906	?	GER	
PLANT DEPOT (HITHER GREEN)	34 / 4A	?	N/A	PRIV	
PLASSER WORKS (WEST EALING)	19 / 4A	?	N/A	PRIV	
PLUMSTEAD	35 / 1A	1859	N/A	SER	
PLUMSTEAD YARD	35 / 1A	?	N/A	?	
Point Pleasant Junction	31 / 4A	1889	N/A	LSWR	"Up" line and flyover dismantled 1990, "Down" line now bi-directional
PONDERS END	5 / 4B	1840	N/A	GER	
PONTOON DOCK	34 / 1B	2005	N/A	DLR	
POPLAR (LBR)	23 / 4B & 48 / 4B	1840	1926	LBR	Passenger service to Blackwall withdrawn 1926
POPLAR (NLR - Did Not Open)	48 / 3A	N/A	N/A	NLR	Platforms constructed 1851 but station did not open
POPLAR (NLR) Poplar (East India Road)	23 / 4B & 48 / 3A	1866	1944	NLR	Passenger service Dalston Junction to Poplar withdrawn 1944
POPLAR (DLR)	23 / 4B	1987	N/A	DLR	
POPLAR DEPOT	23 / 4B & 48 / 3A	1987	N/A	DLR	DLR Depot
POPLAR DOCK GOODS	48 / 4B	1882	1951	MID	
POTTERS BAR	3 / 1A	1850	N/A	GNR	
Potters Bar Tunnel	3 / 2A	1850	N/A	GNR	
Pouparts Junction	31 / 3B	1867	N/A	LBSCR & LSWR	
POYLE ESTATE HALT	27 / 3A	1954	1965	BR	Passenger service West Drayton to Staines West withdrawn 1965
POYLE FOR STANWELL MOOR HALT Stanwell Moor & Poyle Halt	27 / 3A	1927	1965	GWR	Renamed 1927. Passenger service West Drayton to Staines West withdrawn 1965
PRE-ASSEMBLY DEPOT (HITHER GREEN)	34 / 4A	?	N/A	PRIV	Balfour Beatty
PRESTON ROAD (FOR UXENDON)	19 / 1B	1908	1931 / 1932	MET	Southbound / Up platform closed 1931, Northbound / Down closed 1932
PRESTON ROAD	19 / 1B	1931 / 1932	N/A	MET	Southbound / Up platform opened 1931, Northbound / Down opened 1932
PRIMROSE HILL Chalk Farm Hampstead Road	21 / 2B	1851	1992	LNWR	Closed 1917-1922. Chalk Farm renamed Primrose Hill 1950. Closed when Watford Junction to Liverpool Street service withdrawn 1992
Primrose Hill Tunnels	21 / 2B	1837	N/A	L&B	2nd tunnel added 1879, 3rd tunnel added 1922
PRINCE REGENT	24 / 4B	1994	N/A	DLR	
PUDDING MILL LANE	23 / 3A	1996	N/A	DLR	
PURFLEET	16 / 3A	1854	N/A	LTSR	
PURFLEET FOSTER YEOMAN STONE TERMINAL	16 / 3A	?	N/A	PRIV	Deep Water Wharf
PURFLEET RIFLE RANGE HALT	16 / 3A	1911	1948	LTSR	
PURFLEET THAMES TERMINAL	16 / 3A	?	N/A	PRIV	Deep Water Wharf
PURLEY Caterham Junction Godstone Road	47 / 4B	1841	N/A	L&BR	Opened as Godstone Road, closed 1847-1856. Re-opened 1856 as "Caterham Junction". Renamed "Purley" 1888
Purley Chipstead Line Junction	47 / 4B	1856	N/A	LBSCR	
Purley North Junction	47 / 3B	?	N/A	LBSCR	
PURLEY OAKS	47 / 3B	1899	N/A	LBSCR	
Purley South Junction	47 / 4B	1847	N/A	LBSCR	
PUTNEY	31 / 4A	1846	N/A	LSWR	
PUTNEY BRIDGE Putney Bridge & Hurlingham Putney Bridge & Fulham	31 / 3A	1880	N/A	MDR	Opened as Putney Bridge & Fulham 1880 as terminus of extension from West Brompton. Extension to Wimbledon opened 1889 (LSWR), "- & Fulham" replaced by "- & Hurlingham" 1902, "- & Hurlingham" suffix dropped 1932.
QUAKER OATS (SOUTHALL)	29 / 1A	?	?	PRIV	
QUEENSBURY	10 / 4A	1934	N/A	LT (MET)	Opened by LT Metropolitan Line. Transferred to Bakerloo Line 1939, Jubilee Line 1979
QUEENS PARK Queens Park (West Kilburn)	21 / 3A	1879	N/A	LNWR	Served by Bakerloo Line since 1915, terminus 1915-1917. Renamed 1954
QUEENS ROAD	23 / 1A	N/A	N/A	GER	Platforms built 1872 but station did not open
QUEENS ROAD GOODS	13 / 4B	1894	?	MID	
QUEENS ROAD PECKHAM Peckham	33 / 3A	1866	N/A	LBSCR	

NAME: (Previous Names Below)	PAGE / GRID:	YEAR OPENED:	YEAR CLOSED:	OPENED BY:	NOTES:
QUEENSTOWN ROAD BATTERSEA Queens Road Battersea	32 / 3A & 51	1877	N/A	LSWR	Renamed 1980

QUEENSWAY
   Queens Road
	21 / 4A	1900	N/A	CLR	Renamed 1946. Closed 2005 for lift
					   replacement (expected to reopen 2006)

RAINHAM	26 / 3B	1854	N/A	LTSR	
RAVENSBOURNE	44 / 2A	1892	N/A	LCDR	

RAVENSCOURT PARK
   Shaftesbury Road
	30 / 2B	1873	N/A	LSWR	Opened by LSWR. First served District and
					   Metropolitan railways 1877, renamed 1888.
					   Last served Metropolitan Railway 1906, last
					   served LSWR 1916.

RAYNERS LANE	8 / 4B	1906	N/A	MET	Served by District Line Trains 1910-1933,
					   Piccadilly Line thereafter. Goods Yard open
					   1929-1964

RAYNES PARK	40 / 3B	1871	N/A	LSWR	
RAYNES PARK GOODS	40 / 3B	1859	?	LSWR	
Raynes Park Junction	40 / 3B	1859	N/A	LSWR	
Reading Lane Junction	23 / 2A	1986	N/A	BR	Curve opened due to closure of Broad Street. Passenger service withdrawn 1992
RECTORY ROAD	23 / 1A	1872	N/A	GER	
REDBRIDGE	14 / 4B	1947	N/A	LT (CEN)	
REDLAND STONE TERMINAL (CRICKLEWOOD)	20 / 1B	?	N/A	PRIV	
REEDHAM Reedham Halt	47 / 4A	1911	N/A	LBSCR	Closed 1917-1919. "Halt" dropped 1936
REEDHAM SIDINGS	47 / 4A	?	N/A	LBSCR	
REEVES CORNER	47 / 1B	2000	N/A	CTL	
REGENT'S PARK	22 / 4A	1906	N/A	BS&WR	
RICHMOND (1st)	29 / 4A	1846	1848	LSWR	Terminus 1846-1848, later became Goods Station

RICHMOND (2nd)	29 / 4A	1848	N/A	LSWR	Replaced 1846 terminus. First served District &
					   Metropolitan Railways 1877. Last served
					   Metropolitan Railway 1906. Extensively
					   rebuilt 1936-1937

Richmond Bridge	29 / 4B	1848	N/A	LSWR	
RICHMOND GASWORKS	30 / 3A	1882	1933	PRIV	
RICHMOND GOODS	29 / 4B	1848	1936	LSWR	Demolished when station rebuilt
Richmond Junction (1)	29 / 3A	1869	1972	LSWR	Physical connection eliminated 1972
Richmond Junction (2)	31 / 1A & 49	1869	1916	LSWR	Service withdrawn between Addison Road and Studland Road Junction 1916

RICKMANSWORTH
   Rickmansworth High Street
   Rickmansworth
	1 / 4A	1887	N/A	MET	Goods Yard closed 1966

RICKMANSWORTH (CHURCH STREET)
   Rickmansworth
	7 / 1B	1862	1952 *(1966)*	LNWR	Branch from Watford Junction; closed to
					   passengers 1952 and freight in 1966

RICKMANSWORTH NORTH SIDINGS	1 / 4A	?	N/A	MET	Stabling Sidings for Metropolitan Line
RICKMANSWORTH SOUTH SIDINGS	1 / 4B	1966	N/A	MET	Stabling Sidings for Metropolitan Line, On site of former goods yard
RIDDLESDOWN	47 / 4B	1927	N/A	SR	
Riddlesdown Tunnel	47 / 4B	1884	N/A	LBSCR & SER	
RIPPLE LANE FREIGHTLINER TERMINAL	25 / 3B	1972	N/A	BR	
RIPPLE LANE YARD	25 / 3B	1937	N/A	LMS	

RODING VALLEY (LNER)	14 / 1B	1936	1947	LNER	Fairlop Loop closed 1947 to allow electrification
					   and transfer to LT Central Line. Freight traffic
					   remained until 1965

RODING VALLEY (LT)	14 / 1B	1948	N/A	LT (CEN)	First served by LT Central Line Trains 1948

ROMFORD
   Romford for Hornchurch, Upminster & Corbet's Tey
   Romford
	16 / 4B	1839	N/A	ECR	

ROMFORD FACTORY	16 / 4B	1843	?	ECR	Locomotive Works until 1847 then wagon cover factory after 1854

ROTHERHITHE	33 / 1A	1869	N/A	ELR	First served District and Metropolitan Railways
					   1884, last served District 1905. No service
					   Metropolitan Railway 1906-1913. Became
					   "East London Line" in 1980s. Closed
					   1995-1998.

ROYAL AGRICULTURAL SHOW SIDING	20 / 3A	?	?	PRIV	
ROYAL ALBERT	24 / 4B	1994	N/A	DLR	
ROYAL BETHLEM HOSPITAL	43 / 4B	1928	1930	PRIV	¾ Mile siding from Eden Park in use during construction of the Hospital
ROYAL DOCKYARD (WOOLWICH)	34 / 1B	?	?	PRIV	
ROYAL MINT STREET GOODS	23 / 4A & 7 / 3A	1858	1951	LBR	
Royal Mint Street Junction	23 / 4A & 7 / 3A	1991	N/A	DLR	
ROYAL OAK	21 / 4A	1871	N/A	MET & GWR	
ROYAL VICTORIA	24 / 4A	1994	N/A	DLR	
RUGBY ROAD	30 / 1B	1909	1917	N&SWJR	Passenger services withdrawn from Hammersmith & Chiswick Branch 1917

RUISLIP	18 / 1A	1904	N/A	MET	Served by District Line Trains 1910-1933,
					   Piccadilly Line thereafter. Goods Yard
					   closed 1964

RUISLIP DEPOT	18 / 1A	1948	N/A	LT (CEN)	Depot for Central Line and Transplant (Engineering)
RUISLIP GARDENS (GCR / GWR)	18 / 1A	1934	1958	GCR / GWR	
RUISLIP GARDENS (LT)	18 / 1A	1948	N/A	LT (CEN)	

NAME: (Previous Names Below)	PAGE / GRID:	YEAR OPENED:	YEAR CLOSED:	OPENED BY:	NOTES:
RUISLIP GOODS	18 / 1A	1905	1964	MET	
RUISLIP MANOR	18 / 1A	1912	N/A	MET	Served by District Line Trains 1912-1933, Piccadilly Line trains thereafter. Closed 1917-1919
RUSSELL SQUARE	22/ 4A	1906	N/A	GNP&BR	
Salmons Lane Junction	23 / 4B	1880	1962	LTSR	
SANDERSTEAD	47 / 2B	1884	N/A	LBSCR & SER	
SANDILANDS	48 / 1A	2000	N/A	CTL	
Sandilands Tunnels	48 / 1A	1885	N/A	SER	Closed 1983 along with Woodside to Selsdon, but re-opened 2000 by Croydon Tramlink
SELHURST	42 / 4B	1865	N/A	LBSCR	
SELHURST DEPOT	42 / 4B	1911	N/A	LBSCR	
Selhurst Junctions	42 / 4B	1862	N/A	LBSCR	
SELSDON Selsdon Road	47 / 2B	1885	1983	LBSCR & SER	Woodside to Selsdon closed 1916-1935, "Road" dropped 1935, Oxted Line platforms closed 1959. Woodside platforms closed for good 1983
SEVEN KINGS	25 / 1A	1899	N/A	GER	
Seven Kings West Junction	25 / 1A	1903	1956	GER	Link between Newbury Park and Seven Kings dismantled 1956
SEVEN SISTERS	12 / 4B	1872	N/A	GER	Victoria Line station opened 1968
SEVEN SISTERS (Palace Gates Platforms)	12 / 4B	1878	1963	GER	Platforms for Palace Gates Branch, closed to passengers 1963
Seven Sisters Junction	12 / 4B	1880	N/A	GER	Junction with curve to Tottenham & Hampstead Junction Railway
Shacklegate Junction	39 / 2A	1894	N/A	LSWR	
SHADWELL & ST GEORGES EAST Shadwell	23 / 4A	1840	1941	LBR	Renamed 1900. Closed 1916-1919
SHADWELL Shadwell & St Georges-in-the-East	23 / 4A	1876	N/A	ELR	First served District and Metropolitan Railways 1884, last served District 1905. No service Metropolitan Railway 1906-1913. Became "East London Line" in 1980s. DLR platforms opened 1987. East London Line platforms closed 1995-1998.
Sheet Factory Junction	53	1846	1973	ECR	Eastern Curve at Stratford dismantled 1973
SHELL MEX & BP (ANGERSTEIN WHARF)	34 / 1A	?	?	PRIV	
SHEPHERD'S BUSH (CLR)	31 / 1A & 49	1900	N/A	CLR	Terminus of Central London Railway 1900-1908. Sometimes has suffix "Green" added
SHEPHERD'S BUSH (GWR & MET)	49	1864	1869	MET & GWR	Station opened on 1864 Spur from Metropolitan and Great Western Railways' line to Hammersmith. Replaced by Uxbridge Road Station to South in 1869
SHEPHERD'S BUSH (LSWR)	30 / 1B & 49	1869	1916	LSWR	Addison Road to Studland Road Junction abandoned 1916
SHEPHERD'S BUSH (MET) (1st)	30 / 1B & 49	1864	1914	MET & GWR	Replaced by Shepherd's Bush (2nd) to North and Goldhawk Road to South
SHEPHERD'S BUSH (MET) (2nd)	30 / 1B & 49	1914	N/A	MET & GWR	Replaced Shepherd's Bush (1st) to South
SHEPHERD'S BUSH (NR)	31 / 1A & 49	2006	N/A	NR	New Network Rail station on site of former Uxbridge Road Station. Projected opening 2006
SHEPHERD'S BUSH (WLR)	49	1844	1844	WLR	Initial passenger service on West London Railway withdrawn after 6 months When services resumed in 1863 original 1844 Shepherd's Bush Station did not re-open
Shepherd's Lane Junction	32 / 3A	?	N/A	LCDR & LBSCR	
SHEPPERTON Shepperton for Halliford	37 / 4B	1864	N/A	LSWR	
SHERN HALL STREET WALTHAMSTOW	13 / 3B	1870	1873	GER	Terminus of branch from Stratford 1870-1873
SHERWOOD HOSPITAL & POWER STATION	45 / 3A	1918	1950	PRIV	Horton Estate Light Railway opened to supply building materials, later fuel, to hospitals
SHOREDITCH (NLR)	22 / 3B	1865	1941	NLR	
SHOREDITCH (ELR)	23 / 4A	1876	N/A	ELR	To close 2010 when projected northern extension built. Line beyond platforms severed 1966. Closed 1995-1998.
SHOREDITCH (DUNLOE STREET) GOODS DEPOT	23 / 3A	1893	1968	NLR	
SHOREDITCH HIGH STREET	23 / 4A	2010	N/A	LUL (ELL)	Projected to open 2010 as part of East London Line Extension Phase 1
SHORTLANDS New Bromley	44 / 3A	1858	N/A	LCDR	
Shortlands Junction	44 / 3A	1892	N/A	LCDR	Remodelled as a "flying" junction 2003
Silk Stream Junctions	10 / 3B	?	N/A	MID	Junction between Midland Main Line and Freight Flyover
SILVER STREET	13 / 2A	1872	N/A	GER	
SILVERTOWN & LONDON CITY AIRPORT Silvertown	34 / 1B	1863	N/A	ECR	
SLADE GREEN Slades Green	36 / 3B	1900	N/A	SECR	Renamed 1953
SLADE GREEN DEPOT	36 / 3B	1901	N/A	SECR	Converted for EMU use 1924 (previously Steam depot)
Slade Green Junction	36 / 3B	1895	N/A	SER	

NAME: (Previous Names Below)	PAGE / GRID:	YEAR OPENED:	YEAR CLOSED:	OPENED BY:	NOTES:
SLOANE SQUARE	31 / 2B	1868	N/A	MDR	
SMALLBERRY GREEN	29 / 3A	1849	1850	LSWR	Opened as "Hounslow". Terminus 1849-1850.
Hounslow					Replaced by Isleworth Station to West.
SMITHAM	47 / 4A	1904	N/A	LBSCR	Closed 1917-1919. Goods Yard closed 1962
SMITHFIELD GOODS	22 / 4B	1869	1962	GWR	
SMITHS SIDING (FELTHAM)	38 / 1A	?	?	PRIV	
SNARESBROOK (ECR)	14 / 4A	1856	1970	ECR	Majority of Passenger services transferred to LT
Snaresbrook for Wanstead					in 1947. First Trains in the morning
Snaresbrook & Wanstead					remained British Rail services until 1970
Snaresbrook					
SNARESBROOK (LT)	14 / 4A	1947	N/A	LT (CEN)	First served by LT Central Line trains in 1947.
					Goods Yard closed 1949
SOMERS TOWN GOODS	22 / 3A & 54	1877	1975	MID	
SOUTH ACTON (N&SWJR)	30 / 1A & 40 / 1A	1880	N/A	N&SWJR	
South Acton Junction	30 / 1A & 40 / 1A	1869	N/A	N&SWJR	
SOUTH ACTON (MDR)	30 / 1A & 40 / 1A	1905	1959	MDR	South Acton curve opened 1899 in connection
					with construction of South Harrow extension.
					First passenger trains 1905, last freight trains
					1914. Passenger service withdrawn 1959.
SOUTH BERMONDSEY (1st)	33 / 1A & 52	1869	1928	LBSCR	Closed 1917-1919
Rotherhithe					
SOUTH BERMONDSEY (2nd)	33 / 2A & 52	1928	N/A	SR	
South Bermondsey Junction	52	1869	N/A	LBSCR	
SOUTHALL	28 / 1B	1839	N/A	GWR	
Southall West Junction	28 / 1B	1859	N/A	GWR	
SOUTH BROMLEY	23 / 4B	1884	1944	NLR	Passenger service Dalston Junction to Poplar
					withdrawn 1944
SOUTHBURY	5 / 4A	1960	N/A	BR	Opened 1960 on site of former Churchbury
					Station. Goods Yard closed 1970
SOUTH CROYDON	47 / 2B	1865	N/A	LBSCR	
South Croydon Junction	47 / 2B	1884	N/A	LBSCR & SER	
SOUTH DOCK	33 / 1B	1871	N/A	LBR	
South West India Dock					
South Dock					
SOUTH EALING	29 / 1B	1883	N/A	MDR	First served by Piccadilly Line 1933. Last
					served by District Line 1964
SOUTH EASTERN GAS WORKS	34 / 1A	1889	1978	PRIV	
Southern Junction (Stratford)	53	1847	1981	ECR	Western Curve at Stratford dismantled 1981
SOUTHFIELDS	41 / 1A	1889	N/A	LSWR	Putney Bridge to Wimbldeon built by LSWR but
					operated by District Railway from opening.
					Last regular Main Line passenger service
					withdrawn 1941, although services called on
					occasions until 1969. Point Pleasant Jcn to
					Wimbledon still used for empty stock working
					and diversions.
SOUTHGATE	12 / 1A	1933	N/A	LT (PIC)	
SOUTH GREENFORD	19 / 3A	1926	N/A	GWR	
South Greenford Halt					
SOUTH HAMPSTEAD	21 / 2B	1879	N/A	LNWR	Closed in 1917, re-opened and renamed 1922
Loudoun Road					
SOUTH HAREFILED HALT	17 / 1B	1928	1931	GCR & GWR	
Harefield Halt					
SOUTH HARROW (1st)	19 / 1A	1903	1935	MDR	Terminus 1903-1910. First served Piccadilly
					Line 1932. Last served District Line 1933.
SOUTH HARROW (2nd)	19 / 1A	1935	N/A	LT (PIC)	Station relocated 1935
SOUTH HARROW SIDINGS	19 / 1A	1903	N/A	MDR	Stabling sidings (formerly depot) for Piccadilly
					Line (previously District Railway)
South Junction (Mitcham)	42 / 4A	1855	1997	LBSCR & WCR	Junction eliminated when Wimbldeon to
					Croydon line closed 1997
SOUTH KENSINGTON	31 / 2B & 56	1868	N/A	MDR	Initial section of Metropolitan District Railway
					Gloucester Road to Westminster (Bridge)
					opened 1868 but operated by Metropolitan
					Railway. Separate District platforms opened
					1871.
					GNP&BR platforms opened 1907.
SOUTH KENTISH TOWN	22 / 2A	1907	1924	CCE&HR	
SOUTH KENTON	19 / 1B	1933	N/A	LNWR	Served by Bakerloo Line Trains 1917-1982,
					1984-Present
SOUTH LAMBETH FREIGHT DEPOT	32 / 2A & 51	1863	1980	GWR	
SOUTH MERTON	41 / 3A	1929	N/A	SR	
SOUTH METROPOLITAN GAS COMPANY	34 / 1A	?	?	PRIV	
SOUTH QUAY	33 / 1B	1987	N/A	DLR	
SOUTH RUISLIP	18 / 2B	1908	N/A	GCR & GWR	First served by Central Line Trains 1948
South Ruislip & Northolt Junction					
Northolt Junction					
SOUTH SHED (QUEENS PARK)	21 / 3A	1915	N/A	UERL (BAK)	Stabling Shed for Bakerloo Line
SOUTH TOTTENHAM	13 / 4A	1871	N/A	T&HJ	
South Tottenham & Stamford Hill					
South Tottenham Junction	13 / 4A	1880	N/A	GER	Junction between Tottenham & Hampstead
					Junction Railway and curve to GER
SOUTHWARK	32 / 1B	1999	N/A	LUL (JUB)	
SOUTHWARK PARK	33 / 1A & 52	1902	1915	SECR	
Corbett's Lane					
SOUTH WIMBLEDON	41 / 2A	1926	N/A	UERL (NOR)	(Merton) suffix added 1928, but gradually

NAME: (Previous Names Below)	PAGE / GRID:	YEAR OPENED:	YEAR CLOSED:	OPENED BY:	NOTES:
South Wimbledon (Merton)					dropped
South Wimbledon					
SOUTH WOODFORD	14 / 3A	1947	N/A	LT (CEN)	First served by LT Central Line Trains 1947.
South Woodford (George Lane)					On site of George Lane (Woodford) Station
					"George Lane" suffix dropped 1950.
					Goods Yard closed 1964
SPA ROAD, BERMONDSEY	33 / 1A	1843	1915	LGR	Replaced original station to West
Spa Road & Bermondsey					
SPA ROAD & BERMONDSEY	33 / 1A	1836	1843	LGR	Temporary terminus of London & Greenwich
					Railway during 1836. Resited East 1843.
SPENCER ROAD HALT	47 / 2B	1906	1915	SER	
SPITALFIELDS GOODS	23 / 4A	?	1967	GER	
SQUARE GRIP REINFORCEMENTS LTD (COLNBROOK)	27 / 2A	1957	?	PRIV	
Spur Junction	43 / 3A	1862	1972	LCDR	Bromley Spur disused since 1966 but not
					dismantled until 1972
STAINES	37 2A & 3B	1849	N/A	LSWR	"Staines Central" 1923-1966
Staines Central					
Staines Junction					
Staines Old					
Staines					
Staines Bridge	37 / 4A	1856	N/A	LSWR	
STAINES CARRIAGE SIDINGS	37 / 2A	?	N/A	LSWR	
Staines East Junction	37 / 3B	1856	N/A	LSWR	
STAINES HIGH STREET	37 / 2A & 3B	1887	1916	LSWR	
STAINES LINOLEUM WORKS	37 / 3B	1887	1957	PRIV	
Staines Moor Junction	37 / 3A	1940	1947	SR	Established during World War II to provide an
					alternative route in case of bomb damage
STAINES WEST	37 / 2A & 3A	1885	1965	GWR	"West" suffix added 1949. Passenger service
Staines					West Drayton to Staines West withdrawn
Staines West Curve					1965
	37 / 3B	1877	1965	LSWR	
STAINES WEST GOODS	37 / 3A	1885	1953	GWR	Later became oil terminal
Staines West Junction	37 / 3A	1981	1991	BR	Established for access to Staines West oil
					terminal after M25 severed route to West
					Drayton
STAINES WEST OIL TERMINAL (SHELL / BP)	37 / 3A	1964	1991	PRIV	
STAMFORD BROOK	30 / 2B	1912	N/A	MDR	Platforms only built for District Railway
STAMFORD HILL	12 / 4B	1872	N/A	GER	
STANMORE	9 / 2B	1932	N/A	MET	Opened by Metropolitan Railway. Transferred to
					Bakerloo Line 1939, Jubilee Line 1979.
					Goods Yard closed 1936
STANMORE SIDINGS	9 / 2B	1932	N/A	MET	Stabling Sidngs for Jubilee Line (previously
					Metropolitan Railway then Bakerloo Line)
STANMORE VILLAGE	9 / 2B	1890	1952 (1964)	LNWR	"Village" suffix added 1950. Stanmore Village to
Stanmore					Belmont closed to passengers 1952,
					Freight remained until 1964
ST ANNS ROAD	12 / 4B	1882	1942	T&HJ	
STEPNEY GREEN	23 / 4A	1902	N/A	MDR & LTSR	Served by Metropolitan Line since 1936
					("Hammersmith & City Line" since 1990)
STEWARTS LANE (LBSCR)	32 / 3A & 51	1858	1858	LBSCR	Opened by West End of London & Crystal
					Palace Railway, but operated by LBSCR
					from outset
STEWARTS LANE (LCDR)	32 / 3A & 51	1863	1866	LCDR	
STEWARTS LANE DEPOT	32 / 3A & 51	?	N/A	LCDR	
STEWARTS LANE GOODS	32 / 3A & 51	?	1970	LCDR	
Stewarts Lane Junction	51	1862	N/A	LCDR	
ST HELIER	41 / 4A	1930	N/A	SR	Goods Yard closed 1963
St James Road Junction	42 / 4B	1862	1984	LBSCR	
ST JAMES'S PARK	32 / 1A	1868	N/A	MDR	Also spelt "St James' Park"
ST JAMES STREET WALTHAMSTOW	13 / 4B	1870	N/A	GER	
ST JOHN'S	33 / 3B	1873	N/A	SER	
ST JOHN'S WOOD	21 / 3B	1939	N/A	LT (BAK)	Opened by Bakerloo Line, transferred to Jubilee
					Line 1979
STOKE NEWINGTON	23 / 1A	1872	N/A	GER	
ST MARGARETS	29 / 4B	1876	N/A	LSWR	
St Mary Cray Junctions	44 / 3B	1904	N/A	SECR	
ST MARY'S (WHITECHAPEL ROAD)	23 / 4A	1884	1938	MDR & MET	Renamed 1923. Closed due to Aldgate East
St Mary's					being relocated eastwards
STOAT'S NEST	47 / 4A	1841	1856	L&BR	
Stoat's Nest Junction	47 / 4A	1899	N/A	LBSCR	
Stockley Park Flyover	27 / 1B	1998	N/A	RT (HEX)	
STOCKWELL	32 / 3A	1890	N/A	C&SLR	Terminus of City & South London Railway
					1890-1900. Closed 1923-1924.
					Victoria Line platforms opened 1971
STONEBRIDGE PARK	20 / 2A	1912	N/A	LNWR	Served by Bakerloo Line Trains since 1917.
					Terminus of Bakerloo services 1982-1984
STONEBRIDGE PARK DEPOT	20 / 2A	1982	N/A	LT (BAK)	Bakerloo Line Depot
STONEBRIDGE PARK GOODS	20 / 2A	?	?	LNWR	
STONELEIGH	45 / 2B	1932	N/A	SR	
STORA DISTRIBUTION DEPOT (RIPPLE LANE)	25 / 3B	?	N/A	PRIV	
ST PANCRAS	22 / 3A & 54	1868	N/A	MID	New Thameslink platforms projected to open
					2007
ST PANCRAS GOODS	22 / 3A & 54	1865	1975	MID	

NAME: (Previous Names Below)	PAGE / GRID:	YEAR OPENED:	YEAR CLOSED:	OPENED BY:	NOTES:
ST PAUL'S	22 / 4B	1900	N/A	CLR	Renamed 1937
Post Office					
ST QUINTIN PARK & WORMWOOD SCRUBS (1st)	20 / 4B	1871	1893	WLR	Relocated North 1893
Wormwood Scrubs					
ST QUINTIN PARK & WORMWOOD SCRUBS (2nd)	20 / 4B	1893	1940	LNWR	Replaced original station to South
Strand-on-the-Green Bridge	30 / 2A	1869	N/A	LSWR	
STRATFORD	24 / 2A	1839	N/A	ECR	Central Line platforms opened 1946, DLR 1987,
Stratford (West Ham)					Jubilee Line 1999
Stratford					
Stratford Central Junction East	53	1840	N/A	ECR	
Stratford Central Junction West	53	1854	N/A	ECR	
STRATFORD FREIGHTLINER TERMINAL	23 / 2B & 53	?	1998	BR	Disused since 1998
STRATFORD GOODS	24 / 2A & 53	?	?	GER	
STRATFORD INTERNATIONAL	23 / 2B & 53	2007	N/A	L&CR	Under Construction
STRATFORD MARKET	24 / 3A	1847	1957	ECR	"Stratford Bridge" until 1880
Stratford Market (West Ham)					
Stratford Market					
Stratford Bridge					
STRATFORD MARKET	24 / 3A	1879	1988	GER	Fruit & Vegetable Market, Closed 1984.
					Sidings retained for engineering until 1988
STRATFORD MARKET DEPOT	24 / 3A	1999	N/A	LUL (JUB)	Jubilee Line Depot, on site of former Stratford
					Market
STRATFORD TRACTION MAINTENANCE DEPOT (TMD)	53	1841	2001	ECR	Relocated to Temple Mills due to Channel
					Tunnel Rail Link works at Stratford
STRATFORD TRACTION MAINTENANCE DEPOT (TMD)	23 / 1B	2001	N/A	EWS	Relocated due to Channel Tunnel Rail Link
					works at Stratford
STRAWBERRY HILL	39 / 1A	1873	N/A	LSWR	
STRAWBERRY HILL DEPOT	39 / 2A	1916	N/A	LSWR	On site of Fulwell Loco Depot. First used for
					EMUs 1916, exclusively so after 1923
Strawberry Hill Junction	39 / 1A	1864	N/A	LSWR	
STREATHAM	42 / 2A	1868	N/A	LBSCR	
STREATHAM COMMON	42 / 2A	1862	N/A	LBSCR	"Greyhound Lane" suffix dropped 1870
Streatham Common (Greyhound Lane)					
Stretham Common					
STREATHAM COMMON GOODS	42 / 2A	?	?	LBSCR	
Streatham Common Junction	42 / 2A	1886	N/A	LBSCR	
STREATHAM HILL	42 / 1A	1856	N/A	LBSCR	Opened by West End of London & Crystal
Streatham & Brixton Hill					Palace Railway, but operated by LBSCR
Streatham					from outset. "Streatham" until 1868
STREATHAM HILL DEPOT	42 / 1A	1936	N/A	SR	
Streatham Junction	42 / 2A	1886	N/A	LBSCR	
Streatham North Junction	42 / 2A	1868	N/A	LBSCR	
Streatham South Junctions A & B	42 / 2A	1868	N/A	LBSCR	
Streatham South Junction C	42 / 2A	1868	N/A	LSWR & LBSCR	
Streatham Tunnel	42 / 1A	1868	N/A	LBSCR	
STROUD GREEN	12 / 4A	1881	1954	GNR	Closed when Alexandra Palace to Finsbury
					Park service withdrawn 1954. Had been
					intended for electrification and transfer to LT
					Northern Line, but works abandoned
					post-WW2
Studland Road Junction	30 / 2B	1877	1916	LSWR & MDR	Addison Road to Studland Road Junction
					abandoned 1916
SUDBURY & HARROW ROAD	19 / 2B	1906	N/A	GCR	
SUDBURY HILL	19 / 2A	1903	N/A	MDR	First served Piccadilly Line 1932, last served
Sudbury Hill for Greenford Green					District Line 1933
SUDBURY HILL HARROW	19 / 2A	1906	N/A	GCR	
South Harrow					
SUDBURY TOWN	19 / 2B	1903	N/A	MDR	First served Piccadilly Line 1932, last served
Sudbury Town for Horsendon					District Line 1933
SUNBURY	38 / 3A	1864	N/A	LSWR	
SUNDRIDGE PARK	44 / 2A	1878	N/A	SER	Renamed 1894
Plaistow					
SURBITON	39 / 4B	1838	N/A	LSWR	
Surbiton & Kingston					
Kingston Junction					
Kingston					
SURREY CANAL ROAD	33 / 2A & 52	N/A	N/A	LUL (ELL)	Projected to open as part of East London Line
					Extension Phase 2
SURREY QUAYS	33 / 1A & 52	1869	N/A	ELR	First served District and Metropolitan Railways
Surrey Docks					1884, last served District 1905. No service
Deptford Road					Metropolitan Railway 1906-1913. Renamed
					"Surrey Docks" 1911. Became "East London
					Line" in 1980s. Renamed "Surrey Quays"
					1989. Closed 1995-1998.
SUTTON	46 / 2B	1847	N/A	LBSCR	
SUTTON COMMON	46 / 1A	1930	N/A	SR	
Sutton East Junction	46 / 2B	1868	N/A	LBSCR	
Sutton West Junction	46 / 2A	1930	N/A	SR	
SWISS COTTAGE (MET)	21 / 2B	1868	1940	MET	Terminus of branch from Baker Street
					1868-1879
SWISS COTTAGE (BAK)	21 / 2B	1939	N/A	LT (BAK)	Opened by Bakerloo Line, transferred to Jubilee
					Line 1979
SYDENHAM	43 / 2A	1839	N/A	LCR	East London Line projected to serve from 2010
Sydenham Down Junction	43 / 2A	1854	N/A	LBSCR	

NAME: (Previous Names Below)	PAGE / GRID:	YEAR OPENED:	YEAR CLOSED:	OPENED BY:	NOTES:
SYDENHAM GASWORKS	43 / 1B	1878	1971	PRIV	Gasworks ceased production in late 1960's but railway connection not removed until 1971
SYDENHAM HILL	43 / 1A	1863	N/A	LCDR	
Sydenham Up Junction	43 / 2A	1854	N/A	LBSCR	
SYON LANE	29 / 2B	1931	N/A	SR	
Tanners Hill Junction	33 / 3B	1976	N/A	BR	
TARMAC STONE TERMINAL (HAYES)	28 / 1A	?	N/A	PRIV	
TARMAC STONE TERMINAL (STEWARTS LANE)	32 / 3A & 51	?	N/A	PRIV	
TEDDINGTON	39 / 2B	1863	N/A	LSWR	"Bushey" also spelt "Bushy" at times. Goods Yard closed 1965
Teddington for Bushey Park					
Teddington & Bushey Park					
Teddington (Bushey Park)					
TEMPLE	22 / 4A	1870	N/A	MDR	"The" prefix dropped gradually
The Temple					
Temple Mills East Junction	23 / 2B & 53	1862	N/A	GER	
TEMPLE MILLS EUROSTAR DEPOT	23 / 1B	2007	N/A	NR (ES)	Partly on site of Temple Mills Marshalling Yard. Projected to open 2007
TEMPLE MILLS YARD	23 / 1B	1959	N/A	BR	No longer used as a Marshalling Yard; some Engineering use.
THAMES DITTON	39 / 4A	1851	N/A	LSWR	
Thames Tunnel (1)	16 / 3B	2007	N/A	L&CR	Under Construction
Thames Tunnel (2)	33 / 1A	1843	N/A	ECR	Opened to pedestrian traffic 1843, first trains ran through tunnel 1869
THAMES WHARF	24 / 4A	1846	1965	ECR	Midland Railway Depot opened 1870
THAMES WHARF	34 / 1A	N/A	N/A	DLR	Projected station, currently dependant on a road bridge scheme
Thames Wharf Junction	24 / 4A	1847	1965	ECR	
THEOBALDS GROVE (1st)	5 / 1A	1891	1919	GER	Closed 1909-1915
THEOBALDS GROVE (2nd)	5 / 1A	1960	N/A	BR	Opened 1960 on site of former Theobalds Grove Station. Goods Yard closed 1967
THERAPIA LANE	42 / 4A	2000	N/A	CTL	
THERAPIA LANE DEPOT	42 / 4A	2000	N/A	CTL	Maintenance and stabling for Croydon Tramlink
THEYDON BOIS (GER)	6 / 3A	1865	1970	GER	Majority of Passenger services transferred to LT in 1949. First Trains in the morning remained British Rail services until 1970
Theydon					
THEYDON BOIS (LT)	6 / 3A	1949	N/A	LT (CEN)	First served by Central Line Trains 1949. Goods Yard closed 1966
THORNEY MILL SIDINGS	27 / 1A	1943	N/A	GWR	Formerly used for Coal, Oil, Scrap Metal and Stone traffic, today only Stone traffic remains.
THORNEY MILL STONE TERMINAL (AGGREGATE INDS.)	27 / 1A	1986	N/A	PRIV	
THORNTON FIELD CARRIAGE SIDINGS	23 / 3B & 53	?	N/A	GER	
THORNTON HEATH	42 / 3B	1862	N/A	LBSCR	
THORNTON HEATH GOODS	42 / 3B	?	?	LBSCR	
TIDAL BASIN	24 / 4A	1858	1943	ECR	
Tilbury Junction	23 / 3B	1869	1959	NLR	Junction between NLR and curve to LTSR at Bromley
TOLWORTH	45 / 1A	1938	N/A	SR	
TOOTING	41 / 2B	1894	N/A	LSWR & LBSCR	Replaced Tooting Junction Station to West. Closed 1917-1923. Junction severed 1934 and line to Merton Park became a siding accessed from that station
TOOTING BEC	41 / 1B	1926	N/A	UERL (NOR)	Renamed 1950
Trinity Road (Tooting Bec)					
TOOTING BROADWAY	41 / 2B	1926	N/A	UERL (NOR)	
TOOTING JUNCTION	41 / 2B	1868	1894	LSWR & LBSCR	Resited to East (Tooting Station)
TOTTENHAM COURT ROAD	22 / 4A	1900	N/A	CLR	CCE&HR platforms opened 1907 as "Oxford Street", renamed 1908
Oxford Street (CCE&HR only)					
Tottenham Curve Tunnels 1, 2 & 3	11 / 4A	1868	N/A	MID	
TOTTENHAM HALE	13 / 3A	1840	N/A	ECR	Victoria Line station opened and "Hale" suffix added 1968
Tottenham					
Tottenham North Junction	13 / 4A	1868	1961	T&HJ	North curve to Lea Valley Line dismantled 1961
Tottenham South Junction	13 / 4A	1868	N/A	T&HJ	Junction between Tottenham & Hampstead Junction Railway and Lea Valley Line
Tottenham West Junction	13 / 4A	1868	1961	T&HJ	North curve to Lea Valley Line dismantled 1961
TOTTERIDGE & WHETSTONE (GNR)	11 / 1B	1872	1939	GNR	Closed in 1939 to enable electrification and transfer to LT Northern Line
Totteridge					
TOTTERIDGE & WHETSTONE (LT)	11 / 1B	1940	N/A	LT (NOR)	On site of former GNR station. Goods yard closed 1962
TOWER GATEWAY	23 / 4A & 7 / 3A	1987	N/A	DLR	
TOWER HILL	22 / 4B	1884	1967	MDR & MET	Replaced former Tower of London Station to East. Renamed 1946, relocated East 1967
Mark Lane					
TOWER HILL	23 / 4A & 7 / 3A	1967	N/A	LT (DIS)	Replaced Tower Hill (formerly Mark Lane) Station to West. On site of former "Tower of London"
TOWER OF LONDON	23 / 4A & 7 / 3A	1882	1884	MET	Terminus of Metropolitan Railway extension from Aldgate 1882-1884, replaced by Mark Lane (later Tower Hill [1st]) station to West. Present Tower Hill Station on site of Tower of London
TRIANGLE SIDINGS	31 / 2A & 50	1957	N/A	LT (DIS)	Built partially on site of Cromwell Curve. Stabling sidings for District and Circle Lines

NAME: (Previous Names Below)	PAGE / GRID:	YEAR OPENED:	YEAR CLOSED:	OPENED BY:	NOTES:
TRUMPER'S CROSSING HALTE	29 / 1A	1904	1926	GWR	Closed 1915-1920
Trumper's Crossing Halte for South Hanwell and Osterley Park					
TUFNELL PARK	22 / 1A & 11 / 3B	1907	N/A	CCE&HR	
TUFNELL PARK GOODS	22 / 1A	1886	1968	T&HJ	
TULSE HILL	42 / 1B	1868	N/A	LBSCR	
Tulse Hill North Junction	42 / 1B	1869	N/A	LBSCR	
Tulse Hill South Junction	42 / 1B	1870	N/A	LBSCR	
TURKEY STREET	5 / 2A	1960	N/A	BR	Opened 1960 on site of former Forty Hill Station. Goods Yard closed 1966
TURNHAM GREEN	30 / 2B & 40 / 1B	1869	N/A	LSWR	Opened by LSWR. First served District and Metropolitan railways 1877, last served Metropolitan Railway 1906, last served LSWR 1916. Restricted Piccadilly Line service since 1963
TURNPIKE LANE	12 / 3B	1932	N/A	LT (PIC)	
TWICKENHAM (1st)	29 / 4B	1849	1954	LSWR	
TWICKENHAM (2nd)	29 / 4B	1954	N/A	BR	
Twickenham Junction	29 / 4A	1863	N/A	LSWR	
TWYFORD ABBEY HALT	20 / 3A	1904	1911	GWR	
UNITED GLASS	34 / 2A	?	?	PRIV	
UPMINSTER	16 / 2B	1885	N/A	LTSR	Served by District Railway since 1902, no service 1905-1932. Goods Yard closed 1964
UPMINSTER BRIDGE	16 / 2A	1934	N/A	LMS	Station on new Slow Lines opened between Barking and Upminster 1932. Served by District Line trains from opening, Main Line services ceased 1962.
UPMINSTER DEPOT	16 / 2B	1958	N/A	LT (DIS)	District Line Depot
UPNEY	25 / 2A	1932	N/A	LMS	Barking to Upminster quadrupled by the LMS in 1932 and Upney station opened. Served by District Line from opening. Ownership transferred to LT in 1970.
UPPER HALLIFORD	38 / 3A	1944	N/A	SR	
Upper Halliford Halt					
Halliford Halt					
UPPER HOLLOWAY	22 / 1A	1868	N/A	T&HJ	
Upper Holloway for St John's Park					
Upper Holloway for St Johns Park and Highgate Hill					
Upper Holloway					
UPPER SYDENHAM	43 / 1A	1884	1954	LCDR	Closed 1917-1919 and 1944-1946. Nunhead to Crystal Palace (High Level) closed 1954
UP SIDINGS (HAYES)	28 / 1A	?	N/A	GWR	S&T Sidings
Up Slow Flyover (Wimbledon)	41 / 1A	1936	N/A	SR	
UPTON PARK (LTSR)	24 / 3B	1877	1962	LTSR	Main Line services non-stopped since 1962, and Fast Platforms abandoned
UPTON PARK (MDR)	24 / 3B	1902	N/A	MDR	First served by District Railway 1902, line quadrupled 1908, District Trains using Slow Lines. Served by Metropolitan Line since 1936 ("Hammersmith & City Line" since 1990)
UPTON PARK GOODS	24 / 3B	1895	1989	LTSR	
UXBRIDGE (1st)	17 / 2A	1904	1938	MET	Served by District Line 1910-1933, served by Piccadilly Line trains 1933-1938
UXBRIDGE (2nd)	17 / 2A	1938	N/A	LT (MET & PIC)	
UXBRIDGE GOODS (MET)	17 / 2A	1905	1939	MET	
UXBRIDGE HIGH STREET	17 / 2A	1907 (1914)	1939 (1962)	GCR & GWR	Passenger services withdrawn from Uxbridge High Street Branch 1939, freight in 1962
UXBRIDGE ROAD	31 / 1A & 49	1869	1940	WLR	Passenger service withdrawn Willesden Jcn to Clapham Jcn 1940. To re-open as "Shepherd's Bush" in 2006
UXBRIDGE ROAD GOODS	31 / 1A & 49	?	1967	LNWR	
Uxbridge Road Junction	49	1864	1940	WLR & MET	
UXBRIDGE SIDINGS	17 / 2A	1938	N/A	LT (MET)	Metropolitan Line stabling sidings. On site of first station and former Goods yard
UXBRIDGE VINE STREET	17 / 3A	1856	1962 (1964)	GWR	"Vine Street" suffix added 1907. Passenger services withdrawn from Uxbridge Vine Street Branch 1962, freight in 1964
Uxbridge					
VAN DEN BURGHS & JURGENS (PURFLEET)	16 / 3A	?	N/A	PRIV	Margerine Manufacturers
VAN OMMEREN (PURFLEET)	16 / 3A	?	N/A	PRIV	Shipping
VAUXHALL	32 / 2A	1848	N/A	LSWR	Victoria Line station opened 1971
Vauxhall Bridge					
Ventnor Road	46 / 3A	1982	N/A	BR	Point where single track commences on Epsom Downs Branch
VESTRY DEPOT	32 / 2B	?	?	LCDR	
Viaduct Junction	20 / 4B	1917	1964	GWR	
VICKERS WORKS (ERITH)	36 / 1A	?	?	PRIV	
VICKERS WORKS (CRAYFORD)	36 / 4B	1915	?	PRIV	
VICTORIA	32 / 2A	1860	N/A	LBSCR	LCDR Station opened alongside LBSCR Station 1862. District Railway station opened 1868. Two Mainline stations unified 1924 by Southern Railway. Victoria Line platforms opened 1969

NAME: (Previous Names Below)	PAGE / GRID:	YEAR OPENED:	YEAR CLOSED:	OPENED BY:	NOTES:
VICTORIA PARK (1st) Victoria Park Hackney Wick	23 / 2B	1856	1866	NLR	Renamed 1859. Resited South 1866
VICTORIA PARK (2nd)	23 / 2B	1866	1943	NLR	
VICTORIA PARK & BOW	23 / 3B	1849	1850	BER & ECR	Blackwall Extension Railway opened to passengers 1849, closed 1850
Victoria Park Junction	23 / 2B	1854	1984	NLR & ECR	Junction eliminated and NLR Poplar Branch dismantled 1984
Voltaire Road Junction	32 / 3A & 51	?	N/A	LCDR & LBSCR	
WADDON	47 / 2B	1863	N/A	LBSCR	
WADDON MARSH (SR) Waddon Marsh Halt	47 / 1B	1930	1997	SR	Wimbledon to West Croydon closed 1997 prior to conversion to Tramlink
WADDON MARSH (CTL)	47 / 1B	2000	N/A	CTL	On site of former Waddon Marsh Station
WALLINGTON Carshalton	47 / 2A	1847	N/A	LBSCR	Renamed 1868
WALTHAM CROSS (1st) Waltham	5 / 1B	1840	1885	GER	Relocated South 1885

WALTHAM CROSS (2nd)
  Waltham Cross (& Abbey)
  Waltham Cross
	5 / 1B	1885	N/A	GER	

WALTHAMSTOW CENTRAL Hoe Street, Walthamstow	13 / 4B	1870	N/A	GER	Victoria Line station opened and Mainline station renamed 1968. Goods Yard closed 1964
WALTHAMSTOW QUEENS ROAD Walthamstow	13 / 4B	1894	N/A	T&FG	Renamed 1958
WALWORTH ROAD Camberwell Gate	32 / 2B	1862	1916	LCDR	Renamed 1865
WALWORTH ROAD COAL	32 / 2B	1871	1973	MID	
WANDLE PARK	47 / 1B	2000	N/A	CTL	
WANDSWORTH COMMON (1st)	31 / 4B	1856	1858	LBSCR	Opened by West End of London & Crystal Palace Railway, but operated by LBSCR from outset. Temporary terminus on North side of Wandsworth Common
WANDSWORTH COMMON (2nd)	31 / 4B	1858	N/A	LBSCR	Replaced temporary station to North
WANDSWORTH ROAD	32 / 3A & 51	1863	N/A	LCDR	LBSCR platforms opened 1867, LCDR platforms closed 1916
WANDSWORTH ROAD GOODS	32 / 3A & 51	?	?	LNWR	
WANDSWORTH TOWN Wandsworth	31 / 4A	1846	N/A	LSWR	
WANSTEAD	14 / 4A	1947	N/A	LT (CEN)	
WANSTEAD PARK	24 / 2A	1894	N/A	T&FG	
WAPPING Wapping & Shadwell	33 / 1A	1869	N/A	ELR	First served District and Metropolitan Railways 1884, last served District 1905. No service Metropolitan Railway 1906-1913. Became "East London Line" in 1980s. Closed 1995-1998.
WARREN STREET Euston Road	22 / 3A	1907	N/A	CCE&HR	Renamed 1908. Victoria Line platforms opened 1968
WARWICK AVENUE	21 / 4B	1915	N/A	UERL (BAK)	
WARWICK ROAD GOODS	31 / 2A & 50	1863	1967	LNWR & GWR	
Warwick Road Junction	31 / 2A & 50	1872	N/A	MDR	Curve to Addison Road built 1869, no regular use until 1872
WATERLOO	32 / 1B	1848	N/A	LSWR	Waterloo & City Line platforms opened 1898, Baker Street & Waterloo Railway 1906, Northern Line 1926, Jubilee Line 1999

WATERLOO EAST
  Waterloo
  Waterloo Junction
	32 / 1B & 55	1869	N/A	SER	Connection to Waterloo LSWR station removed
					1911 and "Junction" suffix dropped
					"East" suffix added after 1977

WATFORD (L&B)	2 / 3B	1837	1858	L&B	Replaced by Watford Junction Station to South
WATFORD (MET & GCR)	2 / 4A	1925	N/A	MET & LNER	Goods Yard closed 1966
WATFORD HIGH STREET	2 / 4B	1913	N/A	LNWR	Served by London Underground Bakeloo Line Trains 1917-1982
Watford East Junction	1 / 4B	1925	N/A	MET & LNER	
WATFORD JUNCTION	2 / 3B	1858	N/A	LNWR	Replaced earlier Watford Station. Served by London Underground Bakeloo Line Trains 1917-1982
WATFORD NORTH Callowland	2 / 2B	1910	N/A	LNWR	
Watford North Junction	1 / 4B	1925	N/A	MET & LNER	
Watford South Junction	1 / 4B	1925	N/A	MET & LNER	
WATFORD STADIUM	2 / 4A	1982	1996	BR	Opened using funds from Watford FC. Only served on Match Days. Not intended to re-open if Metropolitan Line extended to Watford Junction.
Watford Tunnels	2 / 2A	1837	N/A	L&B	
WATFORD WEST	2 / 4A	1912	1996	LNWR	Croxley Green Branch service suspended 1996. Metropolitan Line proposed to re-open line along with Watford West Station
Watling Street Junction	21 / 2A	?	?	MID	
WELLESLEY ROAD	47 / 1B	2000	N/A	CTL	
WELLING	35 / 3B	1895	N/A	SER	Closed 1917-1935, Goods Yard closed 1962
WELLINGTON SIDINGS	11 / 4A	1867	1962	GNR	Freight & Carriage Sidings. Used by Northern

NAME: (Previous Names Below)	PAGE / GRID:	YEAR OPENED:	YEAR CLOSED:	OPENED BY:	NOTES:
					Line Trains post-1940, now Highgate Wood Depot
WELSH HARP	20 / 1B	1870	1903	MID	For excursion traffic to Brent Reservoir (Welsh Harp)
WEMBLEY CENTRAL Wembley (For Sudbury) Sudbury & Wembley Sudbury	19 / 2B	1842	N/A	L&B	Served by Bakerloo Line Trains 1917-1982, 1984-Present. Renamed "Wembley Central" 1948
WEMBLEY PARK	20 / 1A	1894	N/A	MET	Served by Bakerloo Line Trains 1939-1979, Jubilee Line 1979-Present
WEMBLEY PARK GOODS	20 / 1A	1894	1965	MET	Transferred to LNER 1937
WEMBLEY PARK SIDINGS	20 / 1A	?	N/A	MET	Stabling Sidings for Metropolitan Line
WEMBLEY STADIUM (1st) Wembley Exhibition Exhibition Station, Wembley	20 / 2A	1923	1968	LNER	Renamed "Stadium" 1927. Wembley Stadium Loop last used 1968, officially closed 1969, dismantled 1970
WEMBLEY STADIUM (2nd) Wembley Complex Wembley Hill	20 / 2A	1906	N/A	GCR	Opened as "Wembley Hill", renamed "Wembley Complex" 1978, renamed "Wembley Stadium" 1987
WEST ACTON	20 / 4A	1923	N/A	CLR	North Acton to Ealing Broadway opened by Great Western Railway 1920
WESTBOURNE PARK & KENSAL GREEN	21 / 4A	1866	1871	MET & GWR	
WESTBOURNE PARK (GWR)	21 / 4A	1871	1992	GWR	
WESTBOURNE PARK (MET)	21 / 4A	1871	N/A	MET & GWR	
WEST BROMPTON	31 / 2A & 50	1866	N/A	WLER	District Railway platforms opened 1869. Main Line station closed 1940 but re-opened 1999.
WESTCOMBE PARK Coombe Farm Lane	34 / 2A	1879	N/A	SER	
WEST CROYDON Croydon	47 / 1B	1839	N/A	LCR	Original terminus of London & Croydon Railway 1839-1847. Tramlink station opened 2000. Projected terminus of East London Line Extension Phase 1 (2010)
WEST DRAYTON (1st)	27 / 1B	1838	1884	GWR	Served by District Railway 1883-1884. Relocated East 1884.
WEST DRAYTON (2nd) West Drayton & Yiewsley	27 / 1B	1884	N/A	GWR	Served by District Railway 1884-1885, Renamed 1974
WEST DRAYTON COAL (CELTIC ENERGY)	27 / 1A	1963	N/A	PRIV	
WEST DULWICH Dulwich	42 / 1B	1863	N/A	LCDR	
WEST EALING Castle Hill & Ealing Dean	19 / 4B	1871	N/A	GWR	Opened as "Castle Hill", renamed "Castle Hill & Ealing Dean" 1875. Served by District Railway Trains 1883-1885. Renamed "West Ealing" 1899. Old Goods Yard closed in mid-1960's, Milk Traffic ceased 1978
West Ealing Junction	19 / 4B	1903	N/A	GWR	
WEST EALING NEW GOODS	19 / 4B	1908	1980	GWR	Old Goods Yard on south side of station
WEST END SIDINGS	21 / 2A	1868	1968	MID	
Western Junction (Stratford)	53	1847	1981	ECR	Western Curve at Stratford dismantled 1981
WEST FINCHLEY (LNER) Finchley West	11 / 2A	1933	1939	LNER	Closed in 1939 to enable electrification and transfer to LT Northern Line
WEST FINCHLEY (LT)	11 / 2A	1940	N/A	LT (NOR)	On site of former GNR station
WESTFERRY	23 / 4B	1987	N/A	DLR	
WEST GREEN	12 / 3B	1878	1963	GER	Palace Gates Branch closed to passengers 1963, freight 1965. Goods Yard closed 1964
WEST HAM West Ham Manor Road West Ham	24 / 3A	1901	N/A	LTSR	Served by District Railway since 1902. Served by Metropolitan Line since 1936 (="Hammersmith & City Line" since 1990). "Fast" Platforms abandoned 1940. Low Level (North London Line) Platforms opened 1979. "Fast" (LTS) Platforms re-built 1998. Jubilee Line Platforms opened 1999. "Manor Road" suffix in use 1924-1969
WEST HAMPSTEAD (MET)	21 / 2A	1879	N/A	MET	Last served Metropolitan Line 1940. Served by Bakerloo Line 1939-1979, Jubilee thereafter
WEST HAMPSTEAD (LNWR) West End Lane	21 / 2A	1888	N/A	LNWR	Goods Yard open 1870-1967. Renamed 1975. Closed 1995-1996
WEST HAMPSTEAD THAMESLINK West Hampstead Midland West Hampstead West End & Brondesbury West End (For Kilburn & Hampstead)	21 / 2A	1871	N/A	MID	"Thameslink" suffix added 1988
WEST HAM SOUTH GOODS	24 / 4B	1892	1964	GER	
WEST HARROW	9 / 4A	1913	N/A	MET	
WEST INDIA DOCKS	23 / 4B	1840	1926	LBR	Passenger service to Blackwall and North Greenwich withdrawn 1926
WEST INDIA QUAY	33 / 1B	1987	N/A	DLR	
WEST KENSINGTON North End (Fulham)	31 / 2A & 50	1874	N/A	MDR	Renamed 1877
WEST KENSINGTON GOODS & COAL	31 / 2A & 50	1878	1965	MID	
West Kensington Junction	50	1874	N/A	MDR	
West London Junction	31 / 3B	1993	N/A	BR	Sheepcote Lane Curve originally opened 1863 but dismantled 1936. Re-opened 1993 to allow Eurostar trains access to North Pole Depot from Waterloo
WEST LONDON WASTE WASTE TRANSFER STATION	18 / 2B	?	N/A	PRIV	

NAME: (Previous Names Below)	PAGE / GRID:	YEAR OPENED:	YEAR CLOSED:	OPENED BY:	NOTES:
WESTMINSTER *Westminster Bridge*	32 / 1A	1868	N/A	MDR	Renamed 1907. Jubilee Line platforms opened and station rebuilt 1999
WEST NORWOOD *Lower Norwood*	42 / 1B	1856	N/A	LBSCR	Opened by West End of London & Crystal Palace Railway, but operated by LBSCR from outset. Renamed 1886
West Norwood Junction	42 / 1B	1870	N/A	LBSCR	
WEST PARK HOSPITAL	45 / 3A	1918	1950	PRIV	Horton Estate Light Railway opened to supply building materials, later fuel, to hospitals
WEST RUISLIP *West Ruislip (For Ickenham)* *Ruislip & Ickenham*	17 / 1B	1906	N/A	GCR & GWR	First served by LT Central Line Trains 1948
WEST SIDINGS (SOUTHALL)	28 / 1B	1838	N/A	GWR	
WEST SILVERTOWN	34 / 1A	2005	N/A	DLR	
WEST SUTTON	46 / 2A	1930	N/A	SR	
West Thurrock Junction	16 / 3B	1892	N/A	LTSR	Junction between original Tilbury Line and loop via Ockendon
WEST WICKHAM	43 / 4B	1882	N/A	SER	Goods Yard closed 1963
WEST YARD (RIPPLE LANE)	25 / 3B	?	N/A	?	
WHITECHAPEL *Whitechapel (Mile End)*	23 / 4A	1876	N/A	ELR	District Railway platforms opened 1884 (terminus until 1902). Served by Metropolitan Railway 1906-1913 then again 1936-present ("Hammersmith & City Line" since 1990). East London Railway platforms first served by Metropolitan Line 1913, became "East London Line", closed 1995-1998. "Whitechapel (Mile End)" until 1901, suffix then dropped
WHITE CITY (CEN)	20 / 4B & 49	1947	N/A	LT (CEN)	Replaced Wood Lane Station
WHITE CITY (MET) *Wood Lane (White City)* *Wood Lane (Exhibition)*	30 / 1B & 49	1908	1959	MET	Opened as "Wood Lane (Exhibition)" 1908, closed 1914. Re-opened as "Wood Lane (White City)" 1920, renamed "White City" 1947, closed 1959
WHITE CITY (H&C)	49	N/A	N/A	LUL (H&C)	Projected station between Shepherd's Bush and Latimer Road
WHITE CITY DEPOT	30 / 1B & 49	1900	N/A	CLR	
WHITE HART LANE	13 / 2A	1872	N/A	GER	Goods Yard closed to public traffic 1965, saw some private traffic until 1977
WHITTON	29 / 4A	1930	N/A	SR	
Whitton Junction	28 / 4B	1883	N/A	LSWR	
WILLESDEN BRENT SIDINGS	20 / 3A	?	N/A	LNWR	
WILLESDEN DEPOT	20 / 3B	1965	N/A	BR	
WILLESDEN FREIGHTLINER TERMINAL	20 / 3B	?	N/A	BR	
WILLESDEN "F" SIDINGS	20 / 3A	?	N/A	LNWR	
WILLESDEN GREEN *Willesden Green & Cricklewood* *Willesden Green*	20 / 2B	1979	N/A	MET	"& Cricklewood" 1894-1938. Served by Bakerloo Line 1939-1979, Jubilee thereafter Last served Metropolitan Line 1940.
WILLESDEN GREEN GOODS	20 / 2B	?	1966	MET	
WILLESDEN HIGH LEVEL	20 / 3B	1866	1885	N&SWJR	Second High level station. Abandoned when new spur built from first High level Station to Acton Wells Junction 1885
WILLESDEN JUNCTION (1st)	20 / 3B	1842	1962	L&B	Low Level Platforms on West Coast Main Line. Rebuilt & resited 1866
WILLESDEN JUNCTION (2nd)	20 / 3B	1866	N/A	HJR	Low Level Platforms on LNWR DC Lines added 1912, served by Bakerloo Line since 1917
WILLOW WALK GOODS	33 / 1A	1849	1932	SER	
WIMBLEDON *Wimbledon & Merton*	41 / 2A	1838	N/A	LSWR	First served by District Railway 1889. Rebuilt 1929. Goods Yard closed 1970
WIMBLEDON CHASE	41 / 3A	1929	N/A	SR	
Wimbledon East "A" Junctions	41 / 2A	1868	N/A	LSWR & LBSCR	
Wimbledon North Junction	41 / 2A	1889	N/A	LSWR	
WIMBLEDON PARK	41 / 1A	1889	N/A	LSWR	Putney Bridge to Wimbldeon built by LSWR but operated by District Railway from opening. Last regular Main Line passenger service withdrawn 1941, although services called occasions until 1969. Point Pleasant Jcn Wimbledon still used for empty stock w and diversions.
WIMBLEDON PARK SIDINGS	41 / 1A	1937	N/A	SR	Part of Wimbledon Traincare Depot (SW
Wimbledon South "B" Junction	41 / 2A	1855	1997	LSWR & WCR	Wimbldeon to Croydon line closed 199 preparation for Tramlink constructi
WIMBLEDON S&T SIDINGS	41 / 2A	1916	N/A	LSWR	Disused, originally Durnsford Road
Wimbledon West "C" Junctions	41 / 2A	1929	N/A	SR	
WINCHMORE HILL	12 / 1B	1871	N/A	GNR	Goods Yard closed 1962
Windmill Bridge Junctions	42 / 4B	1862	N/A	LBSCR	
WOODFORD (ECR)	14 / 2A	1856	1970	ECR	Majority of Passenger services in 1947. First Trains in the British Rail services until
WOODFORD (LT)	14 / 2A	1947	N/A	LT (CEN)	First served by LT Central Terminus for Central L Goods yard closed 1
Woodford Junction	14 / 2B	1903	N/A	GER	Divergence of Fairlo from Epping Line
WOODFORD SIDINGS	14 / 2A	1947	N/A	LT (CEN)	Central Line stabling
WOODGRANGE PARK	24 / 2B	1894	N/A	T&FG	

NAME: (Previous Names Below)	PAGE / GRID:	YEAR OPENED:	YEAR CLOSED:	OPENED BY:	NOTES:
Woodgrange Park Junction	24 / 2B	1894	N/A	T&FG	
WOOD GREEN	12 / 3A	1932	N/A	UERL (PIC)	
Wood Green North Junction	12 / 2A	1871	N/A	GNR	Divergence of GNR Enfield Branch (now Hertford Loop) from main Line
Wood Green Tunnels	12 / 2A	1850	N/A	GNR	
WOOD LANE	20 / 4B & 49	1908	1947	CLR	Terminus of CLR 1900-1908 (on terminal loop). Replaced by White City 1947
Wood Lane Junction	20 / 4B & 49	1920	1938	GWR & LT (CEN)	Junction between GWR (Viaduct Jcn to North Acton) and Central Line from Wood Lane
WOODSIDE (SER) Woodside & South Norwood	43 / 4A	1871	1997	SER	Goods Yard in use 1871-1963. Elmers End to Addiscombe closed 1997 prior to opening of Croydon Tramlink
WOODSIDE (CTL)	43 / 4A	2000	N/A	CTL	On site of former Woodside Station
Woodside Junction	43 / 4A	1883	1983	SER	Woodside to Selsdon closed 1983
WOODSIDE PARK (GNR) Woodside Park for North Finchley Torrington Park, Woodside Torrington Park	11 / 2B	1872	1939	GNR	Closed in 1939 to enable electrification and transfer to LT Northern Line
WOODSIDE PARK (LT)	11 / 2B	1940	N/A	LT (NOR)	On site of former GNR station. Goods yard closed 1962
WOODSTOCK ROAD	30 / 1B	1909	1917	N&SWJR	Passenger services withdrawn from Hammersmith & Chiswick Branch 1917
WOOD STREET Wood Street (Walthamstow)	13 / 3B	1873	N/A	GER	Goods Yard in use 1893-1968, Carriage Sidings abandoned 1986
WOOLWICH ARSENAL (SER)	35 / 1A	1849	N/A	SER	
WOOLWICH ARSENAL (DLR)	35 / 1A	2009	N/A	DLR	Projected extension of DLR from King George V Station. To open 2009
WOOLWICH ARSENAL	35 / 1A	?	?	PRIV	
WOOLWICH DOCKYARD Woolwich	34 / 1B	1849	N/A	SER	
WORCESTER PARK Old Malden & Worcester Park	45 / 1B	1859	N/A	LSWR	Renamed 1862. Goods Yard closed 1963
WORCESTER PARK BRICKWORKS	45 / 1B	1898	c.1950s	PRIV	
YEOMAN AGGREGATES (PURLEY)	47 / 3B	?	N/A	PRIV	
YEOVENEY HALT Runemede Halt Runemede Range Halt	37 / 1A	1887	1962	GWR	Renamed "Yeoveney" 1935. Passenger service West Drayton to Staines West withdrawn 1965
YORK ROAD	22 / 3A & 54	1906	1932	GNP&BR	May re-open in connection with King's Cross Redevelopment
York Road Curve	54	1863	1977	GNR	Last regular service 1976